When you need
Your soul calmed
read the Psalms.

Ps. 46:10

Juanita
Purcell

MW01049104

Be Still, My Child

Be Still, My Child

DEVOTIONAL READINGS FROM THE PSALMS

JUANITA PURCELL

REGULAR BAPTIST PRESS
1300 North Meacham Road
Schaumburg, Illinois 60173-4806

BE STILL, MY CHILD: 366 Devotional Readings from the Psalms
© 1997
Regular Baptist Press
Schaumburg, Illinois

Printed in U.S.A.

To my three sons—Frank, Dan, and Cary,
my daughters-in-law,
and my nine grandchildren

"I have no greater joy than to hear
that my children [and grandchildren!]
walk in truth" (3 John 4).

Contents

Preface

The word "psalms" comes from a Greek word that means "song sung to the accompaniment of a plucked instrument." Psalms was the hymnbook of the Hebrews. The individual psalms were written over a period of one thousand years from the time of Moses to the return from exile in Babylon. While David was the primary writer, other writers are also featured.

As you read through Psalms, you encounter a diversity of emotions: fear of the enemy, confidence in God's goodness and power, praise to God, questions to God, cries to God for help and mercy.

This devotional book will take you through the entire book of Psalms in one year. These devotional readings are designed to help you get to know God well enough to trust Him with your finances, your marriage, your job, your children—with everything in your life!

If your faith is weak, it is because your knowledge of God and His Word is weak. The only way to increase your faith and trust in God is to increase your knowledge of God. And you do that by spending time in His Word. *"Be Still, My Child*, and learn of Me," is God's invitation to you in the book of Psalms.

Be still—slow down!
Take time in God's presence;
Listen to His whisper,
"Be still, and know that I am God."

Set aside all your busyness, thoughts, and jobs to be done.
Just be still and quiet before God.
He will not compete with your busyness;
You must choose Him first!
When you put Him first, you finally
Really get to know Him.

In this quietness there is peace;
In this quietness there is fullness of joy;
In this quietness He restores your soul;
In this quietness He strengthens you for the next conflict.

When you truly know how great your God is,
All your doubts and anxieties will begin to fade;
When you truly learn to trust His power and might,

You will never have to fear again.
He is in control of Heaven and earth;
He stands ready to work for those who trust Him;
For those who sincerely believe,
"Nothing is impossible with God!"

He has done all that needs to be done to teach you to trust Him;
He has given you His Holy Spirit to help and strengthen you;
He lifts you up when you utterly fail;
He encourages you when you think,
"There's no use trying again."
He believes in you; do you believe in Him?

Do you really know Him well enough to trust Him?
Slow down; be still!
Take time in God's presence.
Then, and only then, will you understand why He said,
"Be still, and know that I am God."

January 1

Psalm 1

"But his delight is in the law of the LORD; and in his law doth he meditate day and night"
(Psalm 1:2).

PSALM 1 could be called "The Secret of the Happy Life." The firm ground on which we build that happy, blessed life is found in verse 2: "But his delight is in the law of the LORD; and in his law doth he meditate day and night." The law of the Lord is the Word of God.

Are you reading the Word daily? Is it changing your life? I fear that many people who read the Bible each day are only going through the "motions of devotions." Their lives never change. God isn't interested in our getting more information in our souls; He wants us to get more of Him in our souls. He wants us to develop an intimate relationship with Him each day, not just read our Bibles out of habit or duty.

Would you like to quit going through the "motions of devotions" and start getting to know God better? If your answer is yes, I suggest that you keep a journal each day. Here's how I do it. I read the Bible verses suggested in the devotional book I am using. I then read several verses before and after those verses to understand the verses in their context. I select one verse that is especially meaningful to me. Then I read the thoughts in my devotional book. I am now ready to write in my journal. I write down my selected verse, and I write a prayer to the Lord, telling Him I want to use that verse in my life that day.

We're constructing our future thought
    by thought;
To be blessed this year, we must do as
    we ought!

Will you do as you ought and read God's Word each day this year?

"And he shall be like a tree planted by the rivers of water, that bringeth forth his fruit in his season; his leaf also shall not wither; and whatsoever he doeth shall prosper" (Psalm 1:3).

THE WRITER of Psalm 1 is unknown, but the message is clear: the righteous are blessed and the wicked are cursed. The Lord wants to bless us, but we must meet the conditions laid down in verses 1 and 2. We must separate ourselves from the ungodly lifestyle of the world, and we must read God's Word each day.

God promises prosperity to those who will follow these two simple commands: "And he shall be like a tree planted by the rivers of water, that bringeth forth his fruit in his season; his leaf also shall not wither; and whatsoever he doeth shall prosper" (v. 3).

Does this mean we will never fail or have difficulty? Is this a guarantee we will have good health and much wealth? No; this is a promise of spiritual prosperity and growth. There will be a stability about our lives that will result in attitudes and actions that honor God and lead to a blessed life for us.

Would you like to live life with a capital L? If so, let me recommend the "Vine Life." What is the "Vine Life"? It is living out the commands in John 15:1–5. John 15 says Christ is the vine and we are the branches. If you disconnect a branch from the vine, what happens? It withers up and dies. Only as the branch is connected to the vine can the sap keep flowing into the branches. Only as we stay connected to the Vine each day will His life flow through us so we can continue to grow.

How do we stay connected to the Vine? By spending time in His presence each day, reading and meditating on His Word. ("Day and night" in Psalm 1:2 indicates that meditating should be a daily practice.) When we learn to live the Vine Life, our "leaf also shall not wither; and whatsoever he doeth shall prosper."

Will you start living the Vine Life today so you can experience life with a capital L?

"The LORD knoweth the way of the righteous: but the way of the ungodly shall perish"
(Psalm 1:6).

THE LORD knows the destiny of the righteous person and the unrighteous person. The destinies are as different as the lifestyles. The godly person who meditates on God's Word and obeys it will be spiritually prosperous, happy, and holy. The ungodly person who lives to please the flesh and the Devil will be condemned to eternal torment (Revelation 20:11–15).

God not only knows our eternal destiny, He also knows what is going on in our lives right now. Psalm 139 tells us how closely He keeps track of His children. He is behind us and before us, and His hand is upon us. This is the hand that leads us and upholds us. Job 23:10 says, "He knoweth the way that I take: when he hath tried me, I shall come forth as gold."

The way that He takes us is sometimes down a dark path that seems senseless and unreasonable to us. God wants us to learn to walk by faith and not by sight. This kind of faith develops best when things seem fuzzy and foggy to us, even when it seems that God is far away. During these times nothing works like we thought it would, and we wonder if God is still in control. We could call this kind of faith "Job-like" faith. Such faith cannot be shaken because it has developed as a result of our being shaken.

When we begin to look at life with the eyes of faith, we see "things which are not seen: for the things which are seen are temporal; but the things which are not seen are eternal" (2 Corinthians 4:18).

Is it enough for you to know the Lord knows the way even when you don't?

"Let us break their bands asunder, and cast away their cords from us" (Psalm 2:3).

THE PEOPLE in the psalmist's day were just as vocal against God as people are today: "Let us break their bands asunder, and cast away their cords from us" (v. 3). The unbeliever, as well as the believer in rebellion against God, sees the principles of God's Word as strong bands or cords that bind them. These people want to break away from God and His Word so they can be free.

People do not want rules and restraints to repress their feelings and actions. They want to be free to do their own thing. Many groups today tell people that the church and God's rules are outdated.

Some people have fallen for these lies; they are looking for the freedom they believe has been denied them by the "repressive rules" of God's Word. They truly believe that if they can get rid of these cords and bands they will find the peace and joy they are seeking. What a sad disappointment is awaiting them!

Satan will put his cords and bands around them, and they will be chained to their sin.

Every freedom has a bondage. You can be free from your toothbrush, but in time you will be a slave to cavities. Or you can be a slave to your toothbrush and free from cavities. But you cannot be free from your toothbrush and free from cavities. This kind of freedom does not exist in any area of life. A bondage goes with every freedom.

Wise are the people who choose well their bondages and their freedoms. We can choose to be slaves to God and put ourselves under His authority, or we can choose to be slaves to sin and free from God. The latter choice is a dead-end street that leads nowhere. Doesn't it make sense to make ourselves slaves to God? Everything He asks of us is for our good.

Do the bands and cords of God's Word bother you or bless you? Whose slave are you?

"Serve the LORD with fear, and rejoice with trembling" (Psalm 2:11).

THE WORDS "serve," "LORD," "fear," and "trembling" all have a strong emphasis on submission. At first glance the words "fear" and "rejoice" seem to be in the wrong order. Serve and rejoice should go together, and fear and trembling should go together. But God's Word teaches that rejoicing is a by-product of serving the Lord with reverential fear and awe. Psalm 112:1 and 128:1 say the person who fears the Lord is blessed or happy.

Do "fear" and "joy" seem to be contradictory words to you? Some things seem contradictory that are not, such as oxygen and nitrogen. These may be spoken of as contradictory gases; yet when they are combined in right proportions, they make the atmosphere sweet and life-giving.

So it is with fear and joy. These two seemingly contradictory emotions can coexist in the believer's heart when they are combined in the right proportions. God's children have the ability to say yes or no to their Heavenly Father. If we say yes to Him in reverential fear and submission, we will be blessed and experience a life full of joy. On the other hand, if we say no, "Woe unto him that striveth with his Maker!" (Isaiah 45:9).

God wants to do great things in your life, but you have the ability to submit or resist. Which are you doing?

"Blessed are all they that put their trust in him" (Psalm 2:12).

THE WORD "trust" means "to take refuge in." I love the picture of security that the word "refuge" symbolizes. "God is our refuge and strength, a very present help in trouble" (Psalm 46:1); "He is my refuge and my fortress: my God; in him will I trust" (Psalm 91:2); "It is better to trust in the LORD than to put confidence in princes," or those who rule over us (Psalm 118:9).

The leaders of our government cannot give us a sense of security. Social Security is not secure anymore. New inventions and technology do not offer peace and security. We have only one source of true security: God Himself! "Blessed are all they that put their trust in him" (v. 12).

All of us have probably read or heard this statement, "The safest place for a Christian to be is in the center of God's will." "But,"

you may say, "what if I get in trouble, and God doesn't come through for me?" Our problem is that we have already determined how God should come through for us. He never told us *how* He would do it, just that He *would* do it!

God did not promise we would never face danger, but He did promise His help whenever we face danger. (See, for instance, Isaiah 41:10.) He did not promise we would never hurt, but He did promise that whatever happened would be for our good (Romans 8:28). Whatever He allows is for our good if it helps make us more like the Lord Jesus (Romans 8:29). So we have nothing to fear—not even death—because He is our refuge and strength.

Are you trusting God? Are you safe and secure?

"But thou, O LORD, art a shield for me; my glory, and the lifter up of mine head"
(Psalm 3:3).

WHEN David wrote this psalm, he was experiencing one of the most trying circumstances anyone can endure: turmoil in his family. David was alone with God, away from everyone and everything he loved. He was reaping some of the results of his sin with Bathsheba (2 Samuel 11). The rebellion of his son Absalom was one calamity that had fallen upon him (2 Samuel 15). Absalom was threatening to usurp the throne. Not only was David's life in danger, but his honor as a parent was being tested.

Can you imagine the heartache and shame David was experiencing? David may have lost confidence in his son but not in his God. He was confident God would protect him and be his shield. He was confident God would remove the shame and failure he was feeling and replace it with glory. He was confident he would be filled with joy again. His head was bent in sorrow, but he knew he would again lift his head and sing praises to God. "But thou, O LORD, art a shield for me; my glory, and the lifter up of mine head" (v. 3).

We must never doubt in the dark what we know in the light. God is good; God loves me; I will again lift my head and sing. Anyone can sing when the sun is shining brightly, but only confidence in God can give us a song in the night.

Don't lose hope! Hope is admitting that troubles do exist, but believing they won't last forever. Hope believes that God will lead us through the darkness to the sunshine of His love.

Don't give up; don't lose hope! You will lift your head and sing again.

"I laid me down and slept; I awaked; for the LORD sustained me" (Psalm 3:5).

DAVID was chased out of Jerusalem. Who was chasing him? His own son and an army of men who were threatening to kill him (2 Samuel 15:13–17). If anyone had reason to be filled with fear and anxiety, certainly it was David. Yet we read he laid down and slept.

How could a person sleep in a wilderness when he was being chased like an animal? David had a shield of protection around him. The Lord God was his shield, protector, and sustainer. It was not the enemies on the outside that would keep him awake but the agony on the inside.

David slept because he did the same thing we must do: he pillowed his head on the promises of God. He didn't have aspirin or sleeping pills. He had something better: absolute confidence that God would sustain him. "I laid me down and slept; I awaked; for the LORD sustained me" (v. 5).

My husband and I like to go to the Atlantic Ocean and watch the waves toss to and fro. Sometimes it is so peaceful. But when a storm is coming, the mountainous waves are loud and threatening. However, it is always quiet and peaceful on the ocean floor. Scientists say that if you stretched a rope of sand from one side of the ocean floor to the other, nothing would disturb it.

So it is in the midst of the worst storms in the believer's life. When we pillow our heads on the promises of God, our sleep will be sweet for we have perfect peace. In fact, it is a peace that "passeth all understanding" (Philippians 4:7).

Are you pillowing your head on the promises of God or on your problems?

"Hear me when I call, O God of my righteousness: thou hast enlarged me when I was in distress; have mercy upon me, and hear my prayer" (Psalm 4:1).

DAVID may have written this psalm after spending a night in the midst of danger. He cried out for help and mercy: "Hear me when I call, O God of my righteousness . . . hear my prayer" (v. 1).

David acknowledged God's answer: "thou hast enlarged me when I was in distress." David was strengthened and enlarged (grew) because of the trial.

Outward stresses can strengthen us inwardly (spiritually) if we have adequate inner resources to face the outer circumstances.

As hard as outward trials and distresses are to endure, they are never wasted if we accept them with an absolute faith in God, knowing He has everything under control. I have learned that the limitations and distresses in my life have been the very things that have led to my enlargement. I have learned that even childlike faith is enough to sustain me.

I read of a lady who was complaining bitterly about the difficult trial she was experiencing. Her five-year-old child said, "Mommy, it will all work out before too long."

Oh, if we only had that childlike faith and confidence; then we, too, could say, "Thou hast enlarged me when I was in distress."

Yes, outward trials will enlarge us spiritually if we accept them with an open heart that says, "Teach me, Lord, what You want me to learn from this experience." Remember, outward stresses can strengthen us inwardly if we have adequate inner resources to face the outer circumstances.

Do you have adequate inner resources? If not, why not?

"Thou hast put gladness in my heart, more than in the time that their corn and their wine increased" (Psalm 4:7).

DAVID was going through a time of turmoil and anguish—probably the same situation he faced in Psalm 3: running from Absalom (2 Samuel 15). He felt just like we do when we feel the loneliness of a wilderness experience.

How can we make it through these times? Just like David did: keep our eyes on the Lord instead of our circumstances. When we do this, we can have joy in the midst of our circumstances. We can't whip up this joy on our own; only God can put it in our hearts. "Thou hast put gladness in my heart, more than in the time that their corn and their wine increased" (v. 7).

Harvesttime is a happy, prosperous time. Yet prosperity cannot bring joy to the heart when we're hurting. Happiness can disappear in a matter of minutes, depending on the circumstances in our lives. But joy just keeps flowing because it comes from within; it is dependent upon what God is doing in our hearts. This joy gives us unusual strength and power to move through difficult circumstances.

I like Emma Moody Fitt's thoughts on joy: "Happiness is caused by things which happen around us, and circumstances can mar it, but joy flows right on through trouble; joy flows on through the dark; joy flows in the night as well as in the day; joy flows all through persecution and opposition; it is an unceasing fountain bubbling up in the heart; a secret spring which the world can't see and doesn't know anything about. The Lord gives His people perpetual joy when they walk in obedience to Him."

Do you have the joy of the Lord in your life to help you move through your wilderness experience?

"My voice shalt thou hear in the morning, O LORD; in the morning will I direct my prayer unto thee, and will look up" (Psalm 5:3).

IN PSALM 5:3 David pulled back the curtain and gave us a brief glimpse of his prayer life. Before he faced people, he turned his face toward God: "My voice shalt thou hear in the morning, O LORD; in the morning will I direct my prayer unto thee, and will look up."

What a blessing we enjoy when we begin the day in God's presence. Someone has said, "The morning is one end of the thread on which the day's activities are strung; it should be well-knotted with devotion."

Not only did David lift his voice to God, he also lifted his heart. The expression "direct my prayer," in the Hebrew text, implies coming to God with a calmed heart, a heart drawn away from the hustle and bustle of the day, a heart prepared to listen to God.

When we come into God's presence, do we come with a heart prepared to express our love and devotion to God? How often do we rush in and out of God's presence with nothing but our needs' list in mind? Not once do we tell God we love Him. Not once do we praise Him for yesterday's blessings and new mercies for today (Lamentations 3:22, 23). We are so rushed there is no time for God to speak to us.

I am ashamed to say I do not always come to God with a heart prepared to listen to Him speak; I'm too busy speaking. When I sense my need to slow down and quiet my heart before I come into God's presence, I need to pray, "Lord, I want to be open and honest with You right now. I have to admit I often rush in and out of Your presence without realizing I am coming into the presence of the King of Kings. Help me to slow down enough to prepare my heart and mind to hear You speak to me before I speak to You."

Do you need to pray that prayer with me?

"But let all those that put their trust in thee rejoice: let them ever shout for joy, because thou defendest them: let them also that love thy name be joyful in thee" (Psalm 5:11).

THIS PSALM was written by David when he was greatly distressed by the attacks of his enemies. It could have been written at several times in his life because he was continually beset by his enemies. But David rejoiced in spite of his circumstances: "Let all those that put their trust in thee rejoice: let them ever shout for joy, because thou defendest them: let them also that love thy name be joyful in thee" (v. 11).

David sounds like Paul in Philippians 4:4: "Rejoice in the Lord alway: and again I say, Rejoice." Paul, like David, had learned we can't always rejoice in our circumstances, but we can always rejoice in the Lord, Who is in control of our circumstances. We can rejoice in spite of our circumstances because we love and trust our God, Who will be our defense and protector in our difficult circumstances.

When the favor of God is on our lives, we have a defense on every side. As long as we stay under His divine protection, we are safe and satisfied.

Don't run from your trials; face them head-on in the power and might of the Holy Spirit, Who dwells in you.

> "Said the Robin to the Sparrow:
> 'I would really like to know
> Why these anxious human beings
> Rush about and worry so.'
> Said the Sparrow to the Robin:
> 'Friend, I think that it must be
> That they have no heavenly Father
> Such as cares for you and me.' "

Rejoice! God knows exactly what is going on in your life and is allowing it! Do you believe that?

"Have mercy upon me, O LORD; for I am weak: O LORD, heal me; for my bones are vexed" (Psalm 6:2).

WHAT HAPPENED to David's joy and peace? They were gone! We see a picture of a man full of sorrow, fear, and humiliation and a body racked with pain. "Have mercy upon me, O LORD; for I am weak: O LORD, heal me; for my bones are vexed" (v. 2).

Only one thing can cause a man who loves God to fear God's chastening, and that is sin. We're not sure what David's sin was in this case, but we see a man who is in sorrow because of his sin. "O LORD, rebuke me not in thine anger, neither chasten me in thy hot displeasure" (v. 1).

The heart-wrenching discipline of his loving Heavenly Father caused David to cry out in agony, revealing the struggles in his soul. His conscience was troubled, and he was depressed and exhausted. All he could do was weep. David almost lost heart, until he faced his sin and began to pray for mercy. When he knew God had heard his prayer, his trust and confidence returned, along with his joy and peace.

Sin not quickly confessed not only troubles our souls but also our bodies and minds. Sin can lead to depression, and depression can lead to all kinds of ailments. Sin also robs us of a peaceful night's sleep. Sin pays high dividends, and they are all negative.

Is some sin in your life robbing you of joy and peace? What are you going to do about it?

"O LORD my God, if I have done this; if there be iniquity in my hands; . . . Let the enemy persecute my soul" (Psalm 7:3, 5).

DAVID'S heart was in turmoil because of the slanderous accusations against him. His enemies claimed he was trying to kill King Saul and take his throne (1 Samuel 22:8; 24:9; 26:17–20). There was no court on earth to which David could appeal for help. Even those who were closest to him and could have helped him were now his sworn enemies. What could he do?

David appealed to the righteous Judge in the court of Heaven, his God. David knew he was innocent so he could, with confidence, beg God to deliver him and plead his cause: "O LORD my God, if I have done this; if there be iniquity in my hands; . . . Let the enemy persecute my soul" (vv. 3, 5). How dangerous and presumptuous it would be for a guilty person to plead to God for help.

Have you ever been so badly injured by false accusations you wanted to take revenge? I have! How do we handle it? Do we go to the person and ask, "Why are you telling these lies about me?" Do we ask God, "Why are You allowing this to happen?" Or do we ask ourselves, "Is there any truth in this? Have I sinned in any area where I need correction?"

David searched his heart, and that's what we need to do. We need to ask God to restore our reputation and bring justice. Rather than striking back, we must cry out to God, Who promises He will take care of our enemies. "Vengeance is mine, I will repay, saith the Lord" (Romans 12:19).

Don't try to do God's job.

"My defence is of God, which saveth the upright in heart" (Psalm 7:10).

WHEN PEOPLE lie about us and make false accusations, we can either try defending ourselves or let God be our defense, as David did. "My defence is of God, which saveth the upright in heart" (v. 10). It is less destructive when we put our case into God's hands and let Him be our defense. When we try to defend ourselves, our enemy just has more ammunition to use for our destruction. The enemy will take everything we say and do, twist it and turn it around, then use it against us.

A little boy once asked his mother which was worse: lying or stealing. She said both were awful sins. He said, "I think lying is worse. If you steal something, you can return it. If you lie, you may not be able to change that."

Have you been hounded, betrayed, and unjustly accused? Have you been thinking, "It just isn't fair!" Instead of complaining to people, maybe you need to spend more time giving your complaints to God in prayer.

When we know in our hearts we are right, we can put our case into God's hands. We must trust Him to refute the slanderers in His time and in His way. We must follow the example of our Savior, "Who, when he was reviled, reviled not again; when he suffered, he threatened not; but committed himself to him that judgeth righteously" (1 Peter 2:23).

Remember that truth, like cream, always rises to the top.

"O LORD our Lord, how excellent is thy name in all the earth!" (Psalm 8:9).

IN THIS psalm David praised God for His greatness. David's sovereign Ruler was also the powerful Protector of David and all creation.

How magnificent, how great, is His name: "O LORD our Lord, how excellent is thy name in all the earth!" (v. 9). When David said, "LORD our Lord," he was not being repetitious. The first LORD is "Yahweh," the name of Jehovah. "Our Lord" (Adonai) identifies Him as the sovereign or master. "LORD" is His name; "Lord" is His title. Yes, the LORD is our sovereign master.

I can imagine David's heart and mind overflowing with joy when he sang, "O LORD our Lord, how excellent is thy name in all the earth!" Does your heart overflow when you sing these familiar words:

"O, Lord my God, when I in awesome wonder
Consider all the worlds Thy hands have made,
I see the stars, I hear the rolling thunder,
Thy pow'r throughout the universe displayed!
Then sings my soul, my Savior God, to thee;
How great Thou art, how great Thou art!"
(STUART K. HINE).

How wonderful to realize that the Creator and Controller of the universe is also the One Who created and controls us. Nothing touches our lives without His permission.

That should make you want to sing, "How Great Thou Art!"

"What is man, that thou art mindful of him? and the son of man, that thou visitest him?"
(Psalm 8:4).

WHAT is man? He is a sinful, ungrateful, weak, and miserable person who continually forgets God's commands and is prone to wander from His care and protection. Yet God loves him and cares for him. "What is man, that thou art mindful of him? and the son of man, that thou visitest him?" (v. 4).

God said He made us in His image (Genesis 1:26, 27). We have an intellect, emotions, and will. Animals do not have these; only man, who is made in God's image, has them.

God not only made us in His image, He wants us to be conformed to His image (Romans 8:29). He wants us to be holy (1 Peter 1:16). He wants us to be like Him in this world of fallen men.

What is man? Darwin said he is an animal. God said he is His valuable creation.

How awesome to think that the God of this universe is so personally interested in me that He even counts the hairs on my head! (See Matthew 10:30.) That sounds incredible, doesn't it? Max Factor of Hollywood once had someone undertake the tedious job of counting the hairs on a woman's head. The tally showed she had 135,168 hairs on her head. God keeps a daily tally of each of us!

The same God Who keeps all the galaxies in their course each day is the One Who is in charge of every detail of our lives. He is mindful of us! Rejoice in that truth today.

"I will praise thee, O LORD, with my whole heart; I will shew forth all thy marvellous works" (Psalm 9:1).

ONE OF the most common expressions you hear from David's lips in his psalms is "praise the Lord." This expression is found ninety-five times in the Bible; forty times it is in Psalms. David not only praised God with his lips but with his whole heart. "I will praise thee, O LORD, with my whole heart; I will shew forth all thy marvellous works" (v. 1). Someone has said, "All of God's works praise Him, but man is to be the leading singer in the great choir."

God wants us to be wholehearted people for Him. "Thou shalt love the Lord thy God with all thy heart, and with all thy soul, and with all thy mind" (Matthew 22:37). When we love Him with all our heart, we can praise Him with all our heart.

When I find myself in the midst of a heartbreaking trial, I have a hard time praising God. I know God can heal my broken heart, but I must give Him all the pieces. When I give Him all the pieces, I will be filled with wholehearted praise. How do I know this? I've done it, and it works. This prayer can help to heal your broken heart:

> "Thank You, dear God,
> For all You have given me;
> For all You have taken away from me;
> For all You have left me."

Are you giving God all the pieces of your broken heart so He can make you wholehearted again? Are you ready to offer wholehearted praise?

"For thou hast maintained my right and my cause; thou satest in the throne judging right"
(Psalm 9:4).

DAVID celebrated and sang praises to his God for the glorious victory God had given him over his enemies. David knew his cause was right; he was on God's side and God was on his side. "For thou hast maintained my right and my cause; thou satest in the throne judging right" (v. 4).

Does God ever seem partial to certain people from your perspective? It may appear that way to us, but it is not so because God is not a respecter of persons (Romans 2:11). It may appear that the saint is wronged and the sinner triumphant, but God will do what is right. He always judges right. "Shall not the Judge of all the earth do right?" (Genesis 18:25).

Yes, He always does what is right! We sometimes hear a person say, "I cannot forgive God for what He did to me." This is a faulty statement. Why should we forgive a God Who never does anything wrong? If it doesn't look right to us, it is because we don't see it from the same perspective that God sees it. We're not thinking like He is thinking. We do not have all the facts; we don't know all the details. If we did, we would know that the Judge of all the earth always does what is right.

Do you need to change your thinking about God?

"And they that know thy name will put their trust in thee: for thou, LORD, hast not forsaken them that seek thee" (Psalm 9:10).

DAVID was concerned that God's name be held in high esteem. He wanted people to trust God's name and put their confidence in it. "And they that know thy name will put their trust in thee: for thou, LORD, hast not forsaken them that seek thee" (v. 10).

When people mention your name, is it a name they can trust? My husband was taught as a child to honor the Purcell name. When people mentioned that name, his father wanted it to be a name people could trust. My husband taught the same lesson to our three sons and now to his grandchildren. I remember when our teenage grandson came to visit us for a week. As he was leaving for a youth activity, his grandfather said, "Don't forget your name; I'm trusting you to do right."

Do you know God's name well enough to trust it? As I began to think of the names of God, here are are some that came to mind: Savior, Rock, Shield, Fortress, Deliverer, Tower, King of Kings, Messiah, I Am, Wonderful, Counselor, Mighty God, Everlasting Father, Prince of Peace, Lord of Lords, Master.

But what value is a name if you don't know the character traits that belong to that name? Not much! Let's think of the character of our great God and Savior. He is loving, good, kind, long-suffering, forgiving, merciful, holy, righteous, meek, just, faithful, true, tenderhearted, powerful, trustworthy—and the list could go on and on.

You can always trust His name. Can your name be trusted to bring honor to His name?

"Why standest thou afar off, O LORD? why hidest thou thyself in times of trouble?"
(Psalm 10:1).

DAVID seemed perplexed with God. Didn't God care that His people were being persecuted and His name dishonored?

When all signs of escape from our trials seem far from us, we are prone to think God is far from us as well. "Why standest thou afar off, O LORD? why hidest thou thyself in times of trouble?" (v. 1). When all we can see is perplexing circumstances, we become filled with fear and doubt. Our unbelief pulls us away from God, and then we complain that He is standing afar off from us.

Do you ever feel God is standing afar off? Do you ever feel He is not there at all, that He has completely hidden Himself from you? You shout and cry in your time of trouble, and all you hear from God is silence? There is not a yes, no, or even wait—just absolute silence. You have begged God to save your husband, but nothing happens. Your child has a serious addiction, and you beg God to free him, but nothing happens. You feel like your prayers are hitting the ceiling and bouncing back in your face. I know the feeling!

God may be silent, but He is working—working to change you as you wait. He is working to develop your character and to fulfill His plan in your life. When God is silent, we have only one reasonable option—keep trusting and waiting. Just because God seems quiet, doesn't mean He has quit; He is still working!

Will you keep waiting while He keeps working?

"Arise, O LORD; O God, lift up thine hand: forget not the humble" (Psalm 10:12).

DAVID, in his despair, thought God had forgotten him when he said, "Arise, O LORD; O God, lift up thine hand: forget not the humble" (v. 12).

I once heard a lady say, "I needed God's help so badly, but I felt like He was just sitting in Heaven with His hands in His pockets." When God didn't intervene as soon as she thought He should, she took matters into her own hands, trying to help God out a little.

Have you ever felt like God needed your help? I have this note on my refrigerator: "Dear Juanita, I do not need your help today! Love God."

God does not need our help; He needs our helplessness to do His work best. If I'm going to do it, then He can't do it. David said, "Forget not the humble." The humble are the helpless, those who admit they can't handle things by themselves.

When we admit our helplessness over our circumstances, our Lord will arise and lift up His hand. He will do it in His time and in His way.

The next time it seems the Lord is asleep and you feel like crying out, "Carest thou not that we perish?" (Mark 4:37–39), remember, He always arises at the proper time. While waiting for God to do something, I've learned to look for small surprises until I see the big solution.

Can you take your hands off your problem and say, "It's going to be exciting to see what God is going to do"?

"LORD, thou hast heard the desire of the humble: thou wilt prepare their heart, thou wilt
cause thine ear to hear" (Psalm 10:17).

DAVID knew a humble heart never seeks God in vain; he will hear from Him. "LORD, thou hast heard the desire of the humble: thou wilt prepare their heart, thou wilt cause thine ear to hear" (v. 17). David knew God's power and His promises never change. What God had done for him before, He could do again. David was humbly waiting to see what God would do.

The proud heart says, "Lord, work this out for me, and this is how I want You to do it." I'm not sure the Lord even hears that kind of prayer. The humble heart says, "Lord, I need Your help; I don't know what to do. All I want is to know and to do Your will."

We must come into God's presence with a prepared heart, a heart that wants God's will. "Thou wilt prepare their heart."

Do you need God's wisdom and direction in your life? Are you struggling with God's appointment for your life? You have two choices: (1) Turn your problem over to God and receive His strength to keep waiting for Him to work things out; (2) nurse your hurt and disappointment, and demand that God answer your prayer now and in your way.

I encourage you to make the first choice. Ask God to prepare your heart for His answer.

Humbly pray this prayer for a week: "Lord, I don't know what to do; I just want to bring honor to You. I am helpless to know which way I should go. I know it's clear to You, Lord; please make it clear to me."

"In the LORD put I my trust: how say ye to my soul, Flee as a bird to your mountain?"
(Psalm 11:1).

MANY commentators believe David wrote this psalm when Saul first began to vent his jealous resentment against David (1 Samuel 18:11, 12). After Saul tried to kill David **twice**, David was advised to flee to the mountains to save his life. David didn't want to flee, but he did (1 Samuel 19:9–18). He was afraid he would appear as a coward, one who didn't trust God. "In the LORD put I my trust: how say ye to my soul, Flee as a bird to your mountain?" (v. 1).

Do your fears ever override your faith? Have you ever felt like running away from your troubles? I've felt that way often, but only once did it really happen. We had experienced three years of constant turmoil and problems in our church, and my husband and I were both physically and mentally exhausted. My husband gave his resignation, but the deacons would not accept it. They said, "Pastor, we want you to take a month off and just rest and pray about this decision." We followed their directive and fled to the mountains. We trusted God to give us His wisdom, and He did. We did not need to resign; we just needed to rest. Vance Havner said, "If you don't come apart, you WILL come apart."

When we feel like running away, we may not be able to leave and rest in the mountains, but we can flee to God and climb higher with Him. To whom are you fleeing for help?

"I want to scale the utmost height
And catch a gleam of glory bright;
But still I'll pray till heav'n I've found,
'Lord, lead me on to higher ground' "

(JOHNSON OATMAN).

Will you flee to God and climb higher with Him?

"Help, LORD; for the godly man ceaseth; for the faithful fail from among the children of men" (Psalm 12:1).

DURING the reign of Saul, David saw an absence of honesty and godliness. Where had all the faithful, godly men gone? Were there none left? Even those who were supposed to be David's friends were turning against him. David felt a desperate need for help. "Help, LORD; for the godly man ceaseth; for the faithful fail from among the children of men" (v. 1).

When godliness goes, faithfulness is sure to follow. Notice the words in David's prayer, "the godly man ceaseth; the faithful fail." When there is no real love for God, there will be no love for God's Word or His people.

Check your faithfulness in these areas:

1. Are you as faithful as you once were in reading God's Word?

2. Are you as faithful as you once were in attending the services of your church?

3. Are you as faithful as you once were in your service for Christ?

If poor health hinders you, God understands that. If a cold heart hinders you, you need to be alarmed and cry, "Help, Lord! I'm beginning to go under!"

When godliness goes, faithfulness is sure to follow. How did you score in faithfulness?

"The words of the LORD are pure words: as silver tried in a furnace of earth, purified seven times" (Psalm 12:6).

PSALM 12 describes an untamed tongue that is full of double talk, smooth talk, and empty talk. This untamed tongue boasts, deceives, flatters, and manipulates. We all know the result of an evil tongue that can't be trusted.

We can't always trust the words of men, but we can always trust the Word of God. "The words of the LORD are pure words: as silver tried in a furnace of earth, purified seven times" (v. 6).

My wedding ring is fourteen-carat gold. That means it is pure gold, not just gold-plated. In order for metals such as gold and silver to be pure, all the imperfections, or dross, have to be removed in the refining process. There are no imperfections in God's Word; it is as pure and true as silver refined in the furnace. God's Word and His ways are perfect. "As for God, his way is perfect: the word of the Lord is tried" (Psalm 18:30).

God's Word has been tried and tested; and it has been proven to be true. By faith, I have trusted it in the past, and it has never failed me once. By faith, I shall trust it for my future because I have found God's Word and His ways are perfect. Faith is not reasoning, sight, or sense. Faith is just taking God at His Word because you know it is true.

"God said it. I believe it. And that settles it for me!"

Are you living by faith in God's perfect Word?

"How long wilt thou forget me, O LORD? for ever? how long wilt thou hide thy face from me?" (Psalm 13:1).

DAVID was filled with anguish and turmoil. Four times in verses 1 and 2 David asked, "How long?"

Time flies when you're having fun, but a week seems like a month when life goes sour. Sometimes it is not the severity of the trial but the continuance of it that wears us down and causes us to sink into despondency. Our question turns from "Why?" to "How long?"

I remember a night when I was on the edge of despair after three years of continued trials. I couldn't sleep, and I wanted some answers.

"Lord, will these pains and trials never end?
Just when I think it's over, another You send.

You know my heart—how it hurts so bad;
I'm trying to smile, but I feel so sad.
What from these trials do You want me to know?
Oh, I remember; You want me to grow.
Yes, more like Jesus You want me to be;
That's the plan You have in mind for me.
So keep on chipping and banging away;
Don't stop till You're finished, no matter what I say."

God has not forgotten you in your trial. He will give you the strength you need to handle whatever comes.

Will you stretch out your hand to God right now and ask Him to lift you up?

"The fool hath said in his heart, There is no God. They are corrupt, they have done abominable works, there is none that doeth good" (Psalm 14:1).

WHAT DO we call a person who says there is no God? An atheist. The Bible calls him a fool. He is a fool because he ignores, by his own choice, the evidence that God exists and because he refuses to live by God's truths. "The fool hath said in his heart, There is no God. They are corrupt, they have done abominable works, there is none that doeth good" (v. 1).

What would you call a Christian who says no to God? A fool! How foolish to say to God, "No! I don't want to obey You." This is practical atheism. It is living as though God didn't exist.

A loving parent disciplines his child when the child says, "No, I will not obey you." So does a loving Heavenly Father. "Whom the Lord loveth he chasteneth, and scourgeth every son whom he receiveth" (Hebrews 12:6).

How childish and foolish we are to think we know better than our Heavenly Father how we should run our lives. The sun, moon, and stars cannot choose their course, but man can. God does not allow His creation to say no to Him, but His creatures can.

Are you acknowledging God with your lips but saying no to Him in your heart?

"LORD, who shall abide in thy tabernacle? who shall dwell in thy holy hill? He that walketh uprightly, and worketh righteousness, and speaketh the truth in his heart" (Psalm 15:1, 2).

THE SUBJECT of this psalm is the spiritual man. Verses 1 and 2 list some of the positive characteristics of the righteous man. "LORD, who shall abide in thy tabernacle? who shall dwell in thy holy hill? He that walketh uprightly, and worketh righteousness, and speaketh the truth in his heart" (vv. 1, 2). The rest of the psalm lists things that should not be found in a spiritual person: backbiting, mistreating others, breaking promises, misusing money.

If we want to feel comfortable in God's presence, we must obey Him. One author wrote, "It is for the Master of the house to say on what terms He extends hospitality to His guests." If we want to be comfortable guests in God's presence, we must surrender our feet, hands, heart, tongue, eyes, and ears to His control. We must conform to God's standards in our walk, work, and words.

Why not take a spiritual check and see how well you are doing in your walk, work, and words. Read Psalm 15 again and ask yourself these questions: Do I display integrity in my speech and conduct (vv. 2, 3)? Do I have a proper attitude toward sin and worship (v. 4)? Do I faithfully keep my promises (v. 4)? Do I use my money wisely (v. 5)?

Does your walk match your talk? Do you feel comfortable in God's presence?

"I have set the Lord always before me: because he is at my right hand, I shall not be moved"
(Psalm 16:8).

ONCE AGAIN David fled to God for His protection and care. David had learned by experience that those who commit themselves to God's divine care and submit themselves to His divine guidance will enjoy both.

David had a cheerful, believing confidence in God when he said, "I have set the LORD always before me: because he is at my right hand, I shall not be moved" (v. 8).

When I read this verse, the word "always" just jumps out at me. Is the Lord always before you, or do you use Him as you would a spare tire: you only need Him when life goes flat?

I have absolute confidence in God because I have set Him *always* before me.

How do I set Him *always* before me? I read His Word daily and meditate on the thoughts and words throughout the day. Spending time with the Lord each day reminds me "he is at my right hand, I shall not be moved."

I shall not run from my trials because I know He is beside me and I am safe. He will be between me and the trial because it has to pass through His hand before it touches me. Whatever I face, the Lord and I can handle it!

What is your confidence level? If you had to grade yourself on a scale of one to ten, would your confidence in God be high or low?

"Thou wilt shew me the path of life: in thy presence is fulness of joy; at thy right hand there are pleasures for evermore" (Psalm 16:11).

DAVID didn't always have joy in his heart, but he knew he could! He knew that spending time in God's presence could fill him with joy. As long as he lived on this earth, people and things could rob him of his joy, but David knew it would be different in Heaven. In Heaven would be no sin, Devil, or man to take away his joy. On this earth his pleasures could be here today and gone tomorrow. In his heavenly Home his pleasures would not be short-lived but long-lived; they would be forever. "Thou wilt shew me the path of life: in thy presence is fulness of joy; at thy right hand there are pleasures for evermore" (v. 11).

Many times life seems like a long and tedious journey, but remember this isn't home; this is just a necessary part of the journey to our final home. God never intended for us to be satisfied to stay here in our temporary home. The songwriter said, "This world is not my home, I'm just a passing through." God wants us to long for Heaven and His eternal presence.

I can hardly wait for Heaven, to experience that fullness of joy and the pleasures forevermore. Heaven will be happiness and no heaviness, joy and no grief, endless ease and no pain.

Do you want a little bit of Heaven on earth while you're waiting? Spend time in God's presence each day. When He fills your life, you will know true joy and pleasure.

"Thou hast proved mine heart; thou hast visited me in the night; thou hast tried me, and shalt find nothing; I am purposed that my mouth shall not transgress" (Psalm 17:3).

WAS DAVID saying he was sinless? "Thou hast proved mine heart; thou hast visited me in the night; thou hast tried me, and shalt find nothing; I am purposed that my mouth shall not transgress" (v. 3). No; David was stating his relationship with God, not making a statement of his purity. Psalms 32 and 51 are David's admissions of sin and his proneness to sin.

David was constantly being slandered; therefore he needed to keep a check on his tongue to keep from lashing back. Sometimes he passed the test, and sometimes he didn't. In Psalm 17:3 David said that God had searched his heart and knew he was innocent of the evil accusations that were made against him.

We must purpose as David did "that my mouth shall not transgress." We can't control or tame the tongue (James 3:8), but God can. When someone slanders us, it is our word against theirs. That is when we must throw ourselves on the mercy of God and ask Him to examine our hearts.

Remember, only ripe fruit is pecked by the birds! If we are living fruitful lives for God, we can expect outside pecks and attacks from the Wicked One who wants to destroy us.

Have you purposed in your heart ahead of time what you will say when you are attacked? This might be a good prayer to start with: "Set a watch, O LORD, before my mouth; keep the door of my lips" (Psalm 141:3).

"Hold up my goings in thy paths, that my footsteps slip not" (Psalm 17:5).

DAVID knew his tendency to failure. He said, "Hold up my goings in thy paths, that my footsteps slip not" (v. 5). He knew he needed the help of the Lord to hold him up so he would not slip and fall into sin.

Do we realize our tendency to failure? Who of us has not said, "I would never do that"? Peter said he would never fail, but he did. "Peter answered and said unto him, Though all men shall be offended because of thee, yet will I never be offended. Jesus said unto him, Verily I say unto thee, That this night, before the cock crow, thou shalt deny me thrice" (Matthew 26:33, 34).

We must be sure our confidence is not in our flesh but in God's faithfulness. God will hold us up and keep us from slipping when we're holding His hand. It is only when we realize our weakness and our need for His strength that we reach out to take hold of His hand, "for when I am weak, then am I strong" (2 Corinthians 12:10).

When we think we are pretty hot stuff, we will end up as weaklings and failures. When we realize we are weak and prone to fail, we *will* be hot stuff. The literal translation of 2 Corinthians 12:10 is, "For when I am weak, then am I dynamite." That's pretty hot stuff!

Are you slipping? The key to staying on your feet is humility. "Humble yourselves in the sight of the Lord, and he shall lift you up" (James 4:10). Are you willing to humble yourself and cry out for help?

"Keep me as the apple of the eye, hide me under the shadow of thy wings" (Psalm 17:8).

WE OFTEN hear people say, "She is the apple of his eye," meaning, "She is really extra special to him." We take particular care of the people and possessions that are extra special to us, don't we?

David was pleading for extra special care and protection from God: "Keep me . . . hide me." David had been anointed to be king, but for that to be a reality, God was going to have to preserve him against all the attempts of his enemies to destroy him.

David used two pictures of covering in verse 8 to describe God's protection. The "apple of the eye" is the pupil, the most tender part of the eye. God gives this part of the eye special protection. The eyelids are like doors to cover the eyes, and the eyelashes are like strainers to protect them when the doors are open.

The other picture of protection and care is hiding under the shadow of wings. The mother bird protects her little ones from danger by drawing them close to her heart and covering them with her wings.

I often use this illustration to picture how God protects His children: I am in Christ's hand, and God the Father's hand is over Christ's hand (John 10:28, 29). Nothing touches my life unless God opens His fingers to allow it. I can hear some of you saying, "But what if God leaves His fingers open too long?" My answer is, "Then He will stretch out His other hand, lift you up, and care for you."

Can you trust God to hide you under the shadow of His wing?

"The LORD is my rock, and my fortress, and my deliverer; my God, my strength, in whom I will trust; my buckler, and the horn of my salvation, and my high tower" (Psalm 18:2).

YOU WILL find these same words in 2 Samuel 22:2 and 3 as David reflected on all God had done for him. Notice how David delighted in describing what God was to him: "The Lord is *my* rock, and *my* fortress, and *my* deliverer; *my* God, *my* strength, in whom I will trust; *my* buckler, and the horn of *my* salvation, and *my* high tower" (v. 2). Sometimes David was a fugitive, and sometimes he was a fighter. But David knew he never needed to fear with His mighty God beside him, before him, and behind him.

Do you tend to be a bit fearful? Some of you are saying, "No, I'm not a bit fearful, I am full of fear." In fact, if you were honest, you are a full-scale scaredy-cat. I have good news for you! You will never have to fear again when you really understand *Who* walks beside you.

Look at the descriptions of God in verse 2: ROCK—a picture of stability and security; FORTRESS—a place of refuge to run for defense and protection; DELIVERER—one who is mighty and powerful enough to rescue you from everything; GOD—everything I will ever need, my all in all; STRENGTH—a firm support to give continual confidence; BUCKLER—a shield to protect me from the blows of the enemy; HORN of salvation—another picture of strength, with emphasis on God's power and might; HIGH TOWER—a place to flee from the snares on earth. Who can be afraid with Someone like that by her side?

Does this give you confidence to face your fears instead of run from them?

"In my distress I called upon the LORD, and cried unto my God: he heard my voice . . ."
(*Psalm 18:6*).

THE GREATER our distress when we cry to God for help, the greater the deliverance will appear. David cried to God for help: "In my distress I called upon the LORD, and cried unto my God" (v. 6). David could only begin to describe the spectacular way God intervened for him. Listen to some of the graphic words he used in verses 7–17: "The earth shook and trembled"; "He bowed the heavens"; "The LORD also thundered in the heavens"; "He shot out lightnings, and discomfited them"; "He delivered me from my strong enemy." God heard David's distressful cry for help and answered from the heavens.

What is causing distress in your life: pain and misery? danger and trouble? anxiety and anguish? When we are in distress, we usually call on the Lord. Even unbelievers who usually doesn't have time for God need Him in times of distress. I read of a pilot who was experiencing serious problems with his small plane. He called the control tower and gave them the following report: "I'm out of gas, six thousand feet above ground and descending fast. Please advise!" These words came back from the control tower, "Repeat after me: 'Our Father, Who art in Heaven.'"

When we are in distress, we call upon the Lord. When we hear no answer, our calling turns to crying. When we cry and cry and no answer seems to come, we must remember that "no" is an answer. "Heaven" is also an answer.

Are you satisfied with God's answer?

46

"With the merciful thou wilt shew thyself merciful; with an upright man thou wilt shew thyself upright" (Psalm 18:25).

ON MORE than one occasion, David could have killed Saul, but he had been merciful; he wanted to obey God more than he wanted revenge. David knew God was merciful to those who showed mercy, "With the merciful thou wilt shew thyself merciful; with an upright man thou wilt shew thyself upright" (v. 25). Maybe he had learned that life is similar to a boomerang: what you throw out comes back to you.

Christ said in Luke 6:38, "Give, and it shall be given unto you; . . . For with the same measure that ye mete withal it shall be measured to you again." What is the "it" in that verse? "It" is what you give. Give love—you get love back; give mercy—you get mercy back from God and others.

"Bless your false and faithless friend
Just smile and pass along

God must be the judge of it
He knows the right and wrong. . . .
Life is short—don't waste the hours
By brooding on the past
His great laws are good and just
Truth conquers at the last.

Red and deep our wounds may be
But after all the pain
God's own finger touches us
And we are healed again. . . .
With faith restored, and trust renewed
We look toward the stars
The world will see the smiles we have
But God will see the scars"

(PATIENCE STRONG).

If God extended to you the same mercy you extend to others, how much would you receive?

"For thou wilt light my candle: the LORD my God will enlighten my darkness"
(Psalm 18:28).

DAVID knew what it was like to spend the night in darkness, hiding from his enemies. He had also experienced times when his soul was filled with the darkness of sorrow and despair. But David knew that in God's time God's purpose would be accomplished. As David looked back on his life, he could say, "For thou wilt light my candle: the LORD my God will enlighten my darkness" (v. 28).

Darkness can do strange things to people. Children see ghosts and scary things in the dark. Some adults fear the dark. My husband talked to a lady who said she had awful dreams. Ever since she had moved to a new house, she hadn't slept well, and she was disoriented when she awoke. After some discussion, the lady decided her house was too dark. Her former house had a big window that let in the outside streetlights at night. She solved her problem by lighting a little night-light. Just a tiny light can make a difference in a totally dark room.

Do you feel you are walking in darkness? Are you having bad dreams, not sleeping well, or waking up disoriented? Maybe you need more light in your life—God's light, His Word. "Thy word is a lamp unto my feet, and a light unto my path" (Psalm 119:105). He is the only One Who can "enlighten my darkness." "The entrance of thy words giveth light" (Psalm 119:130).

Let the light of God's Word shine into your life each day.

"For by thee I have run through a troop; and by my God have I leaped over a wall"
(Psalm 18:29).

AS DAVID reflected on that long period in his life when Saul was out to kill him, he could hardly believe what he had done. As a shepherd, he had killed a bear and a lion, but he had never trained to be a warrior. God had given him unusual ability and strength to do things beyond himself, things that now seemed impossible. "For by thee I have run through a troop; and by my God have I leaped over a wall" (v. 29).

The headline read, "Woman Pushes Huge Boulder Off Her Child." Incredible! How could she have such strength? When we face a crisis, our bodies produce extra adrenaline. This extra adrenaline gives us superhuman strength, the ability to do things we would never think we can do. Have you ever "run through a troop" or "leaped over a wall"?

The adrenaline to face a crisis is short-lived. What happens the next day when we have to live with the results of the crisis? Where do we get the strength then? David got his strength from his God: "For by thee . . . by my God. . . ."

Do you need strength to keep going? Exchange your puny, weak strength for God's supernatural strength. "But they that wait upon the LORD shall renew their strength; they shall mount up with wings as eagles; they shall run, and not be weary; and they shall walk, and not faint" (Isaiah 40:31).

"As for God, his way is perfect: the word of the LORD is tried: he is a buckler to all those that trust in him" (Psalm 18:30).

DAVID was no longer in the midst of his trial. He was looking back and rehearsing how God had delivered him. When David was running and wondering if God had forgotten him, he may have had a hard time saying, "As for God, his way is perfect: the word of the LORD is tried: he is a buckler to all those that trust in him" (v. 30). No doubt David faced some of the same doubts and frustrations that we experience. Sometimes he must have thought, "Lord, are You sure You know what You're doing?"

God is sovereign. He does as He pleases without asking our permission. "Who is he that saith, and it cometh to pass, when the Lord commanded it not? Out of the mouth of the most High proceedeth not evil and good?" (Lamentations 3:37, 38).

Everything that comes into our lives God either permits or brings about Himself. Does that excite you or frustrate you? Who hasn't been frustrated with God when we realize He could keep everything running smoothly, but He doesn't. The toilet overflows the day company is coming, and the Bible study leader says, "We should thank the Lord for the minor irritations that come into our lives."

What if it isn't a minor irritation but a major interruption in life? The doctor tells you that you have cancer, or your child is born with Down's syndrome. Does your frustration turn to anger?

The sovereignty of God is beyond our understanding and tracing (Isaiah 55:8, 9), but not beyond our ability to trust. Don't forget: We can't always trace God's hand, but we can always trust His heart.

Yes, God's way is always perfect even when it doesn't seem perfect! Do you believe that?

"The heavens declare the glory of God; and the firmament sheweth his handywork"
(Psalm 19:1).

MAYBE David was thinking of the "fools" of Psalm 14:1 when he wrote this psalm. ("The fool hath said in his heart, There is no God.") Only a fool would believe that the perfect order of this world and all the galaxies beyond could just have happened into being. In fact, only a Master Designer could have conceived the idea, much less carried out the plan and brought it to completion. "The heavens declare the glory of God; and the firmament sheweth his handywork" (v. 1).

The sun is 93 million miles from the earth. Is it a coincidence that it is precisely the right distance away to permit life on earth? What if it were closer? We would burn up. What if it were farther away? We would freeze to death. Is it a coincidence that the moon is 240,000 miles from the earth? What

if it were closer? The gravitational pull would be so strong there would be enormous tidal waves.

Truly the heavens are telling us about our magnificent and awesome God. He is absolutely dependable in keeping the universe in perfect order. The meteorologists can tell us exactly what minute the sun will rise and set each day. God is always on schedule—never too early or never too late.

When our lives seem chaotic, we must remember they are right on schedule by God's clock. "For he performeth the thing that is appointed for me" (Job 23:14).

When God interrupts your schedule, it is because He is about to fulfill His appointment in your life. Are you willing to scratch your plan and accept His?

"The law of the LORD is perfect, converting the soul: the testimony of the LORD is sure,
making wise the simple" (Psalm 19:7).

GOD'S ways are perfect; they cannot be improved upon. God's Law (His Word) is perfect; it cannot be improved upon.

When we see the word "law," we usually think of something that keeps us from having fun. Not so with God's Law. What a fun place this world would be if everyone lived by God's ten basic laws, the Ten Commandments (Exodus 20). Just think what this world would be like if everyone honored God by going to His house each week. Wouldn't it be great if children loved their parents, if people didn't kill, didn't steal another's mate or possessions, and didn't covet what others have? Wow! That would almost be Heaven on earth! We all need to get back to the basics in obeying God.

A few years ago I read the book *Everything I Need to Know I Learned in Kindergarten*. It describes how simple life would be if we just practiced some of the basics we learned in kindergarten. Maybe someone needs to write a book called *Everything I Need to Know I Learned in Sunday School!* We learn all the basics in Sunday School as children. Wouldn't it be great if we all practiced the basics we learned?

Some people think they are wise, but they are actually ignorant. The simple person lives by the basics, and God makes this person wise: "The testimony of the LORD is sure, making wise the simple" (v. 7).

Do you need to get back to the basics?

"Who can understand his errors? cleanse thou me from secret faults" (Psalm 19:12).

DAVID shared the secrets of his heart with God: "Who can understand his errors? cleanse thou me from secret faults" (v. 12). David had a hard time calling the secret things in his life sin; notice that he called them "faults." In verse 13 David called willful disobedience "presumptuous sins," but those hidden things were "faults." It is a wise person who doesn't try to hide his sin from God; we can be sure our sin is no secret to Him.

I had a "secret fault." I never saw it as sin until God opened my eyes to what I was doing. Before that time, it was just a weakness, a "secret fault." God hated my secret sin, and He wanted me to hate it as well. God had to humble me in a severe way to give me time to reevaluate my life and see my secret fault as sin.

I wish I could say I have my secret fault completely conquered; I wish it were no longer a problem to me, but that is not true. The only difference is that now my sin is no longer a secret; I have faced it and acknowledged it as sin.

Alexander Smith said, "What strangers we are to ourselves. In every man's nature there is an interior unexplored as that of Africa, and over that region what wild beasts may roam." I was willing to explore the regions within and found a wild beast. I am now working to kill that beast. I will never be completely free of this sin because of my sin nature. However, I am learning that the more I am emptied of self and filled with the Spirit each day, the more I can see God developing His fruit in my life. (See Ephesians 5:18; Galatians 5:22 and 23.)

Do you need to explore the regions within to see if there are any "secret faults"?

"The LORD hear thee in the day of trouble; the name of the God of Jacob defend thee"
(Psalm 20:1).

THE dictionary defines "trouble" as "misfortune or calamity"; it defines "trial" as "a process of testing." When a calamity makes a sudden intrusion into your life, that is your "day of trouble." Most of us can handle anything for one day. But when the days turn into months or years, we may not feel we can handle such a trial. Most of us realize we need help to make it when these times come.

Whom would you call on to help you in your "day of trouble"? What name comes to your mind: Sally, Claire, Mom, your pastor's wife?

Some of you may answer, "I have no close friends, no mother, or pastor's wife who would really care about my calamity." David was in that condition, and he said, "The LORD hear thee in the day of trouble; the name of the God of Jacob defend thee" (v. 1). The Lord often defended and protected David, and He will do the same for you. "Jesus Christ the same, yesterday, and to day, and for ever" (Hebrews 13:8).

When troubles roar like thunder in the storms of life, the believer's voice can be heard above the thunder. "The LORD will hear thee." But remember, He can't hear you unless you call!

On whom are you calling for help?

"Some trust in chariots, and some in horses: but we will remember the name of the LORD our God" (Psalm 20:7).

SOME trust in chariots, and some in horses: but we will remember the name of the LORD our God" (v. 7). David may have been referring to his victory over the Syrians when he wrote this verse. (See 2 Samuel 8:3–6.) The Syrians trusted in earthly sources: chariots and horsemen; David trusted in heavenly sources: "the name of the LORD."

In Biblical times a name always had significance; for instance, Jonathan meant "gift of God." God's name represents His character, His nature. To know His name is to know the basis for peace and tranquillity in your life.

The name "LORD" is more properly pronounced "Yahweh." It occurs 6,828 times in the Old Testament. God revealed Himself as "I AM THAT I AM . . . the LORD . . . this is my name for ever" (Exodus 3:14, 15).

What does "I AM" signify? God is everything you will ever need! "I AM" your peace, your strength, your comfort, your provider, your protector, your friend. "I AM" everything you will ever need!

"The name of the Lord is a strong tower: the righteous runneth into it, and is safe" (Proverbs 18:10).

Now do you understand how the name of the Lord can be a means of comfort for your life? Don't look to earthly sources to provide lasting peace; find your security in the name of the Lord.

"For thou preventest [met or welcomed] him with the blessings of goodness: thou settest a crown of pure gold on his head" (Psalm 21:3).

IN PSALM 21 David described all the gifts he had because he was a child of the King: the desires of his heart (v. 2), rich blessings and a crown of pure gold (v. 3), long life (v. 4), honor and majesty (v. 5), eternal blessings and gladness (v. 6).

Have you counted your blessings lately? Remember, we are the richest people on earth. We are joint heirs with the King; we share His wealth (Romans 8:17).

Many years ago a baby girl was born into the home of a struggling young couple in the foothills of the Ozarks. It was not an influential family; the girl never earned any degrees; she never was wealthy; she married a commoner. Yet today she is part of a royal family. She is a princess! Who is she? It is I! No, I'm not dreaming. I am a princess; I belong to a royal family, and so do you, if you belong to the King of Kings. Being children of the King makes us royalty, doesn't it?

We will have fewer poor-me pity parties when we remember who we are and how rich we are. I can visualize that pure gold crown on my head right now.

Can you see your crown? Are you living like a royal child or a pauper?

"For thou hast made him most blessed for ever: thou hast made him exceeding glad with thy countenance" (Psalm 21:6).

PSALM 21 is David's rehearsing of the blessings he enjoyed because of his relationship with the Lord. Verse 6 summarizes how he felt. The word "him" in the verse refers to David himself. "For thou hast made him [David] most blessed for ever: thou hast made him [David] exceeding glad with thy countenance." The last part of the verse can be translated, "make him joyful with gladness in Thy presence."

Has another person's presence ever put a smile on your face, made you feel glad and full of joy? A daddy's presence can do wonders for a frightened child.

I heard a pastor tell the following story. He and his small son were at an amusement park, and the child kept asking his father to take him on one of the scary rides. Finally the father bought their tickets, and father and son took their places on the ride. The ride started slowly, but soon it was whirling around faster and faster. The child began to cry and cling to his father. The father said, "Actually, I was a little scared myself; but I thought maybe if I started laughing, it would calm his fears." The father started laughing and shouting, "Isn't this fun?" Sure enough! When the little boy looked at his father's face and saw him laughing, soon he was laughing and enjoying the ride. The presence of his smiling father put a smile on the child's face.

Our Heavenly Father takes us on some scary rides in life, doesn't He? When life seems like it is whirling around too fast and you are full of fear, get your eyes off your circumstances and onto your Father, your Heavenly Father. He will make you glad with the joy of *His* presence. "Thou wilt shew me the path of life: in thy presence is fulness of joy" (Psalm 16:11).

In whose presence do you find joy during life's scary rides?

"My God, my God, why hast thou forsaken me? why art thou so far from helping me, and from the words of my roaring?" (Psalm 22:1).

THE PARALLELS between this psalm and Christ's crucifixion are astounding; so much so, that Bible scholars believe David was not writing of himself or any other man but of Christ Jesus, the God-Man. This is a messianic psalm. It finds its fullfillment in Christ.

According to the Crucifixion accounts in Matthew 27:46 and Mark 15:34, Christ quoted Psalm 22:1 at the height of His agony on the cross: "My God, my God, why hast thou forsaken me? why art thou so far from helping me, and from the words of my roaring?"

Do bad things happen to good people? Yes! In fact, to God's people. We are the very ones who may cry out, "My God, my God, why hast thou forsaken me?" When the hoped-for, prayed-for miracle doesn't come, and we know it is too late for deliverance—that is when the whys hound us and cause endless, sleepless nights.

What if we did know why? Would it solve anything or make the pain less intense?

I am learning that the more I can trust God the less I need to understand why. I have also learned that when times of darkness, loneliness, and anguish come, I must remember they will be followed by a sweeter and closer fellowship with God.

Our Savior was forsaken for moments so we would never be forsaken. "He hath said, I will never leave thee, nor forsake thee" (Hebrews 13:5).

Will you learn to trust more so you can say why less?

"My strength is dried up like a potsherd; and my tongue cleaveth to my jaws; and thou hast brought me into the dust of death" (Psalm 22:15).

PSALM 22 has been called the Psalm of the Cross. These words could have been spoken by David when he was going through an agonizing trial. However, the psalm is more than that. It is a picture of Christ in His darkest hours on the cross. Whatever David suffered, Christ suffered a hundred times over when He was crucified for our sins.

Verse 15 is a picture of total exhaustion, feeling like you will die but not dying. "My strength is dried up like a potsherd; and my tongue cleaveth to my jaws; and thou hast brought me into the dust of death."

None of us can even begin to imagine the agony and pain Christ suffered to give us new life. The closest thing some women experience is childbirth. I've often heard that when a woman is in labor and childbirth, she passes through the valley of the shadow of death. She feels like she is at death's door to bring forth new life. But all the suffering and pain are forgotten when she holds her newborn baby.

Christ was willing to go through the darkness and suffering of the cross because He knew the glorious hour that would follow: sinners could be born again. Christ was born to die so that we might live (John 3:16). Christ was brought from life to death; we are brought from death to life (John 5:24).

Have you been born again? Are you alive in Christ?

"The meek shall eat and be satisfied: they shall praise the LORD that seek him: your heart shall live for ever" (Psalm 22:26).

WHAT thoughts passed through Christ's mind as He was hanging on that cross, struggling to breath, before He took His final breath? Could He have been contemplating what His death would accomplish for us? His death would not only give us eternal life in Heaven but an abundant life on earth. "The meek shall eat and be satisfied: they shall praise the LORD that seek him: your heart shall live for ever" (v. 26).

Who are the "meek"? They are people who recognize their spiritual poverty and find a feast in Jesus; they are the submissive ones who love to obey their Savior. Meekness is not weakness; it is power under control. A meek person has the power to do right even when he doesn't feel like it. A humble, submissive person is a beautiful picture of meekness.

I had out-of-town guests coming for lunch. What could I make for them that would be simple but good? I decided on one of my special Italian dishes, a nice salad, hot rolls, and dessert. When I set the casserole on the table, the man turned up his nose and said, "I don't like Italian food." I offered him a sandwich, which he refused. His wife and I were both embarrassed. She kept coaxing him, like you would a little child, saying, "Just take one bite; you may like it." He stubbornly refused! This man was not a picture of meekness.

"The meek shall eat and be satisfied." Meek people do not stubbornly refuse the food the Father serves. They are satisfied and content with His plans and appointments for their lives.

How satisfied are you with what is going on in your life?

"The LORD is my shepherd; I shall not want" (Psalm 23:1).

SOME writers call Psalm 23 the He-and-me Psalm: "He" the Shepherd, "me" the sheep. David may have written this late in his life after years of being battered and baffled by the trials of life. He had gone from shepherd boy to king, but he had made this transition through many years of privation, hardship, and victory (1 Samuel 17—2 Samuel 24). He had been tried and tested in the dark valleys and on the mountaintops.

One value of this psalm lies in the fact that it illustrates David's hopeful, positive, faith approach to life: "The LORD is my shepherd; I shall not want" (v. 1). What David needed, God could provide.

Psalm 23 is one of the most memorized passages in the Bible. With only 118 words, the psalm can be memorized in a short time. But the power of the psalm is not in memo-rizing the words; it is in thinking on the thoughts and concepts being taught. "For as he thinketh in his heart, so is he" (Proverbs 23:7).

The words of this psalm can bring healing to a hurting heart if you think about it all day. Here is Charles L. Allen's prescription in *God's Psychiatry:*

Read Psalm 23 five times a day for seven days at these intervals:

- read it first thing in the morning;
- read it after breakfast;
- read it after lunch;
- read it after dinner;
- read it before bedtime.

For effective results you need to know the Shepherd. Do you know the Shepherd well enough to say, "The LORD is my shepherd; I shall not want"?

"He maketh me to lie down in green pastures: he leadeth me beside the still waters"
(Psalm 23:2).

THE Old Testament shepherd not only cared for his sheep, but he also owned and managed them. So it was with David's Shepherd, Jehovah God, the sovereign God. Psalm 23:2 says, "He maketh me to lie down in green pastures: he leadeth me beside the still waters."

Because God is sovereign and was David's owner, He could *make* David lie down whether he wanted to or not. He also wanted to lead David, to be His manager. As his owner, God could make David lie down, but David had to choose to follow God's leadership, or management, in his life.

I'm sure we all like the idea of our Shepherd caring for us and meeting all our needs.

How does the idea strike you that He is your owner and wants to manage your life? Who is better qualified to manage our lives than the One Who created us with a perfect plan for our lives? "For I know the thoughts that I think toward you, saith the LORD, thoughts of peace, and not of evil, to give you an expected end" (Jeremiah 29:11). God's plans are always for our spiritual good, and we're usually looking for material good.

Do you want Him to lead you "beside the still waters" so you can enjoy His peace? Or do you want to tough out the storms of life alone in anguish and turmoil?

"Who is the King of glory? The LORD of hosts, he is the King of glory" (Psalm 24:10).

THIS PSALM may have been sung as the people brought the ark of the covenant from the house of Obed-edom to Jerusalem (2 Samuel 6:12–15). The entry of the ark was the entry of "the LORD of hosts," Jehovah Himself, into Jerusalem because He dwelled between the cherubim that covered the ark (Exodus 25:20–22). As the ark reached the city, the people may have cried out, "Who is this King of glory? The LORD of hosts, he is the King of glory" (v. 10). Verses 9 and 10 express the people's desire to have God's presence among them.

The first time Christ made His entrance into this world was in humility, as a babe in a manger. The second time He appears on earth will be as King of Kings and Lord of Lords. His Majesty will be riding a white horse, followed by the armies of Heaven on white horses (Revelation 19:11–16). What a glorious day that will be when Christ begins His reign on earth for one thousand years!

Before that event can happen, the Rapture must occur (1 Thessalonians 4:13–18). That could be today! Are we waiting and watching for His appearance in the clouds to catch us up to Heaven? If we are, it will change the way we live. If we really believe Christ could come today, we will want to be ready.

Six-year-old Sally heard the pastor preaching about Heaven and the Rapture. When she got home, she asked her mother if Christ could really come at any time. Her mother said, "Yes." Sally asked, "Could He come today?" Mother answered, "Yes." Sally said, "Mommy, would you comb my hair?"

Would you change anything about your life if you knew Jesus Christ was returning to take us to Heaven today? Let's get cleaned up; we may be leaving soon! Are you ready?

*"Shew me thy ways, O L*ord*; teach me thy paths" (Psalm 25:4)*.

DAVID may have composed this psalm later in life since he mentioned the sins of his youth (v. 7). David had learned the folly of being self-willed; he now wanted God's will more than his will.

Verse 4 shows us the heart of the "man after mine [God's] own heart" (Acts 13:22): "Shew me thy ways, O L*ord*; teach me thy paths."

Are you afraid of God's will for your life? I remember a time in my life when I was afraid to say, "Shew me thy ways, O L*ord*." I didn't want to see God's way; I was sure it would be something awful. I just knew if I said, "I'm willing to do whatever or go wherever," God would send me to Africa or outer Siberia, doing something I hated, for the rest of my life.

Why do we fear the will of God for our lives? Because we do not really believe that it is good, acceptable, and perfect (Romans 12:2). God's will is good; His plan is the best plan for our spiritual good. His will is acceptable; it will be pleasing to us. God's will is perfect; no one could choose a better way for us.

God's plan for His children is good, pleasing, and perfect. Are you ready to say, "Not my will but Thine, O Lord"?

"The meek will he guide in judgment: and the meek will he teach his way" (Psalm 25:9).

GOD had proven Himself to be a trustworthy guide and teacher in David's life. David was more than willing to follow God's leadership. David had a humble spirit, and that made him a good follower. "The meek will he guide in judgment: and the meek will he teach his way" (v. 9).

Have you ever been on a tour in a foreign country? In order to know where you're going and learn anything, you must stay with the tour guide. Christ is our tour guide through life. Every day is a new adventure; every day we cover territory we've never encountered before. Sometimes we come to a fork in the road, and we don't know which way to take. Since Christ is not the author of confusion (1 Corinthians 14:33), we need to seek His guidance in times of decision.

Here are four questions to ask in determining God's leading in a situation:

• Is this in harmony with the teaching of Scripture? We can make a verse say anything we want it to say if we take it out of its context. We must consider the entire teaching of Scripture.

• Is this right? If it is, it will bring glory to God (1 Corinthians 10:31).

• Is this of God? If it is, He will go before and open the door (John 10:4).

• Is this reasonable? God does not ask us to do ridiculous or absurd things. The Christian life is a life of "reasonable service" (Romans 12:1).

The meek are leadable and teachable. Are you a good follower?

"The secret of the Lord is with them that fear him; and he will shew them his covenant"
(Psalm 25:14).

WE TELL our secrets only to those with whom we walk most closely. Only our intimate friends know the things that are tucked away in our hearts. David felt this closeness, this friendship, with the Lord. "The secret of the LORD is with them that fear him; and he will shew them his covenant" (v. 14). The Lord not only wants us to be His servants, but He also wants us to be His friends (John 15:15).

Many people know about the Lord, but few people really know Him as a close, intimate friend. Why? They don't walk with Him each day. As we spend time in His presence daily, we develop a close relationship with the Lord. This relationship enables us to know the Word of God better ("his covenant") and to better discern God's working in our lives.

Noah walked with God, and God revealed to him His plan to judge the earth and sinful mankind (Genesis 6:8–13). Abraham walked with God, and God showed Himself to Abraham as his shield and great reward (Genesis 15:1). One of the secrets I have found in walking with God is "the peace of God, which passeth all understanding" (Philippians 4:7).

What is God showing you as you develop your friendship with Him?

"Mine eyes are ever toward the LORD; *for he shall pluck my feet out of the net"*
(Psalm 25:15).

MINE eyes are ever toward the LORD; for he shall pluck my feet out of the net" (v. 15). These are the words of a man who felt trapped. Listen to the cry of his heart in verses 16–20: "I am desolate and afflicted"; "bring thou me out of my distresses"; "forgive all my sins"; "deliver me." David was not looking to men to help him; his eyes were toward the Lord. He knew the Lord would pluck his feet out of the net. His trust was in the Lord.

Do you feel trapped in a relationship, a sin, a financial crisis? Are you crying, "Please, Lord, get me out of this mess"? God doesn't always remove the difficulty from us; but He will give us the grace and strength to live above our circumstances, instead of under them, if we keep our eyes on Him.

How do we keep our eyes on the Lord? Do we walk around gazing toward Heaven all day? No, that would only result in stumbling. Do we walk around reading our Bibles all day? No, that would result in negligence. The answer is to have God's Word hidden in our hearts so our minds can focus on the precious promises of God. (See Psalm 119:92, 161, and 162; Isaiah 26:3.)

How will that help? Instead of visualizing the *negative* circumstances in our lives, we visualize the *positive* promises of God. I do this by reciting the "Why Sink When You Can Swim" verses that are listed on page 377 of this book. Start hiding these verses in your heart today.

When you take out the negative, you quit living under the circumstances. When you put in the positive, you start living above the circumstances.

"Judge me, O LORD; for I have walked in mine integrity: I have trusted also in the LORD; therefore I shall not slide. Examine me, O LORD, and prove me; try my reins and my heart"
(Psalm 26:1, 2).

SOME PEOPLE think that in this psalm David was declaring his innocence of any participation in the treacherous murder of Ish-bosheth (2 Samuel 4:5–12). He could say to the Lord, "Judge me, O LORD; for I have walked in mine integrity: I have trusted also in the LORD; therefore I shall not slide. Examine me, O LORD, and prove me; try my reins and my heart" (vv. 1, 2). Because David was walking in integrity (honesty), he had nothing to hide, nothing to fear. His heart and life were clean and pure before God, an open book.

When I get my yearly mammogram, I'm not afraid of the results of the x-rays because I do not expect them to find anything. If I thought they would reveal a cancerous tumor, I might be full of anxiety and fear.

The Bible says, "All things are naked and opened unto the eyes of him with whom we have to do" (Hebrews 4:13). Are you afraid of God's x-ray eyes examining you? You won't be if you have nothing to hide.

When you're in the midst of a trial, how do you know if it is a testing to strengthen your faith or a chastening to correct your sin? What do the x-rays show? Is there any hidden sin? God knows—and you know!

"My foot standeth in an even place: in the congregations will I bless the LORD"
(Psalm 26:12).

DAVID was in enemy territory, but he was confident he would not stumble or fall because of his enemies. He was safe on the open land where he could get away from his enemies; they could not hem him in. He was not shaken by those around him. "My foot standeth in an even place: in the congregations will I bless the LORD" (v. 12). David's prayer had been heard. He could confidently and publicly pour out his thanksgiving to God amid the congregation of the righteous.

None of us likes the idea of standing in a shaky place. We like to be on level ground—"in an even place." Level ground suggests confidence and security, a place where we are not so likely to trip and fall over temptations and evil. But external and internal temptations are constantly with us. How can we overcome them? Here are a few tips that might help:

• Expect temptations because Satan wants you to sin—1 Peter 5:8.

• Recognize that God will help you resist the temptation—1 Corinthians 10:13.

• Know your weaknesses, the areas in which you are most susceptible—Romans 7:14, 15, 18.

• Get away from sources of temptation that appeal to your weaknesses—2 Timothy 2:22.

Maybe we need to sing this old hymn more often: "On Christ, the solid Rock, I stand—All other ground is sinking sand."

Are you walking on level ground or in a shaky place?

February 29   **Psalm 27**

"The LORD is my light and my salvation; whom shall I fear? the LORD is the strength of my life; of whom shall I be afraid?" (Psalm 27:1).

DAVID'S personal faith in God is evident in the very first verse of this psalm: "The LORD is my light and my salvation; whom shall I fear? the LORD is the strength of my life; of whom shall I be afraid?"

David used the personal pronoun "my" three times in this verse: *my* light, *my* salvation, the strength of *my* life. "My" is a small word, but it has great implications. This word filled David's heart with faith instead of fear. Since Omnipotence, the God of the Universe, was his guard and his guide, why should he fear? Since God was his light, he didn't fear the darkness. God was his salvation or deliverer, so he said, "Whom shall I fear?" Since God was his strength, he restated his trust, "Of whom shall I be afraid?" Since the Lord of Hosts protected him, a host of puny people or circumstances could not hurt him.

Are you willing to face your fears? None of us are so full of faith that we never fear. What causes fear? (1) The world we live in can cause fear. Any one of us may face the chilling fear of cancer or the thought of being terrorized by a drug-crazed criminal. (2) Personal relationships with people can cause fear and anguish. (3) Our inner thoughts can fill us with fear. Thoughts of rejection, losing control, or being inadequate can terrify us.

But we do not have to be fearful! We, like David, have Omnipotence at our side as our guide and our guard. He does not cause us to be fearful. Fear is from Satan, our enemy. "For God hath not given us the spirit of fear; but of power, and of love, and of a sound mind" (2 Timothy 1:7).

The next time Satan tries to make you fear, shout Psalm 27:1 in his face, and watch him run. Do you need to do some shouting today?

"One thing have I desired of the LORD, that will I seek after; that I may dwell in the house of the LORD all the days of my life, to behold the beauty of the LORD, and to enquire in his temple" (Psalm 27:4).

DAVID was a one-purpose person: *"One thing* have I desired of the LORD, *that* will I seek after" (v. 4). What was that purpose? "That I may dwell in the house of the LORD all the days of my life."

In the Old Testament God's people could only be in God's presence when they were in the tabernacle (or later, the temple). That was where God dwelt. Today the Holy Spirit indwells believers, so His presence dwells with us continually (1 Corinthians 6:19).

David wanted to learn more about God each day: "to behold the beauty of the LORD, and to enquire in his temple." What a great desire! To learn more and more about the beauty of the Lord each day.

Are you a one-purpose person? Several years ago I learned that God has just one purpose for my life. He wants me to become more like His Son each day (Romans 8:29). I told the Lord that if that was His purpose for my life, then I wanted it to become my purpose as well. When the main goal and desire of our lives is to know Christ better, we will begin to see the beauty of the Lord. Then, ever so slowly, His beauty will begin to shine through our lives.

We have a stained-glass window in the front of our church. The true beauty of the glass is only revealed when light shines through the window. Christians are like stained-glass windows. Our true beauty will only be revealed when the light of Christ shines through us.

Are you a one-purpose person? Can the beauty of Jesus be seen in your life?

March 2   Psalm 27

"I had fainted, unless I had believed to see the goodness of the LORD in the land of the living" (Psalm 27:13).

DAVID'S troubles and trials appeared to be endless. Time after time it looked like he went from the frying pan into the fire. When the troubles became overwhelming and he felt his heart would fail, what kept him going? Believing that God is good and that He loved him. "I had fainted, unless I had believed to see the goodness of the LORD in the land of the living" (v. 13).

Do you sometimes feel your life is out of control? Do you feel like everything is falling apart? Sometimes things seem anything but good in our lives. Sometimes even God doesn't seem good, but remember, He is! (Read Psalm 119:68 and Nahum 1:7.)

When life seems out of control, remember that the Master Designer, Jesus Christ, is in full control, working everything into a pattern for good (Romans 8:28). God's work in our lives sometimes seems similar to the making of an oriental rug. The makers of oriental rugs do all their work on the wrong side of the pattern. The rug designer, viewing the right side of the rug, holds the pattern in his hand and gives instructions to the workers who are tying the thousands of knots on the wrong side. The workers do not see the pattern until the rug is completed. Only then do they know what the designer had in mind.

> ". . . The dark threads are as needful
> In the Weaver's skillful hand
> As the threads of gold and silver
> In the pattern He has planned"
> (GRANT TULLER).

Don't forget: God is good and He loves you—even when things don't seem good. He always has your spiritual good in mind! Do you believe that?

"The LORD is my strength and my shield; my heart trusted in him, and I am helped: therefore my heart greatly rejoiceth; and with my song will I praise him" (Psalm 28:7).

WHEN David remembered how much he had, he said, "The LORD is my strength and my shield; my heart trusted in him, and I am helped" (v. 7). When David started counting his blessings, he was helped. Then look what followed: rejoicing and praise: "Therefore my heart greatly rejoiceth; and with my song I will praise him."

The grateful person feels so unworthy and says, "I have so much more than I deserve." The ungrateful person says, "I deserve so much more than I have." Into which category do you fall?

If you are not sure, here is another test for you. How does this verse strike you: "In every thing give thanks: for this is the will of God in Christ Jesus concerning you" (1 Thessalonians 5:18). Your answer may be, "I have nothing to be thankful for." You can never say that if you belong to Jesus Christ. You have your salvation and a Savior Who is your strength and shield. Our old enemy, the Devil, wants to keep us discouraged and ungrateful, but he can't plant his seeds of discouragement in a thankful heart.

Lettie Cowman, author of *Streams in the Desert*, said, "The secret of victory is not praying but praising; not asking but thanking." I have found that to be true; have you?

"The voice of the LORD is powerful; the voice of the LORD is full of majesty" (Psalm 29:4).

DAVID spent many nights sleeping in a cave or under a tree when he was fleeing from Saul. This psalm may have been written at one of those times, perhaps during a thunderstorm. Each clap of thunder reminded David of the power and majesty of His great God. "The voice of the LORD is powerful; the voice of the LORD is full of majesty" (v. 4).

According to the dictionary, thunder is the sound that follows a flash of lightning, caused by the sudden expansion of the air in the path of the electrical discharge. Nothing demonstrates the power of God more dramatically than lightning, that electrifying blast from the sky, along with the accompanying thunder. Thunder is like the voice of God, roaring from Heaven, saying, "See My power!"

It took some adjusting to get used to liv-ing in central Florida, "the lightning capital of the U.S.A." The first time I experienced a storm, accompanied by a torrential downpour and terrible lightning, I thought I must be in the midst of a hurricane. Was it ever scary!

In an instant, as God wills it, one flash of lightning can split a hundred-foot tree or kill the most powerful man. We are powerless when His Majesty, the King of Kings, decides to demonstrate His power.

"The voice of the LORD is powerful." If we don't listen to His still, small voice, He has unusual ways to shout His message from the heavens. "It is a fearful thing to fall into the hands of the living God" (Hebrews 10:31).

Does God have to shout to get your attention?

"For his anger endureth but a moment; in his favour is life: weeping may endure for a night, but joy cometh in the morning" (Psalm 30:5).

EVEN THOUGH this psalm may have been written to use at the dedication of buildings, David talked about what it was like to experience God's chastening hand on his life. This chastening may have followed David's numbering the people in pride (1 Chronicles 21; and the reference to "prosperity" or "pride" in Psalm 30:6), or it may have been God's chastening following David's sin with Bathsheba.

When Nathan confronted David about his sin with Bathsheba, David confessed, "I have sinned against the LORD" (2 Samuel 12:13). Nathan went on to tell David that because he had given the enemies a reason to blaspheme God, the child that resulted from his sin would die.

Soon after Nathan left David, the child became sick. David fasted and wept, but the child still died (2 Samuel 12:15–19). God always keeps His word!

Following the child's death, David rose, ate, and worshiped God. He was not angry with God. Instead, he expressed the confidence that he would see his child again in Heaven (2 Samuel 12:20–23).

David knew the reality of this truth: "For his anger endureth but a moment; in his favour is life: weeping may endure for a night, but joy cometh in the morning" (v. 5).

God is just; we must pay for our sin. "Be sure your sin will find you out" (Numbers 32:23). God is also loving and forgiving when we confess our sin and forsake it (1 John 1:9).

The climb through life is difficult, to say the least. Why make it more difficult by carrying the extra baggage of unconfessed sin? Joy returns when sin is confessed.

Have you lost your joy? Are you carrying extra baggage?

"Into thine hand I commit my spirit: thou hast redeemed me, O LORD God of truth"
(Psalm 31:5).

DAVID wrote Psalm 31 when Saul was chasing him from hill to hill and cave to cave on the hillsides of Judea. At this point in his life, David must have felt sure he was at death's door. "Into thine hand I commit my spirit: thou hast redeemed me, O LORD God of truth" (v. 5).

These living words of David were the dying words of our Savior, Jesus Christ, as He hung on the cross of Calvary: "And when Jesus had cried with a loud voice, he said, Father, into thy hands I commend my spirit: and having said thus, he gave up the ghost" (Luke 23:46).

These same words were repeated by other holy men as they died; e.g., John Huss at his execution; Martin Luther, who repeated the verse three times.

In order to face death with such peace and confidence, we must face life the same way. Paul said in Philippians 1:21, "For to me to live is Christ, and to die is gain." When everything in our lives revolves around our relationship to Christ, we will know peaceful living and glorious dying.

Spurgeon said, "Though life may hang on a thread, and adversities may multiply as the sands of the sea, our soul shall dwell at ease and delight." Only the redeemed can say that!

Are you facing life peacefully? Could you face death gloriously?

"My times are in thy hand: deliver me from the hand of mine enemies, and from them that persecute me" (Psalm 31:15).

SOME writers feel David may have written this psalm at the time he was pursued by the Philistines but escaped death at their hands (2 Samuel 23:8–14). David may have thought, "If it's my time to go, I'm ready." "My times are in thy hand: deliver me from the hand of mine enemies, and from them that persecute me" (v. 15).

My times . . . His hand! There is a time to be born and a time to die (Ecclesiastes 3:2), and God sets the time. He regulates the clock of our lives.

I remember when my father was gravely ill and thousands of miles from me. I prayed for his recovery, but his time of departure from this life was in God's hand. If it was God's appointed time for my father to go to the Father, nothing man could do would reverse that. His times were in God's hand.

My times are in God's hand as well. I cannot do anything to change my final appointment, but I do have a choice in the way I spend my life today. Someone observed, "Life is like a coin. You can spend it anyway you want, but you can only spend it once."

"My times are in thy hand," but I am not a robot. God does not push a button and say do this or do that. I can only spend this day once, so how can I spend it most wisely?

"Only one life—'twill soon be past;
Only what's done for Christ will last!"

Are you spending your time for self or for God?

"Oh how great is thy goodness, which thou hast laid up for them that fear thee"
(Psalm 31:19).

IN THE middle part of this psalm (vv. 9–13), David's feelings of discouragement, grief, despair, and gloom were showing. Look at the graphic words he used to describe his feelings: grief, sighing, consumed, reproach, fear, dead, broken. But once again he affirmed his faith in God, and, in the last part of the psalm, we see him praying and praising again: "Oh how great is thy goodness, which thou hast laid up for them that fear thee; which thou hast wrought for them that trust in thee before the sons of men!" (v. 19).

My compass indicates I am going north, but I feel like I'm going south. Which should I trust: my compass or my feelings? If I am wise, I'll trust my compass. Feelings are not an accurate guide! My Bible says, "Oh how great is thy goodness," but right now I may not feel like God is good. Which should I trust: my Bible or my feelings? Feelings are not an accurate guide in spiritual matters either!

God is good—even when it seems He is against us. If you feel He is against you, think back on all the good things He has done for you in the past. Then try to imagine all the things God has "laid up for them that fear [him]." Let your mind dream about all the laid-up goodness of God that has not yet been lavished upon you.

I'm getting excited; are you?

"I acknowledged my sin unto thee, and mine iniquity have I not hid. I said, I will confess my transgressions unto the LORD; and thou forgavest the iniquity of my sin" (Psalm 32:5).

PSALMS 32 and 51 are the records of David's confession of his sin of adultery with Bathsheba and the murder of her husband, Uriah (2 Samuel 11; 12). God wants us to see the different sides of David's sin and the enormity of it. This psalm includes several related words: "I acknowledged my *sin* unto thee, and mine *iniquity* have I not hid. I said, I will confess my *transgressions* unto the LORD; and thou forgavest the iniquity of my sin (v. 5). Verse 2 mentions the word *guile.*

SIN is missing the mark, falling short of the standard. David knew what the Law taught about purity, but he looked at and lusted for Bathsheba anyway. INIQUITY is perversity or moral fault. It was not wrong for King David to ask a servant to come see him, but when the motive was adultery, that was iniquity. TRANSGRESSION has the idea of trespassing, going into areas where we should not be. David knew he was trespassing into another man's territory when he laid with his wife. GUILE is another word for hypocrisy. David's reason for bringing Uriah home from battle was hypocritical. David pretended it was to give Uriah a rest, but it was really to cover up David's sin.

After a period of time, David quit hiding his sin and confessed it. What a relief to know he was forgiven!

Writer Thomas Watson said, "The hypocrite doth vail [sic] and smother his sin; . . . like a patient that hath some loathsome disease in his body, he will rather die than confess his disease; but a godly man's sincerity is seen in this—he will confess and shame himself for sin."

You'll never find a softer pillow on which to rest your head than a clear conscience. How are you sleeping these days?

*"I will instruct thee and teach thee in the way which thou shalt go:
I will guide thee with mine eye" (Psalm 32:8).*

IN ORDER to get a sense of the weight of sin David was carrying when he wrote this psalm, you must read 2 Samuel 11:1–17. Those verses describe David's sin of adultery and murder. As I reread these verses, I was struck with the thought that David was not listening or looking to God at this point in his life.

David had known what it was to have God instruct him, teach him, and guide him. Why had he stopped? David was about fifty years old. Perhaps he was tired of fighting battles. He should have been at war with the troops; but since he was king, he sent Joab, and David stayed home in the palace (2 Samuel 11:1).

The older I get, the more tempted I am to say, "Let someone else do it; I'm tired; I've done my part." However, God will not let me do that. God's instruction is always to stay in the battle. Don't quit! You and I, like Paul, must keep pressing toward the mark (Philippians 3:14).

If you've decided to sit at home and "let someone else do it," you need to ask God to instruct you, teach you, and guide you into the way He wants you to go.

Don't sit home and do nothing. Remember what happened to David!

"For the word of the LORD is right; and all his works are done in truth" (Psalm 33:4).

THIS is one of David's psalms of praise. David reminds us that God is worthy of our praise because He always does what is right, and His Word will always lead us right. "For the word of the LORD is right; and all his works are done in truth" (v. 4).

"Why should I complain of want or
　　distress,
Affliction or pain? He told me no less;
The heirs of salvation, I know from
　　His Word,
Through much tribulation must follow
　　their Lord" (CHARLES SPURGEON).

God is always right, and He always tells the truth. He has told us time after time that life on planet Earth will not be a bowl of cherries. In fact, most of us have found it can be the pits now and then. God said we would encounter tribulation (John 16:33); trials (1 Peter 4:12; James 1:2; 1 Peter 1:6, 7 [note: "temptations" in these verses is more correctly translated "trials"]); distresses (2 Corinthians 12:9, 10); persecution (2 Timothy 3:12).

Have you faced any of these situations? Sure you have! When the trials get heavy and the way ahead looks cloudy, think about this: The trials of this life make Heaven sweeter and our Savior's face more precious.

That encourages me. What does it do for you?

"The counsel of the LORD standeth for ever, the thoughts of his heart to all generations"
(Psalm 33:11).

OCCASIONALLY some of the verses we have read for many years take on new meaning when we read them in another translation. This is true of Psalm 33:11—"The counsel of the LORD standeth for ever, the thoughts of his heart to all generations." Another translation reads, "The plans of the LORD stand firm forever. . . ."

The psalmist knew God had a plan for his life. In verse 10 he delighted in the thought that God could frustrate and overrule the plans of men and nations. "The Lord bringeth the counsel of the heathen to nought: he maketh the devices of the people of none effect."

This should be an encouraging thought to us as well. Isn't it exciting to realize that today was in God's mind and in His plan before He ever created us? He knew exactly what would be going on in our lives right now. Others may plan to hurt and harm us, but God can thwart "the devices" of these people.

How comforting to know "the plans of the LORD stand firm forever." In other words, nothing can touch our lives unless God allows it as part of His plan for us. Nothing that happens to us is an accident or fate, nor are we the victims of men or Satan. Our sovereign God, Who sits in the heavens and makes the earth His footstool, will permit only those things that work together for our spiritual good to make us more like Christ (Romans 8:28, 29).

Will you turn over the control of your life to the One Who is in control?

"Behold, the eye of the LORD is upon them that fear him, upon them that hope in his mercy"
(Psalm 33:18).

THE psalmist had learned a valuable lesson: God is the only true deliverer. "Behold, the eye of the LORD is upon them that fear him, upon them that hope in his mercy" (v. 18). Many times in the psalms we get the same message: those who fear the Lord and hope in His mercy shall be safe under Jehovah's care.

It's too bad the Children of Israel couldn't remember this valuable truth as they were traveling to the Promised Land. God started their journey with such an awesome miracle (the Passover) you would think they would never again doubt Him. But they did! They were at the Red Sea. They couldn't go forward because they had no boats; they couldn't go backward because the Egyptians were close behind and getting ready to attack. What could they do? Nothing! But Jehovah's eye was upon them. In His mercy, He opened the Red Sea and delivered them from the hands of the enemy (Exodus 14).

"Have you come to the Red Sea place in
   your life,
Where, in spite of all you can do,
There is no way out, there is no way back,
There is no other way but through?
Then wait on the Lord with a trust serene,
Till the night of your fear is gone;
He will send the wind, He will heap the
   floods,
When He says to your soul, 'Go on' "

(ANNIE JOHNSON FLINT).

Do you feel safe and secure under Jehovah's eye?

"Our soul waiteth for the LORD: he is our help and our shield" (Psalm 33:20).

DAVID didn't live in a hurry-up-and-wait society like we do. David's life was free of much of the hustle and bustle that characterizes modern life. David was able to spend time alone—alone with God and waiting. Waiting for what? Waiting to see how God would intervene for him. "Our soul waiteth for the LORD: he is our help and our shield" (v. 20).

My, how hard it is to wait upon the Lord. Everything in my nature goes against the word "wait." I am a type A, let's-get-it-done-now kind of person. Living in this rush-rush, electronic age only encourages my impatient spirit. Fax machines, computers, drive-through banking, instant potatoes, instant puddings—why wait when we can hurry?

But I am learning God is never in a hurry. He seems to love the word "wait." Why? I'm sure one of the reasons is that He wants us to remember "he is our help and our shield."

He says, "Be still, and know that I am God" (Psalm 46:10). How can I be still if I don't take time to wait? I can't!

I'm rather enjoying learning to wait on God and saying, "It's going to be neat to see how God will work out this situation."

What have you learned from waiting?

"I sought the LORD, and he heard me, and delivered me from all my fears" (Psalm 34:4).

THE HEADING of Psalm 34 says, "A Psalm of David, when he changed his behavior before Abimelech; who drove him away, and he departed." The psalm was written when David fled from the rage of Saul and took cover in the land of the Philistines (1 Samuel 21:10—22:1). When the people discovered who David was, he was ordered to go before King Abimelech (Achish). Fearing for his life, David disguised himself as a madman, and the king released him. David then escaped to the cave of Adullam. What extremes we pursue to avoid death!

In fear David cried out to the Lord. God answered, and David wrote, "I sought the LORD, and he heard me, and delivered me from all my fears" (v. 4).

I remember when my dad was near death. I had no fear. I knew where he was going. I knew he would be at home with the Lord: "to be absent from the body, and to be present with the Lord" (2 Corinthians 5:8). Dad had suffered so much. I knew it would be a wonderful relief for him to be released from his struggling to breath and receive his new body.

When I am dying, will I be afraid? No, I don't think so. Why should a child of God be fearful of seeing her Savior and spending eternity in Heaven? What a wonderful place that will be: no more sorrow, no more pain. (Read Revelation 21 and 22.)

Are you afraid of dying? Why not ask the Lord to deliver you from that fear?

"They looked unto him, and were lightened: and their faces were not ashamed"
(Psalm 34:5).

WHEN David looked around him, everything looked dark and dismal. His circumstances brought perplexity and confusion. When he looked to the Lord, God lifted the cloud of darkness and lightened David's life and his load. "They looked unto him, and were lightened: and their faces were not ashamed" (v. 5).

Does Jesus Christ "light up your life"? Does He put a smile in your heart when you have every reason to be filled with stress and turmoil? Your life may be whirling in so many different directions that you almost feel dizzy. How can you keep from staggering and stumbling? Quit looking at the whirling circumstances in your life and get your eyes on a steady object, the solid rock, Christ Jesus.

Look to Christ, and He will light up your life and give you joy in the midst of your circumstances. This joy will allow you to move through your troubles and not get bogged down. This joy flows as well in the dark as it does in the day. This is a joy the world doesn't know anything about. It is the joy you get only when you look unto Him.

Where are you looking: at your circumstances or on Christ?

"The young lions do lack, and suffer hunger: but they that seek the LORD shall not want any good thing" (Psalm 34:10).

NO DOUBT David was familiar with the sight of lions prowling over the mountains and in the caves. Often he heard them growling and roaring as they moved from place to place, looking for food. David had to survive in this wilderness with the lions and other dangers. How did he make it? God provided for him day by day. "The young lions do lack, and suffer hunger: but they that seek the LORD shall not want any good thing" (v. 10).

Have you ever wanted something you thought was good for you, but the Lord didn't allow you to have it? Why didn't He let you have it? Perhaps because He knows whether you're spiritually mature enough to handle your wants. It's as though He says, "You haven't grown enough yet to know how to control this desire." Doesn't that sound like something a loving father would say?

My husband bought our nine-year-old grandson his first pocketknife. It had ten blades and gadgets on it. He was so excited! However, we had a problem. His six-year-old brother also wanted a knife. Grandpa wanted to get one for him, but he knew our grandson was too young to handle such a knife; it wouldn't be good for him to have one yet.

❖

Aren't you glad your loving Heavenly Father is wiser than you?

"Depart from evil, and do good; seek peace, and pursue it" (Psalm 34:14).

I'M SURE David was not always proud of the way he handled the trials of life. He may have felt ashamed as he thought back on the scene with King Abimelech when he acted like a madman in order to save his neck (1 Samuel 21:12–15). In Psalm 34:13 David instructs his readers to keep their tongues from evil and hypocrisy. In verse 14 he instructs the readers to "Depart from evil, and do good; seek peace, and pursue it."

"Have a good day!" Often we give or receive these encouraging words without much thought. Do good days just happen, or do I help determine the outcome of my day?

We all know our attitudes and actions help determine whether we have a good or bad day.

"Depart from evil, and do good; seek peace, and pursue it." I see two things in this verse that are determining factors for a good or bad day. Just as oil and water do not mix, neither do good and bad. If I want to have a good day, I must do good and not evil. I must also seek and pursue peace.

Are you having a good day? If not, why not?

"The eyes of the LORD are upon the righteous, and his ears are open unto their cry"
(Psalm 34:15).

DAVID was often encouraged as he remembered he was under his Heavenly Father's protection. His Father's eyes saw every situation he was in, and His ears heard every cry for help. "The eyes of the LORD are upon the righteous, and his ears are open unto their cry" (v. 15). David knew he was never out of his Father's sight.

Again, I am reminded of my father, who spent time in the intensive care unit of the hospital. What a fascinating place. I am convinced no one gets better care and attention than a patient in intensive care. The eyes of the nurse are constantly watching the monitors connected to her (or his) patient. Her ears are listening to the beeping of the monitors and any cry for help from the patient. Her eyes and ears are totally focused on the one patient in her charge. Every moment she is on duty she can tell you every detail about her patient's physical condition.

How assuring to know that my Heavenly Father cares for me in an even greater way. His eyes and ears are focused on me so intently it is as if I were the only child He had to care for or the only sick patient who needed His care and attention. Jesus Christ has promised never to leave us or forsake us (Hebrews 13:5). He does not protect us *from* the storms of life, but He is a perfect security *in* the storms.

Aren't you glad you are never out of the Father's sight?

"Many are the afflictions of the righteous: but the LORD delivereth him out of them all"
(Psalm 34:19).

DAVID, Job, and Jeremiah could all be listed as men who were acquainted with affliction. They also had another thing in common: they all survived their afflictions and trials; the Lord delivered them. "Many are the afflictions of the righteous: but the LORD delivereth him out of them all" (v. 19).

Life is not a fairy tale where everyone lives happily ever after. In the real world where you and I live, husbands leave their wives, children die, friends forsake us. Sometimes the trials seem to be dumped in truckloads, and it is almost more than we can bear. Most of the time, however, it isn't the size of the trials as much as the frequency. They are often like mosquitoes that just keep tormenting us.

Yes, the pathway of life is filled with thorns and briers, but the Lord delivers us out of them all. The Lord, Who sends the afflictions, will withdraw them when His purpose in the affliction is accomplished. One day, when we are delivered to our final home in Heaven, all trials will end. Maybe we wouldn't be anxious for Heaven if life on earth was trial free.

Are you anxious for Heaven? I am!

"Plead my cause, O LORD, with them that strive with me: fight against them that fight against me" (Psalm 35:1).

WE FIND David in troublesome times again, being falsely accused and slandered by his enemies. Did he lash back at those who condemned him? No; he told his troubles to his closest friend, the Lord.

David was irritated beyond measure by the malicious attacks of his enemies, yet this did not move him from the position of one with a bold heart and a clear conscience. David was more concerned with his character and right standing before God than his reputation before his enemies. I sense a strong confidence in David's heart that if he did right, the Lord would do what was right for him. He wouldn't have to fight against his enemies; the Lord would do it for him. "Plead my cause, O LORD, with them that strive with me: fight against them that fight against me" (v. 1).

God has His way of recompensing those who trouble His children. "Seeing it is a righteous thing with God to recompense tribulation to them that trouble you" (2 Thessalonians 1:6).

What should we do when someone falsely accuses us? Maybe we should follow David's example. Three times in this psalm we see this pattern: complaint, prayer, and praise. When we give our complaint to God in prayer, we'll end up praising God for His deliverance.

To whom are you giving your complaints?

"They rewarded me evil for good to the spoiling of my soul" (Psalm 35:12).

NOT MANY people reward us evil for good as they did to David. "They rewarded me evil for good to the spoiling of my soul" (v. 12). This kind of treatment can fill our soul with bitterness and revenge. David had to fight these destructive feelings just like you and I do.

The world's philosophy is good for good and evil for evil: "You treat me nice, I'll treat you nice; you treat me badly, you can expect the same treatment from me." That is certainly not the kind of life Christ told His followers to live. Jesus taught, "Love your enemies, bless them that curse you, do good to them that hate you, and pray for them which despitefully use you, and persecute you" (Matthew 5:44).

Our first reaction to these words might be, "That's just not natural. How in the world can we do that?" No, it is not natural; it is the supernatural way to act. As believers, we have supernatural power available to us to enable us to act and react like Christ did. The Holy Spirit, that supernatural power Who indwells us, must control us if we are going to be Christlike in our lifestyle (Ephesians 5:17, 18).

Matthew 5:44 challenges us to do four things to our enemies: (1) love them; (2) bless them; (3) do good to them; (4) pray for them. What do we pray? When Stephen's enemies persecuted him, he prayed, "Lord, lay not this sin to their charge" (Acts 7:60). In other words, "Father, forgive them." Forgiveness sets us free; unforgiveness keeps us bound to our enemy.

Have you been set free?

"This thou hast seen, O LORD: keep not silence: O LORD, be not far from me"
(Psalm 35:22).

VERSE 22 seems to be the prayer of a man who is in desperate straits: "This thou hast seen, O LORD: keep not silence: O LORD, be not far from me." David was saying, "Lord, You know what is going on. Why don't You give me some answers? I feel You are so far away from me."

Have you stored up faith for desperate days? We often hear people say, "I'm storing up for hard times." I learned a few years ago the necessity to plan ahead for the hard times in life. I've learned to build an "Ark of Faith." When I encounter the floods and storms of life that would tend to overwhelm me and cause me to drown in despair and hopelessness, my "Ark of Faith" has kept me from sinking.

Are you building your "Ark of Faith"? Do you need help getting started? Start by getting to know Christ better and better each day. You can't have faith in a person unless you really know him. Start building a strong faith and confidence in Christ to take you through those desperate days.

"Will your anchor hold in the storms
    of life,
When the clouds unfold their wings of
    strife?
When the strong tides lift and the
    cables strain,
Will your anchor drift of firm remain?
We have an anchor that keeps the soul
Steadfast and sure while the billows roll,
Fastened to the Rock which cannot
    move,
Grounded firm and deep in the
    Savior's love" (PRISCILLA J. OWENS).

Will your anchor hold in the storms of life? It will if it is fastened to the Rock!

"Thy mercy, O LORD, is in the heavens; and thy faithfulness reacheth unto the clouds"
(Psalm 36:5).

IN THE first four verses of Psalm 36, David described the wickedness of the ungodly—why they sin and how they sin. Sinful men are mean, unfaithful, and unmerciful. God is merciful and faithful to us even when we fail to be merciful and faithful. "Thy mercy, O LORD, is in the heavens; and thy faithfulness reacheth unto the clouds" (v. 5).

What is mercy? It is the opposite of justice. Justice is getting what I deserve; mercy is not getting what I deserve. I don't deserve God's faithfulness to me when I am so unfaithful to Him. I deserve His forsaking me. Still, He is loving, kind, faithful, and patient with me.

Sometimes my patience runs out with people who continually fail me, but not so with God. How long will He keep showing mercy? As long as I'm on this earth. His "faithfulness reacheth unto the clouds." While I am under the clouds, I am in the sphere of God's faithfulness. When I rise to my heavenly Home beyond the clouds, God will still be faithful.

Have you been feeling sorry for yourself lately? Do you feel God has been dealing too harshly with you? Maybe you need to rehearse God's mercies in your life. Get a sheet of paper and write all your "mercies" in one column and all your "miseries" in the other column. You will find that your mercies far exceed your miseries. If you can measure the heavens, you can measure God's mercies.

Have you been counting your mercies or your miseries?

"For with thee is the fountain of life: in thy light shall we see light" (Psalm 36:9).

PSALM 119:105 says God's Word is a "lamp unto my feet, and a light unto my path." Our key verse for today reminds us, "In thy light shall we see light" (v. 9).

God's Word lightens our path and lifts the clouds of darkness. Our circumstances may not change, but our attitude about our circumstances can change as we dwell on the promises of God and walk in the light of His Word.

What are you looking for in life? Doom and gloom or happiness and sunshine? We see what we're looking for. If we train our minds to look for dark and dreary things, we surely shall find them. On the other hand, we can train our minds to look for good, beauty, and happiness. Remember, we'll find what we're looking for. Are you filling your mind with negative, gloomy thoughts or positive "light" from God's Word?

I like this old and simple piece of verse:
"Two men looked out from prison bars,
One saw mud, the other saw stars."

Do you feel imprisoned? Are you looking up or down?

"Fret not thyself because of evildoers, neither be thou envious against the workers of iniquity" (Psalm 37:1).

THIS PSALM may have come out of David's wilderness exile (1 Samuel 22; 23). David's wisdom, patience, and strength were stretched almost beyond endurance; things really looked hopeless. David was encouraged by Jonathan, who "strengthened his hand in God" (1 Samuel 23:16).

In Psalm 37 David has passed on that encouragement down through the centuries to millions of others. He encourages us to not worry about the wicked when they give us a hard time: "Fret not thyself because of evildoers, neither be thou envious against the workers of iniquity" (v. 1).

David encourages us to trust, lean on, rely on, rest in, take refuge in, and be confident in the Lord. David was filled with hope instead of hopelessness; there was no need to worry!

Fret not! Don't worry! Don't get unduly heated; keep cool! It is no help to a train for the axles to get hot; their heat is only a hindrance. Friction heats the bearings, but it does not generate steam. Fretfulness starts when a little grit gets into the bearings of life —some cross words, a selfish spirit of ingratitude, bitterness, and resentment. Friction mounts and so does the heat. Don't let your bearings get hot! The result could be dangerous conditions that require much labor to repair.

Are evildoers causing you to fret and worry? The only thing worry will do is make your headache worse, raise your blood pressure, or help create an ulcer.

Fret not! Pray much! Why not turn every care into a prayer?

"Commit thy way unto the LORD*; trust also in him; and he shall bring it to pass"*
(*Psalm 37:5*).

THE BURDENS David carried for so many years would have destroyed him mentally and physically if he had not learned to give them to the Lord and leave them there. He encourages others to do what he had learned to do: "Commit thy way unto the LORD; trust also in him; and he shall bring it to pass" (v. 5).

The idea of "commit" in this verse is "to roll." The picture is one of rolling our burdens from our shoulders to God's shoulders.

What burdens are you carrying: sorrow over a loss? the pain of a physical need? heartache over a loved one? Give your burden to God and trust Him to do what you can't do.

God won't do for us what needs to be done until we let go of our burdens. If we're going to try to bring things to pass, then God won't do it. God doesn't need our help; our help only interferes and hinders His working things out His way.

When I mail a letter, I commit my letter to the post office and trust postal workers to deliver it to the person to whom it is addressed. However, it will never be delivered if I don't let go of it and drop it into the mailbox.

Commit, roll over, entrust, let go of your burdens; commit them to God. Drop your problems into God's mailbox; trust Him and let Him work.

"Rest in the LORD, and wait patiently for him" (Psalm 37:7).

HAVE YOU learned to walk the path of patient faith? David had to learn, through many trials, to be still before the Lord and just wait. He had to learn to walk in that path of patient faith. "Rest in the LORD, and wait patiently for him" (v. 7). Today we hurry up and wait. David's counsel is better: "be still and wait."

Psalm 37:5 says we are to "commit" and "trust"; verse 7 says we are to "rest" and "wait." The literal meaning of the word "rest" is "be silent" toward the Lord. Once we learn to "commit" or let go of our problems and trust them to God's care and concern, we begin to learn things are safer in His hands than ours. Only then can we rest while we are patiently waiting to see what God is going to do. This is silent resting—no murmuring or complaining. This resting and waiting does not demand answers to questions such as What have I done to deserve this? When is this all going to end?

We must remember God does not grow an oak tree in a day; neither can some prayers be answered in a day. Sometimes God takes time to answer our prayers in order for His purposes to be accomplished.

"Rest in the LORD, and wait patiently for him." Martin Luther translated this, "Be silent to God, and let Him hold thee." As we wait to see what God is going to do, we can be confident He is working in us and on us while He is working for us.

Have you learned to rest while you are waiting?

"The steps of a good man are ordered by the LORD: and he delighteth in his way"
(Psalm 37:23).

DAVID may not have always been pleased with the path of life the Lord ordered for him, but David knew the Lord was pleased with him when he followed His orders. "The steps of a good man are ordered by the LORD: and he delighteth in his way" (v. 23).

Someone wrote, "If a man will choose God for his Friend, he shall travel securely through a wilderness that hath many beasts of prey in it; . . . for he only is safe that hath God for his guide." The man who wrote that statement was not a believer. If an unbeliever can say that, the voice of the believer should ring a thousand times louder and clearer with the same message.

Truly our God is a good guide. He had stop-and-go signals long before someone invented electric ones and put them on street corners. God can clearly give us a green light and say, "Go." Sometimes when we want to keep going, He puts up the red light and says, "Stop." And then there is the yellow light that flashes, "Caution; you better watch out."

God orders our stops as well as our steps. Have you been running any red lights lately?

"Though he fall, he shall not be utterly cast down:
for the LORD upholdeth him with his hand" (Psalm 37:24).

I WOULD not lose the hard things from
  my life—
  The rocks o'er which I stumbled long
    ago,
The griefs, the fears, the failures, the
    mistakes,
That tried and tested faith and patience so.
I need them now; they make the deep-
    laid wall,
The firm foundation-stones on which I raise,
To mount thereon from stair to stair,
The lofty towers of my House of Praise."

David did not write this poem, but it reflects ideas he has shared in his psalms. David was acquainted with failures and mistakes, but the Lord always lifted him up when he fell. "Though he [the good man of verse 23] fall, he shall not be utterly cast down: for the LORD upholdeth him with his hand" (v. 24).

If we are honest, we will admit we have stumbled and fallen; we have failed to be what God wanted us to be. But, praise God, our Father didn't cast us away as failures! His hand held us up and kept us from going under in complete despair and hopelessness. When we were ready to get up and try again, His outstretched hand was there to get us back on our feet, and He whispered, "I still love you, My child."

Abraham Lincoln had thirteen major failures in his life before he became president. Is he remembered for his failures? No! He is remembered as one of our greatest presidents! David had some major failures in his life, yet the New Testament records that he was a "man after mine [God's] own heart" (Acts 13:22).

We are not failures because we fall. We are failures if we don't get up and try again.

Do you need to get up and start again? Why not begin today?

"I have been young, and now am old; yet have I not seen the righteous forsaken, nor his seed begging bread" (Psalm 37:25).

DAVID had experienced the life of a fugitive, living off the land. He had experienced the life of a king, living in luxury. But through the years he had come to realize that his security and wealth didn't lie in material riches but in the Lord Himself. The Lord had been faithful to him through thick and through thin. "I have been young, and now am old; yet have I not seen the righteous forsaken, nor his seed begging bread" (v. 25).

God has promised never to leave us or forsake us (Hebrews 13:5). He will always be there for His children to meet their every need.

You may be saying, "Why isn't God meeting our needs?" My answer is, "Are you sure He isn't meeting your needs?" God promised to meet our needs (Philippians 4:19), not our wishes, whims, and wants. I've often observed, through the years, that people's financial crises are of their own making. They live beyond their income, charge things they can't afford, and then wonder why God doesn't meet their "needs."

God promises to never forsake the "righteous," those who are living right. Are you living right? Matthew 6:33 says, "But seek ye first the kingdom of God, and His righteousness; and all these things shall be added unto you." God will provide the basic things we need if we keep Him first in our lives.

Is Christ first in your life when it comes to your finances?

"The mouth of the righteous speaketh wisdom, and his tongue talketh of judgment"
(Psalm 37:30).

PSALM 37 is a description of the difference between the fate of the righteous and the fate of the unrighteous. Verse 30 is a test by which a righteous man is known: "The mouth of the righteous speaketh wisdom, and his tongue talketh of judgment" (v. 30).

"Let me see your tongue" is sometimes part of determining a person's physical condition. "Let me hear your tongue" plays a big part in determining a person's spiritual condition. "The mouth of the righteous speaketh wisdom."

The word "righteous" means "right living." When you need counsel from someone, do you go to someone whose living is characterized as right or someone who is reckless? I'm sure you have already noticed, but let me remind you again, some "religious" people live reckless lives. There is a big difference between righteous people and religious people.

If your life is righteous, your speech will be right, wise, and full of good judgment because "out of the abundance of the heart the mouth speaketh" (Matthew 12:34).

This proverb is accurate: "A bird is known by its note, a man by his talk."

Are you living a righteous life or a religious, but reckless, life? You may think you are fooling people, but your tongue will reveal the real you.

"The law of his God is in his heart; none of his steps shall slide" (Psalm 37:31).

THE PSALMIST continued to talk about the righteous person, the one living right. "The law of his God is in his heart; none of his steps shall slide" (v. 31).

Righteous people know how to live right because they have God's Word in their hands and in their hearts. People who walk close to Christ won't slide, especially backward.

Do you want to make sure none of your steps slide backward? God has a remedy that cannot fail: keep God's Word in your heart each day. I once read that "backsliding is caused by slack abiding." John 15:5 and 6 talk about abiding: "I [Christ] am the vine, ye [believers] are the branches: He that abideth [stays closely connected] in me, and I in him, the same bringeth forth much fruit: for

without me ye can do nothing. If a man abide not in me, he is cast forth as a branch, and is withered."

Are you withered and dried up spiritually? Do you know how you got that way? You dry up the same way a tree does: lack of water, improper food, or disease.

When we are not abiding in Christ each day, we soon find that we have slidden far from Him. We are spiritually sick. We don't stand still in the Christian life. We are either moving forward or sliding backward.

Is your daily Bible reading a time when you are developing an intimate relationship with Christ, or is it just a time to read a bunch of verses? Remember: "Backsliding is caused by slack abiding!"

"Mark the perfect man, and behold the upright: for the end of that man is peace"
(Psalm 37:37).

CHRIST lived on this earth for thirty-three years. His life span was not long, but it was long enough to leave us an example of how He wanted us to live. He said, "Be ye therefore perfect, even as your Father which is in heaven is perfect" (Matthew 5:48); "Be ye holy; for I am holy" (1 Peter 1:16).

The righteous woman desires to live a perfect life because she wants to be like Christ. She wants to be blameless and upright in all her ways. This kind of lifestyle produces peaceful living.

Is it possible to be Christlike? While we are on this earth, we cannot be as perfect and holy as Christ was. But we should be more like Him today than we were yesterday if we are following His example.

When we strive to live the Christlike life, people will see something different about our lives. We'll do everything "heartily, as to the Lord" (Colossians 3:23). The goals of perfection (completeness, maturity) and holiness will cause us to want to do our best so we can be a reflection of Christ to the world.

What is the end of the perfect and upright woman? Spurgeon summarizes it like this: "Peace without end comes in the end to the man of God. His way may be rough, but it leads home."

Will the way you're walking end in peace?

"I am troubled; I am bowed down greatly; I go mourning all the day long" (Psalm 38:6).

DAVID may have been physically sick when he wrote this psalm. Verses 6–8, for instance, describe physical and emotional pain. We're not sure if David was remembering some sin in his past or repenting of a present sin (see verse 1), but we do know he was hurting. "I am troubled; I am bowed down greatly; I go mourning all the day long" (v. 6) We might say David "felt like he had the weight of the world on his shoulders."

I know what it's like to feel like that. My father hung between life and death for more than a month. At the same time, one of our sons was going through a deep trial. I felt like a lot of things in my own personal life were not going as I had hoped and planned they would. During that time, I had a hard time living above my circumstances and not under them.

Over the entrance to a narrow passage in London is the sign, "No burdens allowed to pass through." If I am to enter into the perfect rest and peace Christ has provided, I must daily erect a mental gate and write over it, "No burdens allowed to pass through." How can I do that? I must give my burdens to the Lord, Who is strong enough to carry them. "Come unto me, all ye that labour and are heavy laden, and I will give you rest" (Matthew 11:28).

Do you need to erect a mental gate? What will you write over it?

"Lord, all my desire is before thee; and my groaning is not hid from thee" (Psalm 38:9).

PSALM 38 is a psalm of grief and complaint. From the beginning to the end, David opened his heart to God: "Lord, all my desire is before thee; and my groaning is not hid from thee" (v. 9). If ever David's groanings were known to God, it was surely during his times of grief.

I remember passing through the valley of grief when my father died. It was the first time I had experienced the pangs of death in our family, other than grandparents. My father was finally released from his suffering body and was at Home with the Lord. What a relief for him and for his family!

My groanings were not hidden from the Lord. My heart had been so heavy as I prayed for God to take him Home and end his suffering. I was both sad and glad. I was sad that I couldn't have been with Mother when Daddy died; but I was glad that I had spent ten days with him while he was in the hospital. I was sad for my mother, brothers, and myself because we will never enjoy Daddy's company again on this earth; but I was glad that our parting is only temporary. One day we will all spend eternity together.

These words were a comfort and encouragement to me: "She [he] is not sent away, but only sent before; like unto a star, which, going out of our sight, doth not die and vanish, but shineth in another hemisphere: ye see her [him] not, yet she [he] doth shine in another country" (Samuel Rutherford).

When you die, will your family know they will see you again in Heaven?

April 6   **Psalm 38:13–22**

"For in thee, O LORD, do I hope: thou wilt hear, O Lord my God" (Psalm 38:15).

AN OLD-TIMER was once asked what his favorite Scripture verse was. He replied, "And it came to pass."

David's hope and confidence in God allowed him to be encouraged that this awful time in his life would not continue; this, too, would pass. "For in thee, O Lord, do I hope: thou wilt hear, O Lord my God" (v. 15).

How is hope strengthened? I don't know about you, but mine is strengthened by my confidence that God not only hears my prayers in the time of adversity, but that He will answer in His time and in His way. He has done it before; He will do it again.

God uses different ways and means to answer our prayers. Sometimes we do not see any evidence to encourage us that He has heard our prayers. Other times we see evidence that we know is answered prayer.

Why do we not always see the evidence that God is hearing and answering? I think He wants us to place our confidence in His Word and not in outward evidences. When we see the evidence of answered prayer, we will appreciate it even more after we have learned to trust Him without such evidence.

"Delays are not refusals; many a prayer is registered, and underneath it the words: 'My time is not yet come.' God has a set time as well as a set purpose, and He who orders the bounds of our habitation orders the time of our deliverance" (author unknown).

Are you learning to trust God without any visible evidence?

"I said, I will take heed to my ways, that I sin not with my tongue: I will keep my mouth with a bridle, while the wicked is before me" (Psalm 39:1).

DAVID said the only way he could keep from sinning with his mouth when his enemies were around was to put a bridle or muzzle on his mouth, which would keep him from speaking at all. "I said, I will take heed to my ways, that I sin not with my tongue: I will keep my mouth with a bridle, while the wicked is before me" (v. 1). David would look funny, but that would be less embarrassing than the words that would fly out of his mouth.

Sometimes unbelievers (and sometimes even Christians) aggravate us so much we can hardly control our emotions. Soon what we're feeling inside comes rolling off our tongues. Maybe we need to put a muzzle on our mouths when we are around people who agitate and provoke us. James 3:8 says, "But the tongue can no man tame; it is an unruly evil, full of deadly poison." If my mouth is full of deadly poison, I'd better quarantine it so the poison doesn't spill out on someone else.

I like this little thought: "Lord, fill my mouth with worthwhile stuff, And nudge me when I've said enough!"

Who agitates and aggravates you the most? Maybe you should wear an invisible muzzle on your mouth when you are around those people.

April 8

Psalm 39

"I was dumb, I opened not my mouth; because thou didst it" (Psalm 39:9).

WE DON'T often use the term "dumb" to refer to someone who cannot speak; the word we more commonly use is "mute." David said he would be mute or silent; he wouldn't complain about what was happening in his life because God did it. "I was dumb, I opened not my mouth; because thou didst it" (v. 9).

God is love, and love always seeks the best for its object. God will not allow any needless suffering. If we keep that in mind, we will not have hard thoughts toward God, even when His hand seems severe.

Why did God allow my father to suffer for a month in intensive care before He took him Home? I don't know why, and I don't need to know why. God was accomplishing His purpose in Daddy's life, not our plans and purposes.

One of the saints of old said, "What a reason for hushing every murmuring thought is the reflection, 'because thou didst it'! It is his right to do as he wills, and he always wills to do that which is wisest and kindest; why should I then arraign his dealings? Nay, if it be indeed the Lord, let him do what seemeth him good."

Can you see God's hand in the circumstances of your life and say "thou didst it"?

"And he hath put a new song in my mouth, even praise unto our God: many shall see it,
and fear, and shall trust in the LORD" (Psalm 40:3).

AS DAVID reflected on what God had done for him (vv. 1, 2), he declared, "And he hath put a new song in my mouth, even praise unto our God: many shall see it, and fear, and shall trust in the LORD" (v. 3).

A music director in our church once said, "I can teach anyone to sing." I didn't want him to have his first failure, so I didn't sign up for lessons. When the Lord passed out talents, He did not include singing among mine. Maybe, just maybe, I could learn, but I've been satisfied to have a song in my heart and not embarrass myself by what might come out of my mouth.

If I have a song in my heart, eventually praise will come from my lips. This praise is not necessarily something people hear, but rather something they see. "Many shall see it, and fear, and shall trust in the LORD."

When I gave a tribute to my daddy at his funeral, my heart was filled with a song but my eyes were filled with tears. Through the tears, I prayed that the many unsaved people who were there would see something different about my life and want to know the Savior Whom I know.

Has the Lord put a new song in your heart? Are you sharing it with others?

"Many, O LORD my God, are thy wonderful works which thou hast done, and thy thoughts which are to us-ward: they cannot be reckoned up in order unto thee: if I would declare and speak of them, they are more than can be numbered" (Psalm 40:5).

MANY, O LORD my God, are thy wonderful works which thou hast done . . . they are more than can be numbered." David spoke these words, but they could also have been spoken by Job. Job experienced great loss and affliction (Job 1:13—2:8), but he is remembered for his great patience ("Ye have heard of the patience of Job" [James 5:11]).

When his wife said, "Curse God, and die," Job answered, "What? shall we receive good at the hand of God, and shall we not receive evil?" (Job 2:9, 10). As time went on and Job's three friends (better known as "miserable comforters") kept insinuating his trials were a result of sin in his life, Job began to question God. "Surely I would speak to the Almighty, and I desire to reason with God" (Job 13:3).

But God never gave Job answers. Instead, He asked Job if he thought he could do a better job of running the universe and keeping things in order (Job 38—41). Finally Job just stood in awe of all God's works and said, "I know that thou canst do every thing . . . things too wonderful for me, which I knew not. . . . I have heard of thee by the hearing of the ear: but now mine eye seeth thee" (Job 42:2–5).

The hard things in our lives should deepen our character and cause us to cry, "Many, O LORD my God, are thy wonderful works . . . they are more than can be numbered."

When was the last time you stood in awe of God's wonderful works rather than questioning His work in your life?

"I am poor and needy; yet the Lord thinketh upon me: thou art my help and my deliverer; make no tarrying, O my God" (Psalm 40:17).

DAVID was feeling low and disheartened because of his sin. In verse 12 he said his sins were more than the hairs on his head. Just the thought of this nearly caused his heart to fail. "I am poor and needy; yet the Lord thinketh upon me: thou art my help and my deliverer; make no tarrying, O my God" (v. 17). David was down, but he was not out because He knew God was his help and deliverer.

My mother may have felt poor and needy after my daddy's death. She was faced with a whole new way of life. She was poorer than she was before. Not only did she lose her husband, but her income was not as much as it was before his death. She was needy. Who was going to do all the things her husband did? Things like mow the lawn, rake the leaves, fix the car.

She may have felt poor and needy, but she wasn't! "The Lord thinketh upon me [on her]: thou art my [her] help and my [her] deliverer."

We never have to feel we are alone. Our Heavenly Father, Who is close at hand, is always thinking about us. What is He thinking about? Jeremiah 29:11 gives us one answer: "I know the thoughts that I think toward you, saith the LORD, thoughts of peace, and not of evil, to give you an expected end." Another translation of "an expected end" is "a future and a hope."

We may feel poor and needy, but we never have to feel hopeless. God's thoughts for our future are full of hope. Does that fill you with hope?

"Yea, mine own familiar friend, in whom I trusted, which did eat of my bread, hath lifted up his heel against me" (Psalm 41:9).

LA FONTAINE said, "Rare is true love; true friendship is still rarer." Queen Elizabeth said, "In trust, I have found treason." "Friends," said Socrates; "there is no friend." David was not the only one who had a friend turn on him. "Yea, mine own familiar friend, in whom I trusted, which did eat of my bread, hath lifted up his heel against me" (v. 9) The Lord Jesus applied this Scripture to Himself on the eve of Judas's betrayal (John 13:18).

Most of us, at some time or another, have had a friend knock us down and stomp on us. What causes someone whom you once loved and trusted to turn on you? Usually the root problem can be traced to selfishness on the part of one or both persons. How can two people who were best friends, or even marriage partners, end up being enemies? Selfishness began to spread like a cancer, and eventually love turned into hatred.

Have you lost confidence in people? Do you need a friend who will never turn on you? "There is a friend that sticketh closer than a brother" (Proverbs 18:24). Jesus knows everything about us, and yet He still loves us. He sticks with us through every situation. In Him our hearts find companionship, confidence, acceptance—all the blessings of a faithful friend.

Have you made Jesus your closest friend?

"Why art thou cast down, O my soul? and why art thou disquieted in me?" (Psalm 42:5).

DAVID was passing through a dark valley of despondency. His soul was fixed on God, but his mind and body were feeling the awful effects of depression and despair.

Have you been there? If not, you may pass through this valley someday. It seems God wanted to emphasize this common weakness of man because this verse is repeated three times: Psalms 42:5 and 11 and 43:5. "Why art thou cast down, O my soul? and why art thou disquieted in me?"

The only ray of light in David's darkness was his confidence that the Lord loved him and would help him.

When we feel down and despondent, we need to do what David did: ask ourselves "why?" Why do I feel so down and discour- aged? Why do I feel no rest or peace? Is it my sin or someone else's sin that is troubling me?

I once heard someone say, "A mother is only as happy as her unhappiest child." I've experienced that; when my children hurt, I hurt. I have also found that the misfortunes of this world (e.g., poor health, loss of a loved one, lack of material possessions) can cause despondency.

What is the cure for despondency? Trust in God for the present and the future. "If the clouds do not disperse until the dark river be past, yet you may walk by God's voice though you see not His face" (author unknown).

Can you trust God to see you through the hard times?

"Hope thou in God: for I shall yet praise him, who is the health of my countenance, and my God" (Psalm 42:11).

DO YOU ever talk to yourself? Maybe you've done something dumb and then asked yourself, "Why did I do that?" I talk to myself quite often.

David may have been in a pit of depression when he wrote this psalm. He asked himself, "Why am I so down? Why is my soul in such turmoil?" (vv. 5, 11).

How did he get out of the pit? He started talking to himself. He might have said something like this, "Soul, I want you to listen to me. You've been whining and moaning long enough. It hasn't solved anything. You've been down long enough. It is time for us to move on." Then he gave his soul an order: "Hope thou in God: for I shall yet praise him, who is the health of my countenance, and my God" (v. 11).

Are you in the pit of depression? Do you need to talk to yourself a little? Do you need to tell yourself to "hope in God"? If you will begin to look at the greatness of your God and remember all His attributes and abilities instead of your failures and troubles, you can begin to move upward. However, it will take an act of your will. Tell God what you are feeling in your soul; say it out loud. Then with your mouth praise Him that He is greater than all your problems. That's what David did.

"Hope thou in God: for I shall yet praise him, who is the health of my countenance, and my God." Nothing brings healing to your countenance like praising God.

Remember, where there is a will there is a way! By an act of your will and with the help of God, get up and move on.

"For thou art the God of my strength: why dost thou cast me off? why go I mourning because of the oppression of the enemy?" (Psalm 43:2).

PSALMS 42 and 43 picture a lonely, despondent man. David felt God had forsaken him: "For thou art the God of my strength: why dost thou cast me off? why go I mourning because of the oppression of the enemy?" (43:2).

The psalmist honestly admitted that he felt restless and insecure. As we look at David's situation, we might feel he had a right to feel lonely and despondent. The ungodly had accused him unjustly (v. 1). David wanted God to vindicate him and prove his innocence. But while he was waiting, he was in turmoil.

Depression and despondency fill a person's heart and mind with all kinds of feelings and emotions. I think a feeling of loneliness might be at the top of the list. Often this loneliness is self-inflicted. Depressed people usually withdraw themselves from other people and sometimes from God. In their lonely state they just keep mulling over and over the difficult circumstance causing the hurt and pain in their lives. These thoughts just keep going round and round in their minds. The more they dwell on their painful circumstances, the more they tend to withdraw.

God could find many reasons why He might cast us off, but—praise God!—He doesn't. We pull away from Him; He doesn't pull away from us. Even though you may feel like a castaway, God never casts off His children. "All that the Father giveth me shall come to me; and him that cometh to me I will in no wise cast out" (John 6:37).

Do you feel forsaken by God? Don't believe your feelings. You have His promise: you're not forsaken!

"We have heard with our ears, O God, our fathers have told us, what work thou didst in their days, in the times of old" (Psalm 44:1).

THIS PSALM is reminiscent of "the good old days" of triumph and victory. "We have heard with our ears, O God, our fathers have told us, what work thou didst in their days, in the times of old" (v. 1). God's favor on His children in the past gave the psalmist great hope for the future.

Jewish parents often shared with their children all the great things their God had done for them. It was the story of one miracle after another: God delivered the Israelites from Egyptian bondage; He opened the Red Sea so they could walk through on dry ground; He led them and fed them in the wilderness; He gave them victories over their enemies and continued to care for them.

After my daddy's funeral, my mother's house was filled with relatives. It was fun listening to them reminisce about "the good old days" and the things they did with Daddy.

God wants us to learn from our parents, grandparents, and the senior citizens we know. If we are wise, we will listen and learn from their failures and successes. Henry Ford once said, "Anyone who stops learning is old, whether at twenty or eighty. Anyone who keeps learning stays young."

Are you getting old before your time? What new things are you learning about godly living that will stretch your mind and your faith?

"All this is come upon us; yet have we not forgotten thee, neither have we dealt falsely in thy covenant" (Psalm 44:17).

IN THIS psalm of national lament, the people remembered what God had done in the past (vv. 1–3) and affirmed their faith in Him in the present. The people had been afflicted and distressed, yet they never gave up on God. "All this is come upon us; yet have we not forgotten thee, neither have we dealt falsely in thy covenant" (v. 17). They fought in the name of the Lord, the One Who had made a covenant with them.

Have you ever thought about what the ancient saints endured for serving Christ? They were thrown into lions' dens, burned at the stake, beheaded, drowned in the sea, and imprisoned. Continuing to the present day, men and women alike have been given courage to live and die for their Lord.

Betty Scott Stam was one of those women. In 1934 Betty and her husband were beheaded by the Communists in China. Betty watched as her husband was killed; then she knelt down and was beheaded.

How could she do that? She never forgot the commitment she had made to Christ nine years before. This was her prayer: "Lord, I give up all my own purposes and plans, all my own desires and hopes and ambitions (whether they be fleshly or soulish) and accept Thy will for my life. I give myself, my life, my all utterly to Thee, to be Thine forever. I hand over to Thy keeping all of my friendships; all the people whom I love are to take a second place in my heart. Fill me and seal me with Thy Holy Spirit. Work out Thy whole will in my life, at any cost, now and forever. To me to live is Christ."

Could you pray that prayer to the Lord?

"Shall not God search this out? for he knoweth the secrets of the heart" (Psalm 44:21).

THE PSALMIST stated a truth that is often repeated in Scripture: We can't hide from God, nor can we hide our sin from God; He knows us inside out. "Shall not God search this out? for he knoweth the secrets of the heart" (v. 21). (See Psalm 139; Jeremiah 17:10; Acts 1:24; Hebrews 4:13.)

Often when God brings trials into our lives, our first question is "Why, Lord?" We need to search our hearts to find the answer to that question. God may not reveal to us what He wants to accomplish through the trial, but we can know why He has sent the trial. We can ask ourselves two questions: Is this a chastening for known sin in my life? Is this a trial to stretch my faith? Usually you know the answer—and so does God.

Thomas Watson said, "A godly man dares not sin secretly. He knows that God sees in secret. As God cannot be deceived by our subtlety, so He cannot be excluded by our secrecy."

Did you really think you could hide something from God?

"My heart is inditing a good matter: I speak of the things which I have made touching the king: my tongue is the pen of a ready writer" (Psalm 45:1).

PSALM 45 is "a song of loves." "My heart is inditing a good matter: I speak of the things which I have made touching the king: my tongue is the pen of a ready writer" (v. 1) The psalmist is saying, "My heart is full and overflowing with many beautiful thoughts. I will write a letter to my king, and the words will just come pouring out."

Have you ever written a love letter to your sweetheart? Did you have a hard time knowing what to say? If your heart is full and overflowing with love, this love will easily flow from your mouth in spoken words and from your heart in written words.

Have you ever written a love letter to the King of Kings, our Lord and Savior, Jesus Christ? I don't think I have ever actually written a love letter to Him, but I do tell Him daily that I love Him. I know this pleases Him, but it pleases Him even more when I demonstrate my love for Him by the way I live.

Jesus said, "Thou shalt love the Lord thy God with all thy heart, and with all thy soul, and with all thy mind. This is the first and great commandment" (Matthew 22:37, 38). If the greatest commandment is to love the Lord with all our heart, soul, and mind, then the greatest sin would be not to love the Lord with all our heart, soul, and mind.

How much do you love the Lord? Have you told Him lately?

"Thou lovest righteousness, and hatest wickedness" (Psalm 45:7).

PSALM 45 is a royal psalm that talks about the wedding of the king. The king, Jesus Christ, is not neutral when it comes to right and wrong, righteousness and wickedness. As much as He loves the one, He hates the other. "Thou lovest righteousness, and hatest wickedness" (v. 7).

If I am to be Christlike, I need to follow His example, both in love and hate. I do not find it difficult to hate wickedness, but I do have difficulty loving the wicked person. Christ wants us to hate wickedness and wicked actions; He does not want us to hate wicked people. "Love your enemies, bless them that curse you, do good to them that hate you, and pray for them which despitefully use you, and persecute you" (Matthew 5:44). That's a large order to fill!

How can we love the sinner but hate his sin? We must look beyond his fault and see his need. Wicked actions usually come from hurting people. George Sweeting gave a good description of many hurting people, "Frustration, loneliness, self-pity, indifference, emptiness, hostility, hatred, closeheartedness, resentment, jealousy, and the resultant criminal acts, all grow like wild weeds to fill the holes gouged in our hearts when nobody seems to care."

God's kind of love as described in 1 Corinthians 13:4–8 is unconditional love. If we want to demonstrate God's kind of love, we must love the unlovely, no matter how they treat us.

Are you following Christ's example in love and hate?

"I will make thy name to be remembered in all generations: therefore shall the people praise thee for ever and ever" (Psalm 45:17).

WHEN Psalm 45 is interpreted prophetically (i.e., as a messianic psalm), we see that the fame of Messiah is not left for men to guard and guarantee. The eternal God guarantees it! "I [God] will make thy [Messiah's] name to be remembered in all generations: therefore shall the people praise thee for ever and ever" (v. 17).

The name of Jesus is always fresh and exciting to those who hear it for the first time; it should become even dearer to those who have known it from one generation to the next. Christ continues to glow as a bright light in a dark world. His memory will never grow dim.

One of the things I remember most about my daddy is that he ended well, loving his Savior and living for Him. "I will make thy name to be remembered in all generations."

Will God's name be remembered by the next generation when your family, friends, children, and grandchildren talk about your life? Will they be able to say you ended well and kept the faith?

If you haven't been living for Christ, it is not too late to start. Life is made up of new beginnings. It is not how we start but how we finish that people will remember.

"Every day is a fresh beginning;
Listen, my soul, to the glad refrain,
And spite of old sorrow and older sinning,
And puzzles forecasted and possible pain,
Take heart with the day, and begin again"

(SUSAN COOLIDGE).

Do you need to make a new start so you can end well?

"God is our refuge and strength, a very present help in trouble" (Psalm 46:1).

PSALM 46 celebrates God as the defender of His people. The psalmist encouraged the people to trust God in the worst of times and troubles, even when they didn't know whether they were coming or going. "God is our refuge and strength, a very present help in trouble" (v. 1).

When I just don't think I can handle any more difficulty, God often reminds me He does not remove the obstacles in my path until I reach them; He does not give help until help is needed; He doesn't make the path ahead clear until I take the first step into the journey. But when I take that first step, He gives me the help and strength I need to keep going. Let me encourage you: Don't be afraid to take that first step! God will be your "refuge and strength."

When difficult times come, I often think of something Corrie Ten Boom's father told her when she was a child and spoke of her fear that he might die. " 'Corrie,' he began gently, 'when you and I go to Amsterdam—when do I give you your ticket?' I sniffed a few times, considering this. 'Why, just before we get on the train.' 'Exactly. And our wise Father in heaven knows when we're going to need things, too. Don't run out ahead of Him, Corrie. When the time comes that some of us will have to die, you will look into your heart and find the strength you need—just in time' " (*The Hiding Place*).

We need not fear the future. God is our refuge, strength, and helper; the ticket will be there. Do you believe that? I do!

"Therefore will not we fear, though the earth be removed, and though the mountains be carried into the midst of the sea" (Psalm 46:2).

THE PSALMIST was so sure of God's help and His presence that he could say, "Therefore will not we fear, though the earth be removed, and though the mountains be carried into the midst of the sea" (v. 2).

A saint of old once said, "With God on our side, how irrational would fear be! . . . Let worst come to worst, the child of God should never give way to mistrust; since God remaineth faithful there can be no danger to his cause or people. . . . Alps and Andes may tremble, but faith rests on a firmer basis, and is not to be moved by swelling seas."

Oh, how I long for that kind of faith and confidence in God when my whole world seems to be falling apart. My biggest fear is usually facing forward saying, "What if?" I can think of a hundred "what ifs" when I am filled with fear instead of faith. I don't always do it, but I'm learning to say, "So what if it does happen? It's okay! If God sends it, He'll also send me the grace and strength to bear it."

"Passive faith but praises in the light,
When sun doth shine.
Active faith will praise in darkest night—
Which faith is thine?"

"God is in the midst of her; she shall not be moved: God shall help her, and that right early"
(Psalm 46:5).

PSALM 46:5 is a great assurance to those of us who make up the church, the Body of Christ. God will never forsake us. "God is in the midst of her; she shall not be moved: God shall help her, and that right early." We have a similar promise in Matthew 16:18: "Upon this rock [Christ] I will build my church; and the gates of hell shall not prevail against it."

You have probably heard of the courage and boldness Martin Luther displayed during the Reformation. However, Luther had his down times as well. It is said that when these hours would come, Luther would say to his friend, "Come, Philip, let us sing the forty-sixth psalm." Martin Luther left this song for us to sing today:

"Did we in our own strength confide
Our striving would be losing,
Were not the right Man on our side,
The Man of God's own choosing.
Dost ask who that may be?
Christ Jesus, it is He—
Lord Sabaoth His name,
From age to age the same,
And He must win the battle."

When the storms come, I may sway but I won't sink because my faith is built on a solid foundation, Jesus Christ, the Rock of Ages, the One Who will win the battle.

Are you swaying, sinking, or standing firm on the Rock?

"Be still, and know that I am God: I will be exalted among the heathen, I will be exalted in the earth" (Psalm 46:10).

THE LORD speaks, "Be still, and know that I am God: I will be exalted among the heathen, I will be exalted in the earth" (v. 10).

Verses 8–10 describe God's triumph at the end of the age. He will be exalted in all His glory and majesty. The world will be still and know that God is God. He is all that will matter in the end.

One day a little boy about three years old was seated behind me on an airplane. Every now and then his mother would say, "Shhh, be still." About thirty minutes from our scheduled arrival time, she said, "We'll be home in just a few minutes." Soon after that, the pilot announced there was a thunderstorm in Tampa and we would be in a holding pattern for fifteen to twenty minutes. The little boy became more and more restless and finally just let out a big scream. I looked at the man seated next to me, and we both smiled. I said, "I feel like screaming too, don't you?" He nodded his head in agreement.

When we are faced with interruptions, aggravations, and detours, we often feel like screaming and running from our problems. God says, "Be still." Psalm 46:2 and 3 speak of earthquakes, floods, and all kind of disasters. In that context God tells us to "Be still."

Why "be still"? So we can get to know God in a more intimate way. Relationships don't start on an intimate level; they develop with time. The more time we spend with the Lord, the more intimate our relationship will become. "Shhh, be still; get to know God better."

How much time do you spend being still in God's presence?

"He shall choose our inheritance for us, the excellency of Jacob whom he loved"
(Psalm 47:4).

GOD CHOSE the portion of land the Israelites should have for their inheritance. "He shall choose our inheritance for us, the excellency of Jacob whom he loved" (v. 4). But their most valuable treasure was not the land the Lord gave them but the Lord Himself, Who loved them and promised to care for them.

An inheritance is something someone else chooses for us and gives to us. After the death of my father, I spent a couple of weeks with my mother. During that visit, she took me through the house and read from a list that identified which of her possessions were to be mine when she died. She told me what she had chosen for my inheritance.

The inheritance God has chosen for us is beyond anything we can even imagine. Peter described it this way: "Blessed be the God and Father of our Lord Jesus Christ, which according to his abundant mercy hath begotten us again unto a lively hope by the resurrection of Jesus Christ from the dead, To an inheritance incorruptible, and undefiled, and that fadeth not away, reserved in heaven for you" (1 Peter 1:3, 4).

When I receive my inheritance from my mother, it will eventually perish. But I look forward to an inheritance that will never perish. It has my name on it. God has reserved it just for me! I'm an heir of God and a joint-heir with Jesus Christ (Romans 8:17).

I don't know about you, but I'm looking forward to claiming my heavenly inheritance!

"God is gone up with a shout, the LORD with the sound of a trumpet" (Psalm 47:5).

THIS PSALM, a hymn to our great King, gives us a vivid picture of the excitement of worship. It was written to stir up praise to God for His majesty, sovereignty, and wondrous works. The Old Testament saints allowed themselves to be caught up in worship to their King. "God is gone up with a shout, the LORD with the sound of a trumpet" (v. 5).

When Jesus Christ, God made flesh, came to earth the first time, the angels announced His birth with shouts of joy and sang, "Glory to God in the highest" (Luke 2:14). When He ascended back into Heaven from the Mount of Olives, there were no angels singing or trumpets blowing on earth. But no doubt the angels welcomed Him back to Heaven with shouts of joy.

In Bible times victorious soldiers returned home to shouts of joy and trumpets playing.

When Christ returned to Heaven, His battle on earth was over; the victory was won. All people could now be set free from Satan's bondage and power. The angels must have rejoiced!

One day our battle on this earth will be over, and the Lord will descend from Heaven with a shout and the sound of the trump of God (1 Thessalonians 4:16). The Bible doesn't tell us what He will shout, but I wonder if maybe He will say, "The battle's over, the victory is won, and I'm taking you home now!"

When the battles of life are raging, don't give up. We may lose a battle now and then, but we know we will win the war.

I've read the last page of the Book! Have you?

"Great is the LORD, and greatly to be praised in the city of our God, in the mountain of his holiness" (Psalm 48:1).

THE PSALMIST starts this psalm praising God for His greatness: "Great is the LORD, and greatly to be praised in the city of our God, in the mountain of his holiness" (v. 1). He ends the psalm with praise to God for His guidance (v. 14). The greatness of God is more than our minds can conceive.

Our Jehovah God is so great He cannot be described with just one name. He has many names. Here are some of them:

Jehovah-nissi—The Lord My Banner;

Jehovah-jireh—The Lord Will Provide;

Jehovah-shalom—The Lord Is Peace;

Jehovah-sabaoth—The Lord of Hosts;

Jehovah-rapha—The Lord That Heals;

Jehovah-shammah—The Lord Is There;

Jehovah-tsidkenu—The Lord Our Righteousness.

God's names represent His character, attributes, and nature. Our great God longs for us to know Him better so we can trust Him to meet our needs. Do you know God well enough to trust Him? Look at His names again. He is everything You will ever need; He is your all-sufficient God.

How great is God in your eyes? How great is your God in the eyes of those who are watching your life?

"We have thought of thy lovingkindness, O God, in the midst of thy temple" (Psalm 48:9).

THE PSALMIST pondered God's loving-kindness, His unfailing love: "We have thought of thy lovingkindness, O God, in the midst of thy temple" (v. 9). God's loving-kindness could best be described by the word *agape* in the New Testament. *Agape* loves no matter what, no strings attached. The psalmist was thankful that God's love was unconditional and persistent.

"His love has no limit, His grace has no
    measure,
His power no boundary known unto men;
For out of His infinite riches in Jesus,
He giveth and giveth and giveth again."

This beautiful poem by Annie Johnson Flint, which has been set to music, reminds me of the loving-kindness of God. These words also remind me of Jeremiah 31:3: "I have loved thee with an everlasting love: therefore with lovingkindness have I drawn thee."

Yes, God's love has no limit, His grace has no measure. His love for me is everlasting and unconditional. He loves me when I am good, and He loves me when I am bad. Oh, what loving-kindness!

We need to meditate on God's loving-kindness in order for the magnitude of it to affect our lives.

Have you stopped long enough lately to think about God's loving-kindness to you? Why not do a little meditating right now?

"For this God is our God for ever and ever: he will be our guide even unto death"
(Psalm 48:14).

THE ISRAELITES knew their God would not change His mind! He would keep His covenant with His people; He would be their God to the end. "For this God is our God for ever and ever: he will be our guide even unto death" (v. 14). He had guided them from the beginning; He would guide them to the end.

Can you say of any of your possessions, "This will be mine for ever"? Houses and other material goods can be here today and gone tomorrow. A spouse can promise to live with you until death, and then change his mind. Blood relationships cannot be annulled on earth (my parents will always be my parents; my children will always be my children), but even these relationships can be emotionally and physically severed.

Only one relationship is eternal: our relationship with Jesus Christ. His blood was shed for us on the cross so that we might become His children through faith in the sacrifice He made for us (John 1:12). When we accept Christ's payment for our sin, we have a Person to help us and strengthen us in our journey on earth. He will be our guide even unto death.

I can guide my children for only a few years. God guides me forever and ever. I never walk alone; He walks beside me—even through the valley of the shadow of death (Psalm 23:4).

Will you let Him be your guide—even unto death?

"They that trust in their wealth, and boast themselves in the multitude of their riches;
None of them can by any means redeem his brother, nor give to God a ransom for him"
(Psalm 49:6, 7).

THIS PSALM pictures the people of the world who put their trust in their wealth. They need nothing else, not even God. Rich people have a tendency to believe money can buy them anything they need. Many of these people, who thought they were going to Heaven because of all the money they gave to God, will find themselves in Hell. They trust in their wealth and boast of their riches, yet no one, though rich as a king, can ransom himself or his brother from the penalty of sin. "They that trust in their wealth, and boast themselves in the multitude of their riches; None of them can by any means redeem his brother, nor give to God a ransom for him" (vv. 6, 7). The Lord Jesus said, "It is easier for a camel to go through the eye of a needle, than for a rich man to enter into the kingdom of God" (Mark 10:25).

Many years ago Queen Elizabeth I of England found out—too late—that her riches could not ransom her soul. As she lay on her deathbed, she cried out, "All my possessions for one moment of time!" She had two thousand costly dresses in her wardrobe, but they were valueless when she cried out for "one moment of time." Her seventy years had been devoted to wealth and pleasure, pride and ambition. Her preparation for eternity was crowded into a few minutes. She was willing to give up everything for just one more "moment of time."

In what are you trusting: material riches or the finished work of Christ?

132

"For he seeth that wise men die, likewise the fool and the brutish person perish,
and leave their wealth to others" (Psalm 49:10).

THE PSALMIST reminds us of something we already know: the accumulation of wealth does not guarantee happiness or immortality. The wise and the wealthy—with all their brains, money, and management skills—cannot outwit death. It will come to them the same as it comes to the poor and foolish who have no skills or craftiness. The fool has nothing to leave others at death, and the wise leaves everything he has to others whether he wants to or not. "For he seeth that wise men die, likewise the fool and the brutish person perish, and leave their wealth to others" (v. 10).

I dare say you have never seen a funeral hearse pulling a U-Haul truck behind it. Neither have I! We brought nothing into this world, and we shall take nothing with us when we leave. The wealthy Astor family was reminded of this some years ago. When one of the family members died, the eager relatives were waiting to hear the reading of the will. They asked the lawyer, "How much did he leave?" "He left it all," was the lawyer's reply. He did not take anything with him.

How would you finish this statement: For me, real living is . . . ? If your answer is anything other than living for Christ, then death will be loss for you. Paul said, "For to me to live is Christ, and to die is gain" (Philippians 1:21). The only way death will be gain for us is if Christ is the center of our lives.

Will death be gain or loss for you?

"For every beast of the forest is mine, and the cattle upon a thousand hills" (Psalm 50:10).

A FAMILIAR chorus says, "He owns the cattle on a thousand hills, The wealth in ev'ry mine; He owns the rivers and the rocks and rills, The sun and stars that shine. . . ." Asaph the psalmist recorded, "For every beast of the forest is mine, and the cattle upon a thousand hills" (v. 10).

Since God already owned all the cattle, why did He require bullocks, lambs, and other animals as sacrifices in the Old Testament? The blood of these animals was a covering for the people's sins until the perfect Lamb, Jesus Christ, shed His blood on Calvary.

God required these sacrifices, but He also required that they be offered in the right spirit. Sometimes the people offered their sacrifices because of tradition rather than because of heart obedience. First Samuel 15:22 says, ". . . To obey is better than sacrifice, and to hearken than the fat of rams."

Does your inward obedience match up with your outward performance? Answer these questions carefully and prayerfully: Am I really what I appear to be and ought to be? Are the secrets of my heart of such quality I would be willing for others to see them? Is my heart and soul at all like what my most intimate friends believe? Would I be fearful to stand before the Searcher of Hearts, the Lord Jesus, to be judged for my heart obedience today?

We need to pray daily, "Search me, O God, and know my heart: try me, and know my thoughts" (Psalm 139:23).

Is God pleased with your inward obedience as well as your outward performance?

"And call upon me in the day of trouble: I will deliver thee, and thou shalt glorify me"
(Psalm 50:15).

THE PSALMIST, Asaph, was familiar with the promises of God, and no doubt this was one he claimed often: "And call upon me in the day of trouble: I will deliver thee, and thou shalt glorify me" (v. 15).

Our troubles are from God. Does that statement shock you? Nothing touches our lives that God does not allow. Our troubles should draw us closer to God, not push us away from Him. "Call upon me in the day of trouble." God didn't say, "If you have trouble"; He said, "In the day of trouble." We are all called upon to pass through various troubles in our journey here on earth. Those troubles take lots of different forms: ailing bodies, inward conflicts, marital problems, rebellious children, unfaithful friends, slanderous accusations, tormenting fears, financial reverses, and the loss of a loved one. If you haven't faced some of these troubles yet, you will.

We are all familiar with 800 toll-free telephone numbers. God also has a toll-free number, and it is never busy. His number is 1-800-PSA-5015 (Psalm 50:15), "And call upon me in the day of trouble."

In the hour of trouble we usually run to those we love. Do you run to God first or last? God has promised to deliver us, but we must remember it will be in His time and in His way so He will get the glory.

Have you used God's toll-free number lately?

"Seeing thou hatest instruction, and casteth my words behind thee" (Psalm 50:17).

ISRAEL was living in full-fledged disobedience to God. While the people were verbally agreeing with the Law, in reality they were breaking it. "Seeing thou hatest instruction, and casteth my words behind thee" (v. 17). They condoned adultery (v. 18), spoke evil (v. 19), and defended dishonesty (v. 19).

The ungodly who live by the wisdom of this world do not want to listen to God's Word. "The Bible is outdated and irrelevant for this day and age," they say. Such people hate God's instruction and cast it aside as useless.

The homosexual community cannot believe God really means it when He says, "For this cause God gave them up unto vile [shameful] affections: for even their women did change the natural use into that which is against nature: And likewise also the men,

leaving the natural use of the woman, burned in their lust one toward another; men with men working that which is unseemly. . . . Who knowing the judgment of God, that they which commit such things are worthy of death, not only do the same, but have pleasure in them that do them" (Romans 1:26, 27, 32).

Are we, as believers, ever guilty of hating God's instructions and casting His Word behind us, trying to ignore what we know we should do? I think so! Have you heard another believer say, "I know what the Bible teaches, but. . . ?"

Have you ever said that? Is it not brazen impudence when we start picking and choosing what parts of God's Word we want to obey?

"Whoso offereth praise glorifieth me: and to him that ordereth his conversation aright will I shew the salvation of God" (Psalm 50:23).

THE JEWS spoken to in this psalm imagined that their ritualistic practices would hide from God the multitude of sins in which they were involved. They needed to choose to live right and glorify God with their speech and their lives. "Whoso offereth praise glorifieth me: and to him that ordereth his conversation [conduct] aright will I shew the salvation of God" (v. 23).

God is not glorified by our murmurings and complainings and fears. God is glorified by our praise. Sometimes true praise will be a sacrifice, an offering to God. We will give up what we want to do (murmur and complain) and offer God praise instead.

First Thessalonians 5:18 says, "In every thing give thanks: for this is the will of God in Christ Jesus concerning you." In *everything* praise God. "Whoso offereth praise glorifieth me."

Do you feel like you are "going from the frying pan into the fire" and the heat in your life is getting too intense? Praise Him that through this experience you can come forth as gold (Job 23:10).

Do you feel like you can't wait much longer to see what God is going to do in your crisis situation? Praise God that His strength can be renewed in your life each day as you wait (Isaiah 40:31).

Does it seem your trials will never end? Praise Him for the patience you can learn through your trials (James 1:2–4).

Thanksgiving glorifies God. Thanksliving glorifies Him even more! Are you praising or pouting?

"For I acknowledge my transgressions: and my sin is ever before me" (Psalm 51:3).

NO SIN is too great for God to forgive! David vividly pictured himself as a man with "FORGIVEN" stamped across his life.

David committed adultery with Bathsheba and then had her husband, Uriah, killed to cover up for his sin (2 Samuel 11:1—12:23). David was truly sorry for his sin and confessed it to God. "For I acknowledge my transgressions: and my sin is ever before me" (v. 3). David knew his sin had dishonored God and hurt many other people. Yet God mercifully forgave David because he repented of his sin.

Do you feel God could never forgive you for what you have done? Have you committed murder? Have you committed adultery? David did! Is your sin greater than David's? I have good news for you: NO SIN IS TOO GREAT FOR GOD TO FORGIVE!

God will forgive any sin when confession comes from a truly repentant and contrite heart. The only thing God may not do is erase the consequences of that sin. You, like David, may have to live with the results of your sin the rest of your life. However, you can live as a free person. You are no longer in bondage to that sin, dragging it around wherever you go.

The New Testament records nothing of David's sin. He is remembered by God, not for his moral failure, but as "a man after mine [God's] own heart" (Acts 13:22).

The sin man uncovers and confesses, God covers and forgives; the sin man covers and hides, God uncovers and judges.

❖

Do you need forgiveness? Why not ask for it today?

"Have mercy upon me, O God, according to thy lovingkindness: according unto the multitude of thy tender mercies blot out my transgressions. Wash me throughly from mine iniquity, and cleanse me from my sin" (Psalm 51:1, 2).

DAVID did not shift the blame for his sin. Notice the words he used: "*my* transgressions," "*mine* iniquity," "*my* sin."

David did not shift the blame to Bathsheba or other circumstances. It was time to be honest with God. He knew God had seen every vile thing he had done. David was full of godly sorrow that led to repentance. "Have mercy upon me, O God, according to thy lovingkindness: according unto the multitude of thy tender mercies blot out my transgressions. Wash me throughly from mine iniquity, and cleanse me from my sin" (vv. 1, 2). David was also full of hope because He knew his God was a God of loving-kindness and mercy.

My heart is so grieved when I counsel with people who have messed up their lives with sin but who shift the blame for their sin from themselves to others. Sometimes it is a mate's fault for not giving the person the time and attention she needed. Sometimes parents are blamed because the person did not feel loved and accepted. Sometimes a person blames her circumstances or a job that is just too stressful. The list could go on and on.

If we want to enjoy the forgiveness David enjoyed, we must quit shifting the blame and start saying, "*my* transgressions," "*mine* iniquity," "*my* sins."

When you are full of godly sorrow that leads to repentance, you will enjoy God's loving-kindness and mercy. Are you ready to quit shifting the blame?

". . . Blot out my transgressions. Wash me throughly from mine iniquity, and cleanse me from my sin" (Psalm 51:1, 2).

BLOT OUT my transgressions. Wash me throughly from mine iniquity, and cleanse me from my sin" (vv. 1, 2). David used three words to picture the process of moving away from God: transgressions, iniquity, and sin.

In Hebrew (the original language of the Old Testament), "transgressions" can mean "rebellion"; "iniquity" can mean "make crooked"; "sin" can mean "led astray."

David knew the rules; he knew God's Word, but he chose to break the rules. He chose to transgress, to rebel against what he knew was right. The next step backward led to iniquity; he had to use crooked words and actions to cover up for his sin. The last step is plain old sin. The more David sinned, the more he was led astray, away from the commands of God.

Why do we call believers who live in sin "backsliders"? Because they have done just that—slid backward from God. They don't turn their backs on God; they walk backward, facing God, knowing exactly what they are doing. They sin because they choose to sin.

When you find yourself beginning to backslide, ask yourself this question, Am I willing to pay the price this sin may cost me? We must never forget the high cost of low living.

Are you moving forward, or are you sliding backward?

140

". . . My sin is ever before me" (Psalm 51:3).

PSALM 51 records the aftereffects of the saddest day in David's life. For a while, at least, after David's sin, he was confronted with it wherever he turned. He never walked on the roof of his house without remembering the day he saw Bathsheba bathing; he never lay on his bed without remembering lying there with Bathsheba; he never took a pen in his hand without remembering the fatal warrant he signed for Uriah's death.

"My sin is ever before me" (v. 3), said David. "I just can't forget what I did. How could I have ever done that? How could I have brought such dishonor to God, myself, Bathsheba, my people?"

You and I may not be able to enter into the horror of David's guilt, but we've all transgressed; we've all done things we knew we shouldn't do. Do you remember the guilt? I'm so thankful for a guilty conscience that makes me feel awful, that says to me, "You were wrong."

I once read that the conscience is a marvelous gift from God. It is like a window that lets in the light of His truth. When we sin, the window begins to get dirty, and not as much truth can filter through. Eventually, the window becomes so dirty that it no longer lets in the light of God's Word. The Bible calls this a defiled or seared conscience (1 Timothy 4:2; Titus 1:15).

It is springtime, window-washing time. Do you need to do some window washing in your soul so you can experience springtime in your heart?

"Against thee, thee only, have I sinned, and done this evil in thy sight: that thou mightest be justified when thou speakest, and be clear when thou judgest" (Psalm 51:4).

DAVID was forgiven, but he lived with the results of his sin the rest of his life. The Lord said, "Now therefore the sword shall never depart from thine house; because thou hast despised me. . . . Because by this deed thou hast given great occasion to the enemies of the LORD to blaspheme" (2 Samuel 12:10, 14).

David never complained and said, "Lord, You are unfair; the judgment is too severe." No, he felt the sentence was just and right. David openly confessed his sin so that God's name might be cleared when the judgment came. "Against thee, thee only, have I sinned, and done this evil in thy sight: that thou mightest be justified when thou speak-est, and be clear when thou judgest" (v. 4). David didn't want anyone saying, "God is unjust and unfair; He is cruel and mean to you."

Whatever trouble came, David knew he deserved it because he had knowingly sinned against God. It was as though David had said, "God, I know You are watching, but I'm going to do it anyway."

"A sin of infirmity may admit apology; a sin of ignorance may find out excuse; but a sin of defiance can find no defence," said Sir Richard Baker, and I say, "How true!"

Are you asking for God's judgment by your defiance?

"Purge me with hyssop, and I shall be clean: wash me, and I shall be whiter than snow"
(Psalm 51:7).

SEVEN times in Psalm 51 David pleaded for cleansing. He felt vile and dirty, as if his sin was a rotten odor to God's nostrils. Notice the expressions he used in describing his need for cleansing: "blot out"; "wash me"; "cleanse me"; "purge me"; "wash me"; "blot out"; "create in me a clean heart."

David was saying, "Wash me and keep washing me until I can stand myself; clean me from the inside out." He wanted to be "whiter than snow." "Purge me with hyssop, and I shall be clean: wash me, and I shall be whiter than snow" (v. 7).

Snow is white and clean all the way through, inside and out. Other things that are painted white may not be white underneath. David wanted to be clean inwardly and outwardly. He wanted to be clean before God and man.

I've never experienced it personally, but I've been told that being sprayed by a skunk is the most "stinkin" thing that can happen to a person. To get rid of the smell is a major undertaking. People don't even bother with their clothes; they just throw them away. Various "remedies" have been given for getting the smell off one's body.

What can wash away skunk odor? I don't know for sure. What can wash away our sin? The blood of Jesus Christ (1 John 1:7). God allowed His Son to die for our sins so He could offer us pardon, forgiveness, and cleansing when we confess our sins (1 John 1:9).

When we confess our sins, Christ wipes the slate clean. Is your slate clean?

"Create in me a clean heart, O God; and renew a right spirit within me" (Psalm 51:10).

DAVID had pleaded several times for God to wash him, cleanse him, or do whatever He had to do to clean him up. David wanted to be pure, unstained, and forgiven. In the cleansing process, God used some harsh "detergents." David probably felt like a limp rag; he needed restoration.

David prayed, "Create in me a clean heart, O God; and renew a right spirit within me" (v. 10). "It was there once, Lord; put it there again. Repair me, fix me so I'll have a right spirit before You now and forever. I don't ever want to go through this experience again." David's sin was great, but the depth of his confession was just as great. David learned his lesson; he hated his sin.

Years ago when my children were small, I used a product call "Rit." In those days I didn't have a clothes dryer, and the sun faded the colored clothes. The laundry detergents were also harsher, not gentle and mild like they are today. When the colored clothes started to look faded and washed out, I would dip them in the hot Rit mixture; their colors would be restored for a while.

To renew the color in my clothes, I followed a two-step formula: (1) wash clothes; (2) dip in Rit and rinse. The color was renewed.

God has a "renewing" formula also. (1) For cleansing: confess your sin (1 John 1:9). (2) For renewing: ask for it (Psalm 51:10).

Do you need to use the "renewing" formula?

"Cast me not away from thy presence; and take not thy holy spirit from me"
(Psalm 51:11).

COULD these solemn words have been going through David's mind: "But the Spirit of the LORD departed from Saul, and an evil spirit from the LORD troubled him" (1 Samuel 16:14)? God had departed from Saul, not because he fell into sin, but because he continued in his sin; not because he did wrong, but because he did not repent. Saul refused God's counsel and departed from God. Therefore, "the Spirit of the LORD departed from Saul."

David pleaded, "Do not leave me as You did Saul. 'Cast me not away from thy presence; and take not thy holy spirit from me' " (v. 11). David knew he had grieved the Holy Spirit, and God could justly say His Spirit would no longer strive with him or work upon him (Genesis 6:3).

Aren't you glad the Spirit of God does not come and go upon us today as He did in Old Testament days? Without the Holy Spirit, we would not have God's wisdom to lead and guide us; we would be left to our own foolish whims and desires. He is our strength. Without Him, we would have to depend upon our own human weaknesses to overcome the world, the flesh, and the Devil.

The moment we trusted Christ as Savior, the Holy Spirit took up permanent residence in our lives (John 14:16, 17; Romans 8:9). We can't lose the Holy Spirit's presence in our lives, but we can lose His power when we quench Him with our own self-will (1 Thessalonians 5:19).

Is the Holy Spirit presiding as well as residing in your life?

"Restore unto me the joy of thy salvation" (Psalm 51:12).

WHAT sin could a believer commit that would cause him to lose his salvation? Would it be adultery? No! Would it be murder? No! David committed both of these sins, and he didn't lose his salvation. What did he lose? The joy of his salvation.

No sin that we can commit can cause us to lose our salvation. If we have truly been born again, we cannot get unborn (John 3:3–7). If we have everlasting life (John 3:16), it is just what the word implies—everlasting; it cannot be terminated. We cannot lose our salvation, but we can lose our joy when sin breaks our fellowship with God. That's why David prayed, "Restore unto me the joy of thy salvation" (v. 12).

Fellowship with God is conditional. Living in sin cuts off fellowship with God. We lose our joy until we confess our sin (1 John 1:6, 9). Fellowship with others is conditional as well. When you offend a mate, a child, a friend, or anyone with your sin, you don't have fellowship with that person until you confess your sin and ask for forgiveness. Then the joy returns.

At this time of the year we especially think of mothers. How's your relationship with your mother? Do you need your joy restored with her? with God? with someone else? Restoration of joy comes by asking for forgiveness. Why not do it now?

". . . Uphold me with thy free spirit" (Psalm 51:12).

HAVE you ever felt you had died a thousand deaths or wished you could have? I'm sure David might have felt like that during that year or more when he carried his secret sin in his heart. But when Nathan the prophet confronted him with his sin, the secret surfaced; there was no more hiding, David stopped lying to God, to himself, and to others. He was guilty and he admitted it!

The last ounce of this sin had been extracted from David's life, and he was left with a feeling of weakness and helplessness. He needed strength beyond his strength. ". . . Uphold me with thy free spirit" (v. 12). He needed help to get going again; he couldn't make it on his own. In fact, he probably never wanted to try to make it on his own again. Having experienced the awful consequences of sin, he never wanted to try living in his own strength again.

Do you feel so weak you can hardly go on? Do you need help to get going again? The Lord will uphold you just like He did David. In fact, He can help us best when we are so weak we feel we can't make it on our own. God said to Paul, "My strength is made perfect in weakness" (2 Corinthians 12:9). When I turn loose and say, "I can't do it," that's when God can take over and do it.

Are you exchanging your weakness for God's strength (Isaiah 40:31)?

"Then will I teach transgressors thy ways; and sinners shall be converted unto thee"
(Psalm 51:13).

WHEN we're in the midst of a trial, we often have a hard time thinking clearly enough to understand what God is trying to accomplish in our lives. However, once the trial is behind us, we can usually look back and see what God was trying to teach us.

David had learned some valuable lessons in his "valley experience," and now he was ready to teach other transgressors what he had learned. "Then will I teach transgressors thy ways; and sinners shall be converted unto thee" (v. 13).

What might David have taught transgressors that would have converted them or turned them back to God? He might have taught them that sin is "seasonal." Hebrews 11:25 mentions "the pleasures of sin for a season." Sin's "fun" is only for a season, a few months, and then you pay the rest of the year, or, as David did, for the rest of your life.

I've learned many lessons as a result of my valley experiences, and I still have many more to learn if I want to keep moving toward the goal of Christlikeness. One thing I have learned is that God is a good teacher. He keeps on the same lesson until I learn it. If I don't pass the test the first time, I will face it again.

I'd like to learn the lesson the first time through, wouldn't you? It's no fun to repeat the course.

*"The sacrifices of God are a broken spirit: a broken and a contrite heart, O God,
thou wilt not despise" (Psalm 51:17).*

BEFORE a house is built, a tree must be "broken" to make logs. Before grain can be planted, the soil must be "broken" and beaten. This is the law of life in the natural realm, and it is the law of life in the spiritual realm as well.

God uses broken things, and He starts with a broken heart. No sacrifice could adequately cover David's deliberate, rebellious sin. He offered the only thing God would accept. "The sacrifices of God are a broken spirit: a broken and a contrite heart, O God, thou wilt not despise" (v. 17).

Many things are useless if they are broken, but not the heart of man. His heart is at its best when it is broken. Not until it is broken can it send forth its sweetest odor. (Read the account of Mary's breaking the perfume box in John 12:1–8.)

If you are broken by disappointment, by weakness or sickness, by loss or pain, by bereavement, do not despair. Broken things appear to us as tragedies, but to God they are opportunities to display His glory. We cast away broken things as junk; but God casts aside unbroken things as useless.

Have you realized your broken heart is an opportunity for spiritual growth?

"Why boastest thou thyself in mischief, O mighty man? the goodness of God endureth continually" (Psalm 52:1).

DO YOU have a friend or relative who seems to delight in hurting you? This person can stab you in the back and kick you in the stomach and almost boast in his or her mischief or malice. This person can somehow justify his/her actions and never apologize or even seem to feel guilty.

David had such a friend—Doeg, a mighty man, the chief over the servants of Saul. Doeg had a wicked and boastful tongue. (Read the account of David and Doeg in 1 Samuel 21 and 22.) David asked him this question, "Why boastest thou thyself in mischief, O mighty man? the goodness of God endureth continually" (v. 1).

Someone in my life has hurt me several times. It seems this person looks for any little word or action to use against me. How can I be victorious when I am the target of this person's hatred, jealousy, and bitterness? I must leave the matter in God's hands and not take matters into my hands. I must focus on God's goodness instead of man's meanness.

That's what David did. He said, "The goodness of God endureth continually." My loving Heavenly Father will always treat me right.

When others mistreat me, I'm learning to conquer my feelings of revenge and resentment with Matthew 5:44: "Love your enemies, bless them that curse you, do good to them that hate you, and pray for them which despitefully use you, and persecute you."

How do you respond to mistreatment? Ask God to help you apply Matthew 5:44.

"The tongue deviseth mischiefs; like a sharp razor, working deceitfully" (Psalm 52:2).

THIS PSALM was written to expose the treachery of a man named Doeg, who was a slanderer and deceiver (1 Samuel 21; 22). The tongue of this clever, self-serving man revealed his corrupt character. His tongue was used to bring disgrace to God and to destroy people. David said his tongue was as sharp as a razor. "Thy tongue deviseth mischiefs; like a sharp razor, working deceitfully" (v. 2).

Have you ever realized what a lethal weapon you carry around with you each day? It is hidden, and seldom do we realize how dangerous it is until someone is destroyed by it. What is this hidden, lethal weapon? The tongue!

The tongue is *subtle*—it "deviseth mischiefs." It is like a snake hidden in the grass, devising its plan of attack. The tongue is *malicious*—"like a sharp razor." It can prick like a needle or cut deep like a razor. The tongue is *cunning*—"working deceitfully." It is sly, crafty, and cunning in the ways it can deceive and destroy people.

James said, "The tongue is a fire, a world of iniquity: so is the tongue among our members, that it defileth the whole body, and setteth on fire the course of nature; and it is set on fire of hell" (James 3:6).

I don't know if you are for or against gun control, but we had all better be for "tongue control."

We either learn to control our tongues, or our tongues will control and destroy us and others. How is your "tongue control"?

"Lo, this is the man that made not God his strength; but trusted in the abundance of his riches, and strengthened himself in his wickedness" (Psalm 52:7).

WE COULD predict the end of the story for the person who "made not God his strength." It is described in Psalm 52:5, "God shall likewise destroy thee . . . and pluck thee out of thy dwelling place."

Doeg learned, too late, that great riches, obtained at the expense of destroying others, will not stop God's judgment. Doeg's ruin was inevitable; he put his trust in the wrong thing. "Lo, this is the man that made not God his strength; but trusted in the abundance of his riches, and strengthened himself in his wickedness" (v. 7).

When the storms of life come, when it looks like our whole world is falling apart, where do we put our confidence? Is it in our own self efforts? Is it in what our money can do for us? Or is our confidence in God?

We can predict the end of the story for the person who "made not God his strength," whose trust is in self effort or money. Read Matthew 7:26 and 27 to see the outcome for the foolish man: "And the floods came, and the winds blew and beat upon that house; and it fell: and great was the fall of it."

Have you made God your strength? When the storms of life come—and they will come!— will your end be that of the wise man or the foolish man? It is never too late to start building on a solid foundation!

"I will praise thee for ever, because thou hast done it: and I will wait on thy name; for it is good before thy saints" (Psalm 52:9).

WHAT a contrast we see in this psalm between Doeg, the wicked man, and David, the righteous man; Doeg, the traitor, and David, the man of faith. David could praise the Lord for what He had done for him: "I will praise thee for ever, because thou hast done it: and I will wait on thy name; for it is good before thy saints" (v. 9).

"God did it!" With a voice of excitement and joy, my friend shared with me what God had done for her. She is a single mother with financial problems. As she left for work that day, she told the Lord she needed some answer from Him. That very day God provided in a way only He can do. My friend praised God because *He did it!*

I've been waiting for several years for God to answer a prayer of mine. Sometimes I get panicky and think, "God, You've waited too long; things can never be reversed now." Then I'm reminded of something Vance Havner said: "God does not operate by our timetable, and sometimes it does not add up on our computers." When this prayer is answered, I will shout, "God did it!"

"I know not by what methods rare,
But this I know, God answers prayer;
I know that He has given His word,
Which tells me prayer is always heard,
And will be answered, soon or late;
And so I pray, and calmly wait."

Are you full of panic or full of praise?

"The fool hath said in his heart, There is no God. Corrupt are they, and have done abominable iniquity: there is none that doeth good" (Psalm 53:1).

THE MESSAGE of Psalm 53 and Psalm 14 is similar: man is universally wicked and corrupt. Modern-day man says mankind is inherently good; God says he is inherently bad. "The fool hath said in his heart, There is no God. Corrupt are they, and have done abominable iniquity: there is none that doeth good" (v. 1).

Several years ago the president of a large university said, "We no longer take anything for granted, not even the existence of God." Many people would consider this educator a brilliant man because of his advanced degrees. In the eyes of God he is a fool. One wise man said, "If fifty million people say a foolish thing, it is still a foolish thing."

The foolish atheist says, "There is no God." The foolish Christian says, "No, God! You cannot have Your way in my life; I will do as I please." It is a dangerous thing to say, "No, God!" When you shut God out of your life, your conscience becomes hardened. You may do corrupt and abominable things you never thought you could do. It is also dangerous because "it is a fearful thing to fall into the hands of the living God" (Hebrews 10:31).

If you truly belong to God, you can only run from Him so long. Eventually He will prepare a circumstance to stop you like He did for Jonah. "Now the LORD had prepared a great fish to swallow up Jonah. And Jonah was in the belly of the fish three days and three nights" (Jonah 1:17).

Have you been saying, "No, God" in some area of your life? Learn a lesson from Jonah and return to the place of obedience.

"There were they in great fear, where no fear was" (Psalm 53:5).

THE UNGODLY people who say, "There is no God," are suddenly filled with a needless panic. Those who were fearless boasters are now trembling like leaves on a tree. "There were they in great fear, where no fear was" (v. 5). Spurgeon wrote, "He who denies God is at bottom a coward, and in his infidelity he is like the boy in the churchyard who 'whistles to keep his courage up.'"

We sometimes describe fearful people as being afraid of their own shadow. Maybe little Johnny fits that description. His mother asked him to get some jelly out of the pantry. He hated that pantry with no light in it. His flashlight could only light one little place in that deep, dark pantry. He said, "Mommy, I'm scared to go in there; would you get it?"

She said, "Oh, Johnny, don't be afraid; Jesus will be in there with you." Fearfully, Johnny took his flashlight and opened the door. He then said, "Jesus, if You're in there, will You hand me the jelly?"

Could this be written over your life, "In great fear, where no fear is." Are you full of fear or full of faith? People who are full of fear fill their minds with "what ifs": What if this happens? What if that happens? People who are full of faith fill their minds with, "God said it, I believe it, and that settles it for me!" The promises of God fill us with faith.

It is hard to listen to God while listening to your fears. Are you filled with faith or fear?

"For he hath delivered me out of all trouble" (Psalm 54:7).

GOD HAS never failed yet! I think that was the theme of David's heart when he said, "For he hath delivered me out of all trouble" (v. 7). Notice two words in particular in this sentence: "hath" and "all." David didn't say, "he will"; he said, "he hath." He didn't say "most trouble"; he said "all trouble."

As David looked back, he knew God had never failed him, not even once. God had delivered him out of every trouble he had passed through. David didn't say he was "delivered from all trouble"; he said he was "delivered out of all trouble." God doesn't keep us from trouble, but He does help us out of our troubles.

The next time you feel you are about to drown in your troubles, ask yourself, Has God ever failed you? You may feel He did because He didn't work things out according to your plan. But God never fails us; He will deliver us out of our troubles in His time and in His way. God has not failed us in the past; He will not fail us in the future. "Take therefore no thought for the morrow" (Matthew 6:34).

> "I know not if tomorrow's way
> Be steep or rough;
> But when He is guiding me,
> That is enough."

Are you trusting our unfailing God to deliver you?

"And I said, Oh that I had wings like a dove! for then would I fly away, and be at rest"
(Psalm 55:6).

I CAN remember several occasions in my life when I could hardly wait for the next day to come. However, I can also remember times when my heart was so heavy I wished tomorrow would never come. I, like the psalmist David, just wished "I had wings like a dove! for then would I fly away, and be at rest" (v. 6).

Have you ever felt like you just couldn't take it anymore? "Oh, if the Lord would just return and take us to Heaven, then this would all be over!" Most of us have felt that way at some time or another. If you haven't, you will someday when the storms of life beat on you. David wasn't concerned with victory; he just wanted to escape, to get away from the storms and trials. Verse 7 says he wanted to wander away and remain in a wilderness. He wanted a quiet place; he needed some rest and peace.

When the trials of life wear us down, we need to ask ourselves if we need physical rest or spiritual rest. A couple of times I have been so mentally and physically exhausted that I have had to rest physically for a while. But most of the time I just need the spiritual rest that only God can give.

I have learned that you can't run away from your problems; wherever you go, they go with you. This has taught me to face my problems head-on and, with God's help, to rise above them as if I had eagles' wings (Isaiah 40:31).

Don't run from your problems; run to the Lord for rest. I agree with my friend who said, "There are times when God asks nothing of His children except silence, patience, and tears." Have you learned that? I have!

"For it was not an enemy that reproached me . . . but it was thou, a man mine equal,
my guide, and mine acquaintance" (Psalm 55:12, 13).

STICKS and stones may break my bones, but words can never hurt me!" Only a child would babble such words. Adults know that just isn't true. Words can hurt; they can break our hearts—especially if uttered by a dear friend or family member.

The person who was abusing David was not just a friend, but a very special friend: "For it was not an enemy that reproached me . . . but it was thou, a man mine equal, my guide, and mine acquaintance" (vv. 12, 13). This person knew David well, "a man mine equal." This friend was his "guide," one whom he had asked for advice and with whom he shared the secrets of his heart. This friend was not just an acquaintance, but an intimate acquaintance, "mine acquaintance."

The best part of this friendship was the fact that David and he enjoyed spiritual things together. "We took sweet counsel together, and walked unto the house of God in company" (v. 14). David had put his trust in this friend, and then the friend treated David treacherously; he hated David (v. 3). David said, "My heart is sore pained" (v. 4); his heart was breaking.

People can look and sound so good; but if they are not good from the inside out, eventually what is on the inside comes outside, and it isn't very pretty. Someone has said that "Piety outside and corruption inside is a revolting mixture."

Has a friend let you down? Put your trust in the "friend that sticketh closer than a brother" (Proverbs 18:24), our Lord Himself.

"Evening, and morning, and at noon, will I pray, and cry aloud: and he shall hear my voice" (Psalm 55:17).

DAVID'S enemies were relentless in their attacks on him (v. 10), so he was relentless in his petitions for help from his Heavenly Father. "Evening, and morning, and at noon, will I pray, and cry aloud: and he shall hear my voice" (v. 17).

Day and night David's enemies were busy planning how they could weaken him. Day and night he planned to stay strong. David knew God would hear him and help him. He constantly turned every care into a prayer.

Prayer should be a daily practice, just as eating is a daily practice. Prayer is talking to God and listening to God. The more you talk to a person and listen to him, the better you get to know him. And the better you get to know a person, the better you can judge his trustworthiness.

God is worthy of my trust and confidence. Therefore, when I pray, I know He will answer my prayer either yes, no, or wait. Even when the answer is no, I have peace in my heart because I know He has a better plan than my plan. I can handle yes and no answers easier than I can handle wait.

When we pray morning, noon, and evening about a matter, we are probably waiting for God to answer. Maybe that's why God sometimes seems to wait so long. He wants to teach us to pray and trust!

How is your prayer life?

"Cast thy burden upon the LORD, and he shall sustain thee: he shall never suffer the righteous to be moved" (Psalm 55:22).

DAVID knew God heard his cries of distress—morning, noon, and evening—so he just kept unloading them on Him. He knew this was the only way he would survive the agonizing attacks of the enemy and the heartbreaking betrayal of his friend. David knew that, though all others might forsake him, God would be with him and hold him steady. "Cast thy burden upon the LORD, and he shall sustain thee: he shall never suffer the righteous to be moved" (v. 22).

Someone handed me a card with this statement written on it: "Pitch your cares upon the Lord; He is a good catcher." I whispered a silent "amen" as I read it.

We all have cares from time to time that disturb our peace of mind and cause us to be fatigued and frazzled. The sooner we cast these cares back on the Lord, the less damage they will do in our lives. These burdens are appointments from God to help us, not hurt us. They draw us closer to Him so we will learn how He can sustain us and carry us through our trials. When we try to carry these burdens alone, they hurt us.

Have you ever strained your back because you tried to carry too much weight alone? Carrying our own cares will strain our minds, hearts, stomachs, and other vital organs. We weren't made to carry that much weight alone.

Remember, nothing is too heavy, too secret, or too sacred to give to God to carry for you. When you are just too tired to go on, He will only carry you as well as your burden. He will never leave you or forsake you (Hebrews 13:5). He is your care-bearer!

"What time I am afraid, I will trust in thee" (Psalm 56:3).

I ONCE read that Psalm 56 and a penny have one thing in common. What do you think it might be? They both bear this same message: "In God We Trust."

What is it in your life that causes you to be afraid and lack faith? For David it was people: "Man would swallow me up"; "mine enemies would daily swallow me up" (vv. 1, 2).

Who were David's enemies? King Saul was pursuing him. David made his way to the city of Gath, the hometown of the Philistine giant, Goliath, whom David had killed (1 Samuel 22). Gath was a Philistine stronghold, and David's name was probably on the "most wanted" list. We might say David was in double-trouble. What did he do? Doubled up on his faith. "What time I am afraid, I will trust in thee" (v. 3).

What causes you to fear and makes you feel insecure, uncertain, and sometimes full of alarm? Most of our external fears fall into one of the four big *P* categories: people, problems, perplexities, and possibilities. People and problems can cause fear in any number of ways. Perplexities are those circumstances that seem to have no answer. Possibilities are the "what ifs" with which we burden ourselves and that may never happen.

Which big *P* causes fear in your life? How do you face fear: with trembling or trust?

"When I cry unto thee, then shall mine enemies turn back: this I know;
for God is for me" (Psalm 56:9).

HOW did David get rid of his enemies? He cried unto the Lord, and his enemies turned back. "When I cry unto thee, then shall mine enemies turn back: this I know; for God is for me" (v. 9). Notice David said, "This I *know; for God is for me.*" David knew God was for him; he knew God would help him! Is anyone or anything as powerful as God? No! David had the greatest power in the universe on his side and so do we!

Who is your enemy? You may be a kind, sweet, gentle person who has no enemies that you know of. But do you have internal enemies?

I've had a few external enemies, but I have many internal enemies that would love to destroy me. Doubt, discouragement, anger, resentment, and fear are all my enemies. I have no control over my external enemies, but I do over the internal ones. I daily choose whether or not I want these enemies to reside within me.

I once told a very dear friend, "You are your own worst enemy." When I let my internal enemies stay, I become my own worst enemy. The longer I let these enemies stay, the more they feel at home, and the less I think of them as enemies.

The best way to fight your spiritual enemies is on your knees. Are you your own worst enemy?

"In God have I put my trust: I will not be afraid what man can do unto me"
(Psalm 56:11).

IN GOD have I put my trust: I will not be afraid what man can do unto me" (v. 11). David had absolute confidence in the Lord and in His Word. He was so confident, in fact, that he spoke as if his deliverance had already come. Verse 13 can be translated, "You have delivered my soul from death, and you have delivered my feet from stumbling" (v. 13). David wasn't victimized by the people causing the difficult circumstances in his life. He made a conscious choice to trust God and to not fear men.

"I will not be afraid what man can do unto me." What can people do to us? A lot! They can humiliate, antagonize, scandalize, and criticize. They can make us feel like a real ZERO! That is, if we let them. Praise God, I have learned my self-esteem is not dependent on man's evaluation of me but on God's evaluation.

One writer defines self-worth this way: "A healthy self-image is seeing yourself as God sees you—no more and no less." My feelings of self-worth stem from the knowledge that I have fundamental value because I was created in God's image and because Christ died for my sins. Who am I? I am a child of God. What am I? I am a trophy of God's grace.

Trophies are usually put on display as symbols of honor and praise. My life will not bring much praise to God if I lack trust and am full of fear. However, when the world sees a Christian who is full of confident trust in God and not fearful of men, that person becomes a symbol of honor and praise to her Savior.

Is your life a symbol of honor or dishonor to God?

"Be merciful unto me, O God, be merciful unto me: for my soul trusteth in thee: yea, in the shadow of thy wings will I make my refuge, until these calamities be overpast"
(Psalm 57:1).

DAVID was hiding from Saul again. Saul was determined to find David and kill him. While hiding in a cave, David pleaded again for God to have mercy on him and protect him.

David was hiding in a cave made of rock to take refuge from Saul, but David's confidence was not in that rocky shelter. His confidence was in the Rock of Ages, his God. "Be merciful unto me, O God, be merciful unto me: for my soul trusteth in thee: yea, in the shadow of thy wings will I make my refuge, until these calamities be overpast" (v. 1).

Notice where David's refuge was: "in the shadow of thy wings." Just as a mother hen hides her chicks under her wings during a storm, so David wanted God's protection during this storm or calamity in his life.

David wrote this psalm when the things going on in his life were enough to wear down the strongest of men. It was not a single calamity but many calamities that surrounded him: "until these calamities be overpast."

Our family has been passing through a calamity that has gone on and on. I was so encouraged by those words, "until these calamities be overpast." The calamities or storms of life come and go. Someone once said his favorite Bible verse was, "and it came to pass." (Don't try to find that verse; it is part of 446 verses.)

It is not always fair weather in your life, but, praise God, it isn't always stormy either. Don't give up! This too shall pass!

"My heart is fixed, O God, my heart is fixed: I will sing and give praise" (Psalm 57:7).

DAVID said, "My heart is fixed, O God, my heart is fixed: I will sing and give praise" (v. 7). David's heart was steadfast, unwavering, unbending; it could not be moved. What song did he sing? Of course, we don't know; but perhaps he sang Psalm 40, which starts like this: "I waited patiently for the LORD; and he inclined unto me, and heard my cry. He brought me up also out of an horrible pit, out of the miry clay, and set my feet upon a rock, and established my goings. And he hath put a new song in my mouth, even praise unto our God: many shall see it, and fear, and shall trust in the LORD" (vv. 1–3).

Many years ago, after struggling with the matter of complete dedication to Christ, a song helped "fix my heart" and seal my decision. The song was "I Have Decided to Follow Jesus." One line in that song still echoes in my mind when I get discouraged and feel like quitting, "No turning back, no turning back."

It is easy to sing when everything is going right, and the sun is shining; but it takes a fixed, steadfast faith to sing in times of trouble and darkness.

Only a fixed heart has a God-given song in dark days. Do you have a fixed heart or a faint heart?

*"The wicked are estranged from the womb: they go astray as soon as they be born,
speaking lies" (Psalm 58:3).*

THERE was no doubt in David's mind: man is born a sinner! "The wicked are estranged from the womb: they go astray as soon as they be born, speaking lies" (v. 3).

Man is born a sinner, separated from a holy God. Man doesn't become wicked; he is born wicked. If he continues to follow this inborn nature, he will ruin himself and others. "As it is written, There is none righteous, no, not one: There is none that understandeth, there is none that seeketh after God. They are all gone out of the way, they are together become unprofitable; there in none that doeth good, no, not one. . . . For all have sinned, and come short of the glory of God" (Romans 3:10–12, 23).

What is the trademark of a wicked person? The last two words in today's verse tell us: "speaking lies." The wicked person seems to have no conscience at all; he can lie to anyone and everyone and seem to feel no guilt.

Most people are on guard around a person who is known to be wicked; it's the hypocrite that fools us. He can fool us for a while, but eventually his tongue reveals his wickedness. The lying tongue always, eventually, exposes the hypocrite. A wise, old, godly man once said, "None but cowards lie." And such a person will never be believed—even when he does tell the truth.

Let none of us be known by the trademark of a wicked, lying tongue. What is your trademark?

"So that a man shall say, Verily there is a reward for the righteous: verily he is a God that judgeth in the earth" (Psalm 58:11).

DAVID rejoiced in the knowledge that the wicked would not triumph forever; they would be defeated. A judgment day is coming, and God is the judge. "So that a man shall say, Verily there is a reward for the righteous: verily he is a God that judgeth in the earth" (v. 11). The wicked will be judged, and the righteous will be rewarded. In the end, justice will be served.

"And they lived happily ever after." I love stories that have happy endings. Because we have read the last page of the Book, we know the righteous shall live happily ever after in Heaven. Yes, there is a "reward for the righteous," but we may have to wait awhile for it. We may not see our reward until we stand at the judgment seat (2 Corinthians 5:10) when we are given our crowns for faithful service here on earth.

Will you receive a crown when you stand before Christ and see Him face to face? Many Christians won't! All their works have been wood, hay, and stubble; "he shall suffer loss: but he himself shall be saved; yet so as by fire" (1 Corinthians 3:11–15).

When you get to Heaven, will you stand there scorched and empty-handed, or will you have a crown in your hand to place at the feet of Jesus?

A person may say, "Oh, I don't care if I get any rewards or not, as long as I get there." You won't feel that way when you see your Savior, Who died for you. If you have nothing to give back to Him in appreciation for all He did for you, you will be ashamed to look Him in the face.

I want to hear, "Well done, good and faithful servant" (Matthew 25:23); don't you?

*"Slay them not, lest my people forget: scatter them by thy power; and bring them down,
O Lord our shield" (Psalm 59:11).*

DAVID hid from Saul in the caves and mountains—and even in his own house (1 Samuel 19:8–18). David made a strange request of the Lord: "Slay them not, lest my people forget: scatter them by thy power; and bring them down, O Lord our shield" (v. 11). David asked the Lord to destroy his enemies gradually, not swiftly. Why? Swift destruction would startle people for a while, but they would soon forget. Gradual punishment would continually remind the people of God's displeasure with sin.

When my husband preached a series of messages on Hebrews, one verse particularly stood out in my mind: "Therefore we ought to give the more earnest heed to the things which we have heard, lest at any time we should let them slip" (Hebrews 2:1). We need to be reminded of the things we already know lest we let them slip, lest we forget.

How soon we forget God's commands. How soon we forget the promises we make to God. How soon we forget God has the power to scatter and to bring down.

One of the things I dislike the most about getting older is that my memory is not as good as it once was. I may forget some things, but I pray I will never forget God's plan and purpose for my life. What is it? To be like His Son, Jesus Christ.

That's His plan and purpose for your life as well, in case you have forgotten. Is God's plan being fulfilled in your life?

"Unto thee, O my strength, will I sing: for God is my defence, and the God of my mercy"
(Psalm 59:17).

BIBLE scholars believe this psalm was written at the beginning of Saul's persecution of David. David fled from his home by night (1 Samuel 19:11–13); he left the city to wander in the mountains and caves. At the very beginning of a long series of trials, we see a picture of David's faith and courage as he spoke of God as his strength and defense. "Unto thee, O my strength, will I sing: for God is my defence, and the God of my mercy" (v. 17). David was spiritually prepared for the storms in his life; he had built his "ark of faith."

I was challenged to start building my ark of faith one day after I heard someone say that each one of us is like Noah. God calls down from Heaven, "Noah, build your ark of faith. The sun's shining in your life today. There's no tragedy yet; but Noah, there's a great flood coming. While there's still time, build your ark of faith so that when the flood comes, you stay on top of the flood not under it."

To build an ark of faith we must fortify our lives with the Word of God. Then we will have a shelter to keep us from sinking during the storm.

Are you building your ark of faith?

"Thou hast given a banner to them that fear thee, that it may be displayed
because of the truth" (Psalm 60:4).

WHEN the Israelites went out to battle, the leader of the group carried a banner. I wonder what was written on that banner? Could it have been "The Lord of Hosts Fights for Us"?

Moses knew what it was like to have God fight for him. Exodus 17 records the battle between the Israelites and the Amalekites. Moses was on the mountain with Aaron and Hur; Joshua was in the trenches with the people. As long as Moses held up his hands, Israel prevailed; when he put them down, Amalek prevailed. Eventually Aaron and Hur helped hold up Moses' hands, and in the end, Israel won. But Moses recognized that the victory was really God's, and he named the altar he built "Jehovah-nissi"—The Lord Our Banner.

Our verse today tells us that people who fear God have a banner over them: "Thou hast given a banner to them that fear thee, that it may be displayed because of the truth" (v. 4). Isaiah, like Moses, identified that banner: "And in that day there shall be a root of Jesse, which shall stand for an ensign [banner] of the people" (Isaiah 11:10).

The banner we follow is none other than the Lord Jesus Himself. Lots of other banners are out there, and they would seek to distract us from Him. But as we keep following His leading, we will experience victory in the battles of life.

Are you following Jehovah-nissi, the Lord Our Banner, and experiencing the victory He longs to give?

"Through God we shall do valiantly: for he it is that shall tread down our enemies"
(Psalm 60:12).

DAVID believed that God's power would overrule natural resources. He did not say, "We shall do valiantly because of our mighty weapons and crafty strategies." He said, "Through God we shall do valiantly: for he it is that shall tread down our enemies" (v. 12).

The Bible contains 366 "fear nots"—one for each day of the year, even leap year! We need never fear because our God is with us continually. Furthermore, He will guide us continually if we will let Him. "And the LORD shall guide thee continually" (Isaiah 58:11). With God at our side, before us, and behind us, we can face life valiantly, courageously, bravely. "Through God we shall do valiantly."

Are you fearful of the days ahead? If so, you are lagging too far behind your Guide. Or could it be that you have not been following your Guide at all? If this is true, you do have reason to fear!

> "Shall I tell you why my foes no longer
>   vex me,
> And my cares and fears and doubtings
>   all are o'er?
> 'Tis because I've given my burdens all
>   to Jesus,
> And He leads me forth in triumph
>   evermore" (A. B. SIMPSON).

Are you staying close to your Guide or lagging behind?

". . . When my heart is overwhelmed: lead me to the rock that is higher than I"
(Psalm 61:2).

WHAT did David do when he felt overwhelmed? ". . .When my heart is overwhelmed: lead me to the rock that is higher than I" (v. 2).

How unwise to put our trust in things lower than ourselves, such as money and other material things. We need to place our confidence in something higher than ourselves. David's confidence was in the Rock of Ages, his God, the Rock that is higher than you or I. This Rock cannot be overwhelmed by the crashing waves and storms of time.

My husband and I enjoy going to the ocean or gulf a couple of times a year. We don't like getting in the water as much as we like listening to the water. The waves never cease rolling and crashing onto the beach. It is relaxing just to sit and listen. However, getting in the water can be anything but relaxing if you don't know how to ride the waves. If you try to just stand in the water, you'll soon find yourself under the water. The powerful waves can overwhelm and knock down the strongest of men.

Sometimes the trials of life seem to come in on us like waves. It seems we just get up again and get our feet on solid ground when another wave of problems comes along and knocks us down. How are we going to stay on top of our problems instead of under them? We must climb higher on the Rock, get closer to Christ.

Are you under the waves or riding on top of them?

"For thou, O God, hast heard my vows: thou hast given me the heritage of those that fear thy name" (Psalm 61:5).

FOR THOU, O God, hast heard my vows: thou hast given me the heritage of those that fear thy name" (v. 5). What was David's heritage? David enjoyed the temporal and spiritual blessings that God gave His Chosen People in the Promised Land. David knew how God had taken care of his forefathers. The remembrance of those past experiences was an encouragement to the psalmist to trust God in his present trials and dangers. David enjoyed a great heritage!

Every believer has been adopted into the family of God and has a great heritage. What is the inheritance of those that fear God? Here is a sample: supply in the time of need (Philippians 4:19); comfort in the time of trouble (Psalm 23:4); victory in the time of conflict (1 John 5:4); an inheritance reserved in Heaven (1 Peter 1:3, 4). Are you enjoying your heritage?

I once knew a young lady who enjoyed all the privileges of a great life. Not only had she been adopted by her parents, but she also professed faith in Christ, adoption into the family of God. But she turned away from all that she had and chose a life of sin and rebellion. Her parents loved and feared God, but she chose a different path in life. She had no desire to stand in awe of God's authority in her life; she was not fearful of offending God. Rivers of living water were offered to her, but she only took a sip. The bread of life was before her, but she only ate crumbs. The treasury of Heaven was open to her, but she was empty-handed. Rather than appreciating her heritage and enjoying it, she turned her back on it.

Your spiritual heritage has been passed down from God to you through Jesus Christ. Are you enjoying it?

"My soul, wait thou only upon God; for my expectation is from him" (Psalm 62:5).

DAVID may have been giving himself a little pep talk: "Keep waiting on God; keep expecting Him to come through for you, David." His total confidence was in God, not in man. "My soul, wait thou only upon God; for my expectation is from him" (v. 5).

David's son failed him; his friends failed him; other people failed him; but God never failed. David had learned not to expect much from others but everything from God. John Trapp said, "They trust not God *at all* who trust him not *alone*. He that stands with one foot on a rock, and another foot upon a quicksand, will sink and perish, as certainly as he that standeth with both feet upon a quicksand."

We expect so much from people, but they seldom live up to our expectations. We expect a husband to be a Prince Charming, and he may not come close to the expectations. We expect our children to appreciate everything we do for them, but they may be ungrateful. Fallen people in a fallen world can never satisfy all our needs. Only God can quench a thirsty soul. The most perfect person can't meet all our emotional, physical, or spiritual needs.

Can you say, "My soul, wait thou only upon God; for my expectation is from him," or have you placed your expectations in other people?

"O God, thou art my God; early will I seek thee: my soul thirsteth for thee, my flesh longeth for thee in a dry and thirsty land, where no water is" (Psalm 63:1).

THIS POEM, written many years ago, echoes the words of David in Psalm 63:

"How strange to kneel so lonely, so afraid

And then to rise refreshed and undismayed!

You gave no outward sign that I could see,

And yet I felt Your love surrounding me.

And now my wilderness is filled with bread,

And I may walk as one divinely led"

(EUGENIA FINN).

David was in the lonely, barren wilderness of Judah, where water was scarce. He was going through a desert experience. Whatever the situation was (running from Saul [1 Samuel 23] or fleeing from his son [2 Samuel 15]), his circumstances were causing him to seek God even more earnestly. "O God, thou art my God; early will I seek thee: my soul thirsteth for thee, my flesh longeth for thee in a dry and thirsty land, where no water is" (v. 1).

On one of my bathroom mirrors I have placed these words, "Our trials are custom-made by God to draw us closer to Him." God often puts us in desert places to bring us to our knees. Then we will cry out, as David did, "O God, . . . my soul thirsteth for thee." Remember, no water can satisfy like the Water of Life (John 7:37, 38).

Are you in a desert place? If you are thirsting for God, you will be refreshed and strengthened!

175

"Hear my voice, O God, in my prayer: preserve my life from fear of the enemy"
(Psalm 64:1).

DAVID was in enemy territory again. Perhaps this psalm was written while he was being hounded by Saul and his company who wanted to kill him. David used the most powerful weapon he had, which was prayer. "Hear my voice, O God, in my prayer: preserve my life from fear of the enemy" (v. 1).

Prayer was David's most trusted resource in the hour of need. We have seen in past psalms how David turned to prayer when he was in the presence of his enemies. Only God could cause him not to be fearful in enemy territory.

Have you ever been in enemy territory and feared for your life? Most of us probably haven't. Most of us live relatively safe and secure lives with no fear of enemy attacks.

As far as I know, I only have one real enemy, and I need not fear him if I keep my armor on each day. Who is my enemy? The same enemy you have: Satan! He wants Christians to live ineffective lives for God. If I don't put on my armor each day, I will not be ready for his attacks. Read Ephesians 6:10–18 for a full description of the Christian's armor.

This world is Satan's playground, and lazy Christians are his playmates. We must be strong and on guard daily because we are in enemy territory. We are in a war with someone who is as slick as an ice cube and just as hard and cold.

Have you put on your armor today?

*"Blessed is the man whom thou choosest, and causest to approach unto thee,
that he may dwell in thy courts: we shall be satisfied with the goodness of thy house,
even of thy holy temple" (Psalm 65:4).*

THE ISRAELITES were a special group of people, chosen by God to be a holy people (Deuteronomy 7:6). They were permitted to enjoy the outer courtyard of the tabernacle. Only the Israelites from the tribe of Levi were able to serve in the tabernacle itself, and only the high priest could enter the Holy of Holies where the presence of God resided above the ark of the covenant (Leviticus 16; Numbers 3). "Blessed is the man whom thou choosest, and causest to approach unto thee, that he may dwell in thy courts: we shall be satisfied with the goodness of thy house, even of thy holy temple" (v. 4).

Those of us who belong to the family of God are a special people, a chosen people.

The Bible says God chose us in Christ before the world began (Ephesians 1:4). Our salvation was totally dependent on God; He chose us; we didn't choose Him. I cannot understand why God would love and choose a sinner like me and accept me just as I was, but He did. And because He did, I now stand holy and blameless in His sight, just as if I'd never sinned (Romans 3:24, 25). He bids me to come boldly into His presence to present my needs to Him (Hebrews 4:16). "Blessed [happy] is the man whom thou choosest. . . . we shall be satisfied with the goodness of thy house."

I am so happy God chose me, and I am satisfied with His goodness to me! Are you?

"For thou, O God, hast proved us: thou hast tried us, as silver is tried" (Psalm 66:10).

ISRAEL as a nation had come through a severe purification process, much like the refining of silver and gold. "For thou, O God, hast proved us: thou hast tried us, as silver is tried" (v. 10). God had brought the people through the Red Sea, through the wilderness, and finally into the Promised Land, only to be faced with enemies who wanted to kill them. David had his trials and times of purification as well. He just seemed to live from one trial to another.

Psalm 66:10 reminds me of Job 23:10: "But he knoweth the way that I take: when he hath tried me, I shall come forth as gold." Written beside this verse in my Bible are these words: "A crisis does not make a man; it shows what a man is made of."

God tries and tests us to prove to us what stuff we're made of. He doesn't do it to prove it to Himself; He already knows us inside out. The surest way to prove to us what we're made of is to put us in the fiery furnace of testings.

Silver and gold ores become usable metals only after they have been in the fiery furnace and the dross has been removed. The fiery furnace has a refining effect on the precious ores, and the fiery furnace of testing has a refining effect on God's precious ones, His children. God is refining us, making us more like the Lord Jesus.

Are you concerned with comfort or character? Can you accept the fiery furnace of testing in order to be refined as precious silver?

"If I regard iniquity in my heart, the Lord will not hear me" (Psalm 66:18).

DAVID had learned that nothing hinders prayer more than sin harbored in the heart. "If I regard iniquity in my heart, the Lord will not hear me" (v. 18).

Holding one hand up to God and hanging on to sin with the other hand just doesn't impress God. One old theologian wisely said, "For God to accept our devotions, while we are delighting in sin, would be to make himself the God of hypocrites, which is a fitter name for Satan than for the Holy One of Israel."

Some people live by the philosophy "What they don't know won't hurt them." These people think, "As long as I look good and act good, it doesn't matter what I do that people can't see." But God knows otherwise. God's evaluation of this kind of thinking is,

"Woe unto you, . . . hypocrites!" (Matthew 23:25).

As I was studying this passage, I had to ask myself, "Is there some secret sin in my heart that only I know about?" My answer to myself was yes, and immediately I knew why one particular prayer in my life was not being answered. "If I regard iniquity [sin] in my heart, the Lord will not hear me."

We can look good and act good before others but be so rotten inside it is disgusting to God—so disgusting that He doesn't even want to hear our voice.

I want this to be the prayer of my life: "Cleanse thou me from secret [hidden] faults. Keep back thy servant also from presumptuous sins; let them not have dominion over me" (Psalm 19:12, 13). Will you pray that prayer?

"God be merciful unto us, and bless us; and cause his face to shine upon us" (Psalm 67:1).

GOD BE merciful unto us, and bless us; and cause his face to shine upon us" (v. 1). This verse is a reference to the blessing God gave the nation of Israel when He prepared the people for the wilderness march: "The LORD bless thee, and keep thee: The LORD make his face shine upon thee, and be gracious unto thee: The LORD lift up his countenance upon thee, and give thee peace" (Numbers 6:24–26).

If you were to ask me what I like best about living in Florida, my first answer would be, "The sun shines almost every day." In fact, one Tampa newspaper is so sure the sun will shine it offers free newspapers if the sun doesn't shine sometime during the day. One weatherman often says, "We have an another BDIP [Beautiful Day In Paradise]." It is great living in the Sunshine State if you enjoy the sun shining every day.

However, I can think of no greater blessing than to have God's face shine on us each day. How can we be assured of this? God treats us just like we do our children. All they have to do to see our faces shine with love and approval is obey! It sounds so simple: obedience = blessing; disobedience = chastening. Oh, how it must grieve our Father's heart when He cannot look on us with pleasure and approval.

Are you living in such a way that His face shines upon you with approval?

"A father of the fatherless, and a judge of the widows, is God in his holy habitation"
(Psalm 68:5).

DAVID directed his thoughts to the fatherless and the widows: "A father of the fatherless, and a judge of the widows, is God in his holy habitation" (v. 5). The fatherless are those who are helpless and sometimes forsaken; the widows are the sorrowful and lonely ones. They are used to illustrate those who have lost their protector and helper.

David left his father when David was just a young shepherd boy, but his Heavenly Father had been his protector, helper, and provider for many years. Therefore, David never had reason to ever feel alone.

At this time of the year we are reminded of Father's Day when many people will think about their fathers. Some will reflect back with fond memories; for others the memories will be filled with bitterness and resentment.

Some people have no memory of their birth fathers, although other people may have filled a father role for them.

As I think back on my father's life, I realize he had many virtues worthy of copying. Some of his values and virtues have been absorbed into my life. In some ways I am like my father. This thought brought another striking challenge to my heart: In what ways am I like my Heavenly Father? Not only do our lives live on through our children, but our Heavenly Father wants His life to live on through us.

Today is a good day to thank God for your earthly father if he was a positive influence in your life. It's always appropriate to thank God for the unconditional love of your Heavenly Father.

"Blessed be the Lord, who daily loadeth us with benefits, even the God of our salvation"
(Psalm 68:19).

WHEN the psalmist meditated on the goodness of God, he realized he had much to be thankful for each day. "Blessed be the Lord, who daily loadeth us with benefits, even the God of our salvation" (v. 19). His blessings were more than he could fathom, and they were poured out daily.

Have you counted your blessings lately? Some of you may be saying, "What blessings?" All of us are daily loaded with benefits from God. However, we live in such a materialistic society that we often get caught up in this world's thinking and philosophies. Many people think of blessings in terms of how many things they have.

We've all heard the saying, "Stop and smell the roses." We need to slow down and see all the blessings around us each day: air to breath; water to refresh and cleanse our-selves; clothes to wear; houses to live in; family and friends; a mind to think with; senses to see, hear, taste, and feel; and the list goes on and on.

The list gets even longer if you belong to Jesus Christ. We have the Holy Spirit dwelling in us to guide and strengthen us and help us understand the Word of God; we have a Savior Who loves us unconditionally and is preparing an eternal home for us in Heaven.

The next time you feel God is unfair and has shortchanged you, take a few minutes to count your blessings. And don't forget, even burdens are blessings in disguise. Many times the clouds God puts in our lives bring showers of blessings. Are you counting your blessings?

"Thy God hath commanded thy strength: strengthen, O God, that which thou hast wrought for us" (Psalm 68:28).

IN THIS PSALM David put a song on the lips of the people, a song foretelling future victories by the Lord Jehovah. Their God had made them strong in the day of conflict; He would do it again. "Thy God hath commanded thy strength: strengthen, O God, that which thou hast wrought for us" (v. 28). God's power was the constant source of strength that would carry them into the future.

God has told us time and time again where to get our strength to fight the battles of life. One of my favorite reminders is Isaiah 40:31. If we wait on the Lord, He will renew our strength so that we can run and not get weary and walk without fainting.

" 'The Lord is my strength' *to go on.* He gives us power to . . . walk the long lane that seems never to have a turning. . . . 'The Lord is my strength' *to go up.* He is to me the power by which I can climb the Hill Difficulty and not be afraid. . . . 'The Lord is my strength' *to go down.* It is when we . . . begin to come down the hill into closer and more sultry spheres, that the heart is apt to grow faint. . . . 'The Lord is my strength' *to sit still.* And how difficult is the attainment! . . . Just to sit still and wait requires tremendous strength. 'The Lord is my strength!' 'Our sufficiency is of God' " (*Streams in the Desert,* vol. 1).

Do you need to go on, to go up, to go down, or to sit still? Are you depending upon God for the strength?

"Ascribe ye strength unto God: his excellency is over Israel, and his strength is in the clouds"
(Psalm 68:34).

GIVE HONOR to whom honor is due! David said, "Let us give back to God the honor and praise due to Him. Remember how He demonstrated to the Children of Israel His presence and power in the clouds." "Ascribe ye strength unto God: his excellency is over Israel, and his strength is in the clouds" (v. 34). Each day the Israelites were fed from the clouds and led by the cloud.

Summer thunderstorms in Florida remind me of the awesome power of God in the clouds. When the storm is raging and the lightning and thunder are crashing, I get a little scared! I feel like hiding, but there is nowhere to go to get away from the noise of the thunder and the flashes of lightning. Several times the lightning has hit a power line behind our house, and all our lights have gone out. We have been without electricity for hours. When this happens, things I have started come to a halt because I can't do them without electricity.

This reminds me that God has the power to stop us in our tracks; "his strength is in the clouds." God may not use clouds to lead us and feed as He did for the Israelites, but we are surrounded by countless signs of His awesome power in nature and in our lives individually. His majesty and unlimited power should leave us humble in His presence.

When was the last time you bowed in His presence and just thought of His power? He can stop you in your tracks if need be.

"Let not them that wait on thee, O Lord GOD of hosts, be ashamed for my sake: let not those that seek thee be confounded for my sake, O God of Israel" (Psalm 69:6).

DAVID was a hero in the eyes of many Israelites. He knew this; therefore, he didn't want to do anything that would bring shame on God's name or on his own name. He didn't want people to be disappointed in God because of him. He prayed, "Let not them that wait on thee, O Lord GOD of hosts, be ashamed for my sake: let not those that seek thee be confounded for my sake, O God of Israel" (v. 6).

A famous football player, once a hero in the eyes of many people, has fallen from his pedestal. The world watched the drama unfold day by day on national television.

Some people are ashamed that they held him up as such an ideal role model. His reputation and credibility—his name—have been tarnished. To many people he is now a "fallen" star.

You may not feel you are a hero in anyone's eyes; but if you fall into sin, you will disgrace your name and your Savior's name.

Will you pray this prayer with me?
"Dear Father, Please hold my hand;
Without You I will fall;
Your part is to keep me;
My part is to let You—that is all."

"Reproach hath broken my heart; and I am full of heaviness: and I looked for some to take pity, but there was none; and for comforters, but I found none" (Psalm 69:20).

REBUKE and criticism affect people in different ways. Some people are crushed, and some are challenged—they are ready to fight. David was devastated. "Reproach hath broken my heart; and I am full of heaviness . . ." (v. 20). He needed someone to come alongside him, put an arm around him, and say, "I care; can I help you?" But no one came. "I looked for some to take pity, but there was none; and for comforters, but I found none" (v. 20).

When I heard a sad story about a pastor and his wife, I couldn't begin to imagine the shame and reproach they were feeling. I tried to think how I might feel if I were in this situation. I wondered what people would say. I was sure plenty of people would rebuke and criticize, but I wondered if anyone would offer comfort to the broken hearts. God challenged me to be a comforter to my friend. There was nothing I could say to heal her broken heart, but maybe just knowing someone cared helped her endure the pain and embarrassment.

Whom could you comfort with a call or note today?

"Pour out thine indignation upon them, and let thy wrathful anger take hold of them"
(Psalm 69:24).

EVEN people who seem "perfect" in our eyes have imperfections. David is a good example for us. God referred to him as "a man after mine own heart" (Acts 13:22), but God did not cover up the stains in his life. David had a bitter, revengeful spirit toward his enemies. He cried out to God, "Pour out thine indignation upon them, and let thy wrathful anger take hold of them" (v. 24). In this regard David stands before us as an example to shun rather than one to be imitated.

God never covers up the sins of His servants. This is just another evidence of the trustworthiness of His Word. God wanted us to see the heart and character of holy men and women. He tells us their joys and their sorrows, defeats and triumphs, their holy desires and their sinful passions. They were just like us—saved sinners!

What can we learn from David's weakness? None of us is perfect! We need to be transparent and real with other people. They need to know we fail and struggle with the same sins they wrestle with. We don't want to glorify our sin, but neither do we want to hide it. God's Word says, "He that covereth his sins shall not prosper: but whoso confesseth and forsaketh them shall have mercy" (Proverbs 28:13).

Are you transparent with God and others?

"But I am poor and needy: make haste unto me, O God: thou art my help and my deliverer;
O LORD, make no tarrying" (Psalm 70:5).

IT SEEMS we're always in a hurry, but God never is. David needed immediate help. He pleaded for God to "hurry up." He started this psalm with this cry for help, "Make haste, O God, to deliver me; make haste to help me" (v. 1). He repeated the cry in verse 5, "Make haste unto me, O God . . . make no tarrying."

David knew that God was his help. Again and again God had been his help in the time of need. However, the stress and strain of his affliction were so great that he knew he could not endure much longer without God's intervention.

Have you ever cried out to God, "Hurry up, Lord! Why don't You do something now?" At times when I have prayed this way, God has answered right away. Other times God didn't seem to be in a hurry to answer.

How can we handle these delays and disappointments? We must remember that delays are not necessarily refusals. God may have written beside our prayer, "It is not My time yet!" God has set the time of our deliverance.

Are you in a hurry to get an answer, and God doesn't seem to be in a hurry to answer? Take heart! God is never late!

"In thee, O LORD, do I put my trust: let me never be put to confusion" (Psalm 71:1).

DAVID seemed to look backward and forward in this psalm. In rehearsing the past, he said of his sovereign God, "Thou hast taught me from my youth" (v. 17). As he looked toward the future, he wrote, "When I am old and greyheaded, O God, forsake me not" (v. 18). David may have been thinking, "God, You've never failed me in the past; You won't fail me in the future, will You?"

David established his confidence and trust in God by starting the psalm with these words: "In thee, O LORD, do I put my trust: let me never be put to confusion" (v. 1). God had never failed David, but when David started looking into the future, he became fearful. He didn't want to be full of fear and confusion and be a shame to God; he wanted to be full of faith and trust.

Can you relate to David's feelings? I can! When we look back over our lives and see how God has taken care of us step-by-step along the way, we wonder how we could ever fail to trust God again. And yet we do! We forget the blessings of the past so fast; and we don't always enjoy the blessings of the present because we are so worried about the years ahead. These kinds of thoughts fill us with confusion and fear.

George Mueller left these wise words for us: "The beginning of anxiety is the end of faith, and the beginning of true faith is the end of anxiety."

Do you need to refresh your memory about God's care in the past so that you can trust Him more fully for the present and the future?

"Thou, which hast shewed me great and sore troubles, shalt quicken me again, and shalt bring me up again from the depths of the earth" (Psalm 71:20).

DAVID had people in his life who caused him great problems, but not without God's being aware of the situations. In fact, these things could only happen because God allowed them, and David realized this when he said, "Thou, which hast shewed me great and sore troubles" (v. 20).

God had allowed David to sink so low he felt he might die. "Thou . . . shalt quicken me again, and shalt bring me up again from the depths of the earth" (v. 20). In other words, David knew God could restore his life to him once again.

Have you ever been in such depth of despair you thought surely you would die—or you wished you could die? It is not a pleasant place to be; it is dark and lonely. But—praise the Lord!—no matter how low we may sink,

God has set the limit to how low He will allow. In His time and in His way, He will bring us out of the pit of despair. We will feel alive once again.

> "Hope, then, though woes be doubled,
> Hope, and be undismayed;
> Let not thy heart be troubled,
> Nor let it be afraid.
> This prison where thou art,
> Thy God will break it soon,
> And flood with light thy heart
> In His own blessed noon"
>
> (PAUL GERHARDT).

If you are struggling, do not give up hope. God will "bring me up again from the depths of the earth." Fix your eyes on Christ rather than the depths.

"In his days shall the righteous flourish; and abundance of peace so long as the moon endureth" (Psalm 72:7).

THIS PSALM was either written by Solomon or for him. The commentators differ on this point, but they agree that the psalm pictures the Messiah during His millennial reign on earth.

Solomon, David's son, reigned in Israel's golden age; the land rested in peace. Yet Solomon's kingdom, even at its greatest, could not transcend the glories of the millennial Kingdom. When Christ reigns on earth, the land will not only rest in peace, but there will be peace in the hearts of men. The King of both righteousness and peace will reign, and men will be at peace. "In his days shall the righteous flourish; and the abundance of peace so long as the moon endureth" (v. 7).

Before Christ's glorious reign on earth begins, He will take His Bride, the church, to Heaven. The rapture of the church is the next thing to occur on God's timetable of coming events. It could be today!

"Jesus is coming to earth again—
What if it were today?
Coming in power and love to reign—
What if it were today?
Coming to claim His chosen Bride,
All the redeemed and purified,
Over this whole earth scattered wide—
What if it were today?" (LELIA N. MORRIS).

Isn't that an exciting thought? Christ could come today! No more wars; no more worries; just righteousness and peace forever. What if it were today? Are you looking up in joyful expectation?

"His name shall endure for ever: his name shall be continued as long as the sun: and men shall be blessed in him: all nations shall call him blessed" (Psalm 72:17).

PSALM 72 is a messianic psalm. Some of the references in it will be fulfilled in Jesus Christ. This psalm refers to the millennial Kingdom when "all nations shall call him blessed" (v. 17). The psalm describes the One Who is to come, the Prince of Peace, the King of Kings, the Lord Jesus Christ. This King and His kingdom shall never pass away. "His name shall endure for ever: his name shall be continued as long as the sun: and men shall be blessed in him: all nations shall call him blessed" (v. 17).

Can you identify these names: Shammua, Shaphat, Caleb, Igal, Oshea, Palti, Gaddiel, Gaddi, Ammiel, Sethur, Nahbi and Geuel? If you are like me, the only name in that list you may recognize is Caleb. Who were these men? They were the twelve spies who went into the land of Canaan (Numbers 13:1–16). Most of these names have not endured. Some of the people about whom we read in newspapers today will be forgotten in just a few short years; their names will not endure.

The name of Jesus will endure forever. In addition, "God also hath highly exalted him, and given him a name which is above every name: That at the name of Jesus every knee should bow, of things in heaven, and things in earth, and things under the earth; And that every tongue should confess that Jesus Christ is Lord, to the glory of God the Father" (Philippians 2:9–11).

The precious name of Jesus is the "hope of earth and joy of Heaven." Bow before Him in submission today.

"Truly God is good to Israel, even to such as are of a clean heart" (Psalm 73:1).

THIS PSALM, and the next ten, were written by Asaph or the sons of Asaph. In this psalm we see the conflict the psalmist had with a strong temptation to envy the prosperity of the wicked. He expressed his confidence in God in the first verse before he started recounting his inward conflict in verse 2. Asaph seemed to say, "No matter what is going on all around me, I know *God is good* to Israel and all those who are pure in heart toward God."

Many years ago Thomas Watson made this statement about God's goodness: "Purity of heart is the jewel which is hung only upon the elect. As chastity distinguisheth a virtuous woman from an harlot, so the true saint is distinguished from the hypocrite by his heart-purity. . . . God 'is good' to the pure in heart." "Truly God is good to Israel, even to such as are of a clean heart" (v. 1).

God is good! This is a truth we believers must be willing to live and die by. Remembering God's goodness will fortify us when Satan whispers in our ears, "If God loves you, why is He allowing this to happen to you?" Truly *God is good* even when situations aren't good. We may not be able to understand all the workings of His providential hand in our lives, but we know He understands and has a plan. Nothing is out of control from His perspective. Spurgeon's words are a constant encouragement to me in dark days: "When you can't trace God's hand, trust His heart."

Are you having a hard time trusting God? Maybe you need to dust your truster!

"But as for me, my feet were almost gone; my steps had well nigh slipped" (Psalm 73:2).

VERSES 1–3 present a man in turmoil. In verse 1 Asaph said, "God is good" to me; in verse 3 he said, "I was envious . . . when I saw the prosperity of the wicked." Asaph's heart and mind were doing battle. He knew in his heart that God was good to him, but his mind was thinking, "God treats the wicked better than He treats me."

As Asaph looked at wicked people and all the things they owned, he decided that they lived more comfortably and had less trouble in their lives than people who loved God and tried to live righteously. His final analysis was that the wicked had an easier life and more pleasure. He had forgotten one thing: outward comforts and pleasure do not bring inward comfort and contentment. You cannot buy happiness and peace. Asaph realized his state of mind was dangerous. He was about to fall for Satan's lies and tricks. "But as for me, my feet were almost gone; my steps had well nigh slipped" (v. 2).

We, too, will slip and fall if we begin to doubt the goodness of God. A doubting mind leads to falling feet. When we keep our eyes on the world too long, we begin to forget that inward character is more valuable than outward comfort. When we forget this, we are walking on thin ice and heading for a disgraceful fall.

Have you been looking with envy and interest at this world and its value system? You'd better get your eyes back on Christ and His value system. Are you slipping and haven't even noticed it?

"When I thought to know this, it was too painful for me; Until I went into the sanctuary of God; then understood I their end" (Psalm 73:16, 17).

ASAPH had served what he thought was a good God; "Truly God is good" (v. 1). Now he was not so sure; he was beginning to wonder if God was unfair. These thoughts were about to put him into a pit of depression. "When I thought to know this, it was too painful for me" (v. 16).

These thoughts were almost the downfall of Asaph. His mind was in a mess! "My steps had well nigh slipped" (v. 2). How did he get his mind cleared and his feet back on solid ground? The pressure and tension began to fade when he "went into the sanctuary of God" (v. 17). He realized he had made a terrible mistake in ever thinking of trading places with the wicked; "then understood I their end" (v. 17). When Asaph entered the sanctuary, he remembered that the final end of the wicked was Hell—"thou castedst them down into destruction" (v. 18).

Once Asaph got his mind off of the prosperity of the wicked, he could remember the prosperity of the righteous. He reflected on some of his riches in verses 23 and 24: God was always with him; God held him up; God guided him; his final end was Heaven—deliverance to Glory instead of destruction in Hell.

We don't have to be in a church sanctuary to meet with God. The rocking chair in the family room is my sanctuary. There I meet with the Lord each day and remember His goodness to me.

Have you, like Asaph, felt God was unfair? Maybe you need to find a sanctuary and start counting your blessings. Ask God to help you get the right perspective.

*"But it is good for me to draw near to God: I have put my trust in the Lord GOD,
that I may declare all thy works" (Psalm 73:28).*

ASAPH was having a poor-me pity-party in the first part of this psalm. Have you ever been there? The Devil can discourage most anyone when a person dwells on the inequities of life and the things that don't seem fair. That's what Asaph was doing, "until I went into the sanctuary of God, then understood I their end" (v. 17).

We see a complete change of attitude from verse 17 to the end of the psalm. The difference came when the discouraged psalmist went into the sanctuary where he shifted his eyes from the world back to the omnipotent God, Whom he loved and trusted.

Asaph reminded himself that the best thing he could do for himself was to draw near to God. He said, "But it is good for me to draw near to God: I have put my trust in the Lord GOD, that I may declare all thy works" (v. 28). So why did he doubt if he had put his trust in the Lord God? He forgot the Source of his confidence and trust. This world's system is constantly enticing us with money and things, and, if we're not careful, we'll find ourselves trusting in them instead of the Lord.

> "Oh, I long for a flawless trust
> My dear Savior, in Thee,
> Unwavering faith, that never doubts
> You choose what's best for me."

Are you doubting in the dark what you knew in the light? Not until you learn to trust will you be able to tell others about our wonderful Savior; "that I may declare all thy works" (v. 28). Are you shouting God's works or doubting that God works?

"Why withdrawest thou thy hand, even thy right hand? pluck it out of thy bosom"
(Psalm 74:11).

THE JEWISH people had endured a great loss. Their enemies had destroyed their city and temple. Psalm 74 reveals the feelings of the brokenhearted psalmist, Asaph. "They have cast fire into thy sanctuary . . . they have burned up all the synagogues of God in the land" (vv. 7, 8).

Why would God do such a thing? The people's lives were so full of sin that they were defiling the temple and turning it into a den of thieves (Jeremiah 7:11). God would not allow this to continue, so He withdrew His hand of blessing. "We see not our signs: there is no more any prophet" (v. 9). God removed the visible signs of His blessing, and one of these signs was the spirit of prophecy. There were no more prophets to guide the people and instruct them. Asaph wondered how long God's right hand of power would be withdrawn; when would He take His hand out of His pocket? "Why withdrawest thou thy hand, even thy right hand? pluck it out of thy bosom" (v. 11).

Why did God delay His deliverance? For the same reason He delays deliverance in our lives. He wants the chastening to fulfill the mission for which He intended it. He delays until suffering has done its work and the waiting itself has blessed us.

We must not interpret God's silence as powerlessness. He does not have His hands in His pockets; His hand is accomplishing His purpose, in His time and in His way.

Has God withdrawn visible signs of blessing from your life? What does God want His chastening to accomplish in your life?

"The day is thine, the night also is thine: thou hast prepared the light and the sun. Thou hast set all the borders of the earth: thou hast made summer and winter" (Psalm 74:16, 17).

ASAPH asked, " 'Why withdrawest thou thy hand' of blessing from us?" (v. 11). He went on to encourage himself in how God had shown His power in the past. He felt confident God's blessing would return again. If God is faithful to His Word and brings the sun and the moon each day and changes the seasons each year as He has ordained, He will keep His promise to His Chosen People and not cast them aside forever. "The day is thine, the night also is thine: thou hast prepared the light and the sun. Thou hast set all the borders of the earth: thou hast made summer and winter" (vv. 16, 17).

As Asaph remembered past blessing and God's faithfulness, it made the present miseries more bearable and fanned into a flame the spark of confidence that the future would be like the past.

God knows we need variety in our lives. Wouldn't it be boring if every day were the same? He gives us night and day, winter, spring, summer, and fall. He also gives us trouble and peace, prosperity and adversity. He reminds us that He wants us to live lives full and overflowing with joy (John 15:11) and that our lives will be full of trouble (Job 14:1). We have as much reason to expect trouble as we do night and day. But we also have as much reason to expect comfort to return as we do for spring to return after the cold, dreary days of winter.

Are you in the winter right now? Don't give up; spring will come!

"Unto thee, O God, do we give thanks, unto thee do we give thanks: for that thy name is near thy wondrous works declare" (Psalm 75:1).

THE ENEMIES had come against God's people, and there were no visible signs of a soon deliverance. Yet this psalm begins and ends with praise and thanksgiving. "Unto thee, O God, do we give thanks, unto thee do we give thanks: for that thy name is near thy wondrous works declare" (v. 1); "I will sing praises to the God of Jacob" (v. 9). The people remembered God's help in the past; this gave them confidence to praise Him in advance for His deliverance. Their expectation was so vibrant and enthusiastic it made deliverance appear as though it had already happened. By faith, they believed God would come at the very best time and "judge uprightly" (v. 2). Praise for promised blessings blesses those who offer it and those who hear it; it is a double blessing.

I love to be around grateful people. They praise and thank God regardless of the circumstances encircling their lives. I remember a dear lady who frequently said, "I'm just praising God; He is so good."

Gratitude enriches man and is well-pleasing to God. The ungrateful person grabs all he can get and holds all his blessings in his hand. The grateful person holds his blessings in his hand and in his heart. "Nothing more detestable," said an old writer, "does the earth produce than an ungrateful man." If mankind feels this way about ingratitude, I wonder how God feels about it?

Are you a double-blessed person? Do you praise God for past, undeserved favors and confidently praise Him for promised blessings for the future?

"Surely the wrath of man shall praise thee: the remainder of wrath shalt thou restrain"
(Psalm 76:10).

PSALM 75 is a psalm of faith and thanksgiving sung in anticipation of triumphant deliverance from the enemy. Psalm 76 is a song of victory; Israel was celebrating the defeat of her enemies. God did it; He stopped the enemy. "Thou didst cause judgment to be heard from heaven; the earth feared, and was still, When God arose to judgment, to save all the meek of the earth" (vv. 8, 9).

The Israelites had sinned, and God had withdrawn His hand of blessing from them. God used the wrath of their enemies to accomplish His divine will in their lives. "Surely the wrath of man shall praise thee: the remainder of wrath shalt thou restrain" (v. 10). The suffering the Israelites endured from the enemy brought them to their knees, praising God for His faithfulness to them. The enemy meant the wrath for hurt, but God used it for help.

Are you enduring suffering from an enemy? Did you know this could be God's way of accomplishing His divine will in your life? God uses suffering to get our attention and shake us out of our complacency. When my husband returned from a week in Russia, he said, "The churches were packed with people. They stood along the walls and outside." There was no spirit of complacency, but, on the contrary, a strong desire for the Word of God and companionship with other Christians.

Richard Pearson wrote these words in 1684; I think they still apply today: "Till they have suffered something for it, truth is too apt to grow cheap and be less prized many times, even by those that are good men."

Will God have to use the wrath of our enemies to bring America to her knees?

"I remembered God, and was troubled: I complained, and my spirit was overwhelmed"
(Psalm 77:3).

ASAPH wrote this psalm during a time of personal distress. He used the pronoun "I" fourteen times in the first twelve verses. Even his memories of God were distressing. "I remembered God, and was troubled: I complained, and my spirit was overwhelmed" (v. 3).

This is a sad state for a child of God to be in, yet some of us have known what it is like to be in a pit of depression. However, all of us are acquainted with trouble in some form or another. God never promised we would travel through life under unclouded skies, enjoying refreshing breezes, surrounded by delightful scenery, with enchanting companions, on pleasant and easy paths. At times we have to walk in sorrow and loneliness, beneath dark clouds, and in the midst of blasting storms. The child of God is not exempt from the sorrows and trials of life. Asaph was passing through one of those dark, stormy times in his life as he shared his heart with us.

I've learned that my troubles can make me bitter or better. God says He wants to use them to make me better. He says they are better for me than gold that will pass away (1 Peter 1:7).

How we respond to trouble is far more important than the trouble itself. Are your troubles making you bitter or better?

"I will remember the works of the LORD: surely I will remember thy wonders of old. I will meditate also of all thy work, and talk of thy doings" (Psalm 77:11, 12).

THIS PSALM started with the cries of a man in deep distress of heart and mind. The last part of the psalm reflects a complete change of mood. How did Asaph move from deep distress to victorious calmness? The answer is in verses 11 and 12: "I will *remember* the works of the LORD: surely I will *remember* thy wonders of old. I will *meditate* also of all thy work, and *talk* of thy doings."

Notice three key words in these verses: remember, meditate, talk. Asaph started recalling all the wonderful things He knew about God. He let his mind dwell on these things until he was so excited he was talking to others about how great his God was.

What worked for Asaph will work for us. We must quit thinking about our circumstances with a "poor-me" attitude. We must focus our minds on the goodness of God instead of the awfulness of our circumstances. I once heard someone say, "Winter must be cold for those with no warm memories."

Do you have warm memories in your heart when you recall the past and dwell on the good things you know about God? If your memories about the goodness of God don't warm your heart, maybe you need to know God better.

"Thou leddest thy people like a flock by the hand of Moses and Aaron" (Psalm 77:20).

THE MEMORIES of God's miracles and faithfulness to Israel sustained Asaph during the time of distress in his life (vv. 1–3, 11, 12). He seemed to be rehearsing one incredible miracle that each generation remembered. Look at verses 16–19. What miracle do you think Asaph remembered? I think it was the parting of the Red Sea. "Thy way is in the sea, and thy path in the great waters" (v. 19).

Under God's direction, Moses and Aaron led the "flock" of Israelites (two million or more people) to the Red Sea. When the enemy closed in behind them, they had no way to escape. God made a way to escape that was contrary to human reasoning. He opened the sea, and they walked through on dry ground (Exodus 14:21, 22).

Asaph was encouraged that even though his troubles might seem as deep as the Red Sea, God could make a way through them. "Thou leddest thy people like a flock by the hand of Moses and Aaron" (v. 20).

God doesn't usually take us away from our troubles or around our troubles; He takes us through them. "When thou passest *through* the waters, I will be with thee . . . when thou walkest *through* the fire, thou shalt not be burned" (Isaiah 43:2).

God doesn't take us through trials to drown us but to develop us. Don't run from your troubles; face them head on, with a firm grip on God's hand as He leads you through.

"For he established a testimony in Jacob, and appointed a law in Israel, which he commanded our fathers, that they should make them known to their children" (Psalm 78:5).

IN PSALM 77 Asaph, for his own encouragement during a difficult time in his life, reflected on God's wonders in days past. However, he seemed to end the psalm rather abruptly. Some writers feel he resumed his reflections of "the good old days" in Psalm 78. "For he established a testimony in Jacob, and appointed a law in Israel, which he commanded our fathers, that they should make them known to their children" (v. 5).

Israelite parents were instructed to recount past events and pass on this heritage to their children. "Take heed to thyself, and keep thy soul diligently, lest thou forget the things which thine eyes have seen, and lest they depart from thy heart all the days of thy life: but teach them thy sons, and thy sons' sons" (Deuteronomy 4:9). God also commanded the fathers to tell their children those things they had learned from their parents regarding the "testimony" and the "law." The fathers were to write on their children's hearts the wonderful works of God. If they were written on paper, they could perish; however if they were written on their hearts, neither time nor wear could destroy them (Deuteronomy 6:6, 7).

Parents are instructed to "train up a child in the way he should go" (Proverbs 22:6). It is not the responsibility of the Sunday School or the Christian school; it is the responsibility of parents to teach their children the wonderful works of God.

What are you doing to pass on the wonderful works of God to the next generation?

July 13

Psalm 78:10–20

"In the daytime also he led them with a cloud, and all the night with a light of fire"
(Psalm 78:14).

GOD GAVE the Children of Israel a visible sign of His presence with them: the cloud and the fire. "In the daytime also he led them with a cloud, and all the night with a light of fire" (v. 14). The cloud was a shade for the day, and the fire was as the sun for the night.

Wouldn't you think it would have been an automatic response on the Israelites' part to obey God after He demonstrated His power in such visible ways? He opened the Red Sea, and they walked across on dry ground; He led them each day with the cloud and the fire; and He fed them little angel food cakes (v. 25) from heaven each day. Wow, what miracles! Surely they would never doubt or disobey God again, but they did. "They kept not the covenant of God,

and refused to walk in his law" (v. 10). It seems incredible, but God's visible presence did nothing to produce lasting faith in His children.

If God spoke to us in an audible voice and gave us visible signs of His guidance in our lives, would we be more likely to love and trust Him? It didn't work for the Children of Israel; God knows it wouldn't work for us either. He wants His children to learn to walk by faith, not by sight (2 Corinthians 5:7). "The just shall live by faith" (Romans 1:17). The essence of faith is trusting in unseen realities (Hebrews11:1).

A special blessing is given to those who believe without seeing (John 20:29). Are you walking by faith?

"For all this they sinned still, and believed not for his wondrous works" (Psalm 78:32).

HAVE YOU ever been around a spoiled brat? Anger builds up inside me when such a person demonstrates his or her ungrateful, rebellious spirit. I just feel like grabbing and shaking the person.

That's the way I feel about the Children of Israel as I read Psalm 78. They were a bunch of ungrateful, rebellious, spoiled brats. After everything God had done for them, how did they respond to Him? "For all this they sinned still, and believed not for his wondrous works" (v. 32). In spite of everything God had done for them, they were ungrateful and unbelieving. They continued to sin, and they continued to doubt God's goodness and power.

Continuance in sin and continuance in unbelief seem to go hand in hand. If the people had believed God, they would not have continued to sin; and if they had not continued to sin, they would have believed God.

Can a believer live in unbelief? I think so. When I disobey God and live in rebellion against Him, it is as if I am saying to Him, "I know what Your Word says, but I don't want to believe it. I'll just pretend like I never heard it." I choose to live like an ungrateful, rebellious, spoiled brat. Hebrews 10:31 says, "It is a fearful thing to fall into the hands of the living God." The Children of Israel paid for their rebellion, and we will too.

If we live by sin, we will eventually be ruined by sin. What kind of choices are you making?

"But he, being full of compassion, forgave their iniquity, and destroyed them not: yea, many a time turned he his anger away, and did not stir up all his wrath" (Psalm 78:38).

HOW OFTEN did the Children of Israel provoke God in the wilderness (v. 40)? Maybe seventy times seven? In the New Testament Peter asked Christ how many times he had to forgive a brother when he sinned against him, and Christ's answer was, "Until seventy times seven" (Matthew 18:22). When you read that verse, your first reaction might be, "No one keeps forgiving that many times." God does!

For forty years the Children of Israel wandered in the wilderness, sinning and asking forgiveness, sinning and asking forgiveness. God kept forgiving. "But he, being full of compassion, forgave their iniquity, and destroyed them not: yea, many a time turned he his anger away, and did not stir up all his wrath" (v. 38). Had He poured out all His wrath and anger on them, as they well deserved, they would all have perished in a moment. They were never permitted to enter the Promised Land and enjoy all the good things God had planned for them, but He let them live long enough to raise the next generation that entered the land.

Time after time throughout the Bible we see the abundance of God's compassion, but not until the Great White Throne Judgment (Revelation 20:11–15) will men see the abundance of His wrath.

We act like men when we judge one another. We act like animals when we kill one another. We act like Christ when we forgive one another. To forgive 491 times will take supernatural power!

Do you want to be like Christ? "But he, being full of compassion, forgave their iniquity." Do you show compassion or condemnation?

"They remembered not his hand, nor the day when he delivered them from the enemy"
(Psalm 78:42).

I WONDER if God ever looks at His children and says, "Promises, promises—all I ever hear is promises. I'd like to see some walk that matches the talk"? People can make great promises when they are in trouble, but most "foxhole prayers" fade out when the war is over.

Psalm 78:34 and 35 record the Children of Israel turning back to God when they were in trouble. They may have prayed like this, "Lord, if You'll get us out of this mess, we'll serve You the rest of our lives."

I've heard prayers like that many times, but I've seen very few of them materialize into obedient, faithful living for Christ. Most of the people who prayed those prayers are like the Israelites. "Nevertheless they . . . lied unto him with their tongues. For their heart was not right with him" (vv. 36, 37). Talk is cheap! The Israelites followed God with their words, but not with their hearts. Over and over they said they would follow Him, but then they turned away from Him and forgot their promises to Him. "They remembered not his hand, nor the day when he delivered them from the enemy" (v. 42).

We are strange creatures! We forget what we should remember and remember what we should forget. Just as the Israelites were never to forget the day they were delivered from Egyptian bondage (vv. 43–51), so we must never forget the day we were saved—delivered from Satan's bondage.

Are you remembering what you should be remembering and forgetting what you should be forgetting?

"For they provoked him to anger with their high places, and moved him to jealousy with their graven images" (Psalm 78:58).

DO CHILDREN learn from their parents' mistakes and blunders? Sometimes, yes; but many times, no. The Children of Israel didn't! The next generation of Israelites entered Canaan, the Promised Land, and set up the tabernacle at Shiloh (v. 60), but they repeated the sins of their parents. They "turned back, and dealt unfaithfully like their fathers" (v. 57).

Unfaithful, disobedient parents produced children who were even more unfaithful than they were; they started imitating the idolatrous Canaanites. Their spiritual adultery moved God to jealousy and anger. "For they provoked him to anger with their high places, and moved him to jealousy with their graven images" (v. 58). Finally God had enough of their sin; He forsook them and delivered them into the hands of their enemies (vv. 60, 61). Their sins drove God away from them.

God never withdraws His blessing from His children until we have driven Him from us. Our God is a jealous God. He wants to have first place in our lives. The very first commandment reminds us of this (Exodus 20:3). God once said this of Ephraim: he is "joined to idols: let him alone" (Hosea 4:17). God also said, "Take heed, brethren, lest there be in any of you an evil heart of unbelief, in departing from the living God" (Hebrews 3:12).

Do you have gods or idols in your life that are more important to you than the living God? Take heed! God may withdraw His blessing.

"So he fed them according to the integrity of his heart; and guided them by the skilfulness of his hands" (Psalm 78:72).

DAVID was on the throne when Asaph wrote this psalm, but Asaph reminded the people of David the shepherd. Could Asaph have wanted the people to remember that God had chosen a man of humble position to fill an exalted position? God does not choose people because of their appearance or position; God is looking for character and ability. David had both of these. "So he fed them according to the integrity of his heart; and guided them by the skilfulness of his hands" (v. 72).

God is more concerned with our inner condition than our outward appearance. "Man looketh on the outward appearance, but the LORD looketh on the heart" (1 Sam-uel 16:7). We may not have a great many skills, but we can all have "integrity of heart." What is integrity of heart? An honest and sincere heart.

Someone has said that the greatest ability is dependability. When you tell someone you will do something, can they depend on your doing it? Are you so full of integrity you will stay up late, go in early, or do without in order to keep your word? For the Christian honesty is not the best policy, it is the only policy.

Are you known as a person of integrity? Do you keep your word? God looks for integrity, not intentions.

"O remember not against us former iniquities: let thy tender mercies speedily prevent us:
for we are brought very low" (Psalm 79:8).

ISRAEL'S enemies had destroyed Jeru-salem and had demolished Solomon's temple (v. 1). This never would have happened if the Israelites, God's Chosen People, had not first desecrated the holy place with their sins (2 Chronicles 36:14–21). God once again abandoned His people and turned them over to their foes.

We see the effects of sin passing from one generation to another. The people pleaded for mercy and asked God to remove from them the judgment of their parents' sins. Their sins, added to their parents' sins, had brought them low. "O remember not against us former iniquities: let thy tender mercies speedily prevent us: for we are brought very low" (v. 8). The people knew their only hope was God's mercy. Matthew Henry said, "As God's mercies are new every morning toward his people, so his anger is new every morning against the wicked."

Have you been brought low, pleading for mercy? Is it your sin or someone else's sin that is causing such turmoil in your soul? Other people's sin can cause havoc in our lives. Your husband's sin will affect you; your child's sin will affect you; when anyone you love sins, it will affect you. What can you do? Cry out to God for His tender mercy to speedily meet your need for peace and comfort.

Are you seeking help from the right source?

211

"Turn us again, O God, and cause thy face to shine; and we shall be saved" (Psalm 80:3).

WHEN MY husband preaches about repentance, he often says we are born with our backs toward God. We continue walking away from God until we turn around, face God, and repent of our sins. When that happens and when we believe that the Lord Jesus paid the penalty for our sins, we are born again and become new creations (2 Corinthians 5:17). However, because we don't lose our sin natures when we are born again, we will need more repentance experiences (Romans 7:19, 20).

We see this in David's life. David didn't lose his salvation when he sinned, but he lost the joy of his salvation. Not until he repented of his sin was that joy restored (Psalm 51:3, 12). In Psalm 80 we see a similar prayer of repentance: "Turn us again, O God, and cause thy face to shine; and we shall be saved" (v. 3). Three times the psalmist asked God to "turn us again," or restore or quicken us again (vv. 3, 18, 19).

When a person turns away from God, the pattern for turning back is always the same: repentance, restoration, and forgiveness. Only as we turn around can His face shine upon us again. When we are facing God, we can clearly see our sin and be saved from a life of destruction.

"The LORD bless thee, and keep thee: The LORD make his face shine upon thee, and be gracious unto thee: The LORD lift up his countenance upon thee, and give thee peace" (Numbers 6:24–26).

Are you facing God and enjoying His blessing or walking away from God and facing destruction?

"So will not we go back from thee: quicken us, and we will call upon thy name"
(Psalm 80:18).

IN THIS psalm the nation of Israel is described as a vine planted in the land of Canaan. God had driven out many of the other nations to make room for His Chosen People. The vine had taken root and was beginning to bear fruit, but the people started to backslide again. They began practicing the gross sin of idol worship.

The Israelites wanted to be like the other nations, so they started visiting heathen altars and sacrificing to heathen gods. God had departed from His people, and they knew it. They promised anew not to backslide again. "So will not we go back from thee: quicken us, and we will call upon thy name" (v. 18). If God would deliver them, they would faithfully worship Him; "we will call upon thy name." But they would need God's help; He would have to "quicken," or revive, their cold hearts. Their interest in God and the things of God was dying, their spirits were drooping.

Is your interest in spiritual things as keen as it once was? Have you slowly moved into a backslidden condition without even realizing it? Have you lost your joy? Do you need to be revived? Christ tells us how we can have a life full of joy in John 15:1–11. "These things have I spoken unto you, that my joy might remain in you, and that your joy might be full" (John 15:11).

Read John 15 for the next seven days and see what happens. Wouldn't it be exciting to have a life overflowing with joy again?

"Hear, O my people, and I will testify unto thee: O Israel, if thou wilt hearken unto me; There shall no strange god be in thee; neither shalt thou worship any strange god" (Psalm 81:8, 9).

THIS PSALM is called a holiday hymn by some writers. It may have been sung at the Feast of Tabernacles much as we sing Christmas carols to remind us of the birth of our Savior. The song celebrated Israel's exodus from Egypt, reminding the people of God's goodness and their waywardness.

In verses 8 and 9 God spoke through the psalmist to the Israelites and reminded them of the first commandment, "Thou shalt have no other gods before me" (Exodus 20:3). "Hear, O my people, and I will testify unto thee: O Israel, if thou wilt hearken unto me; There shall no strange god be in thee; neither shalt thou worship any strange god"

(vv. 8, 9). Surely a golden calf or any other carved image would be a strange god for anyone who knew the true and living God. How could these strange gods meet the people's needs, answer their desires, or make them happy?

What strange gods do we need to cast out of our lives? The world, the flesh, and the Devil are constantly pulling us toward themselves, wanting us to make them gods in our lives. Our Lord reminds us in 1 John 5:21, "Little children, keep yourselves from idols."

Is there anyone or anything more important to you than God? Have you made it an idol? God wants first place in your life.

"Oh that my people had hearkened unto me, and Israel had walked in my ways!"
(Psalm 81:13).

ONE DAY my husband and I had lunch with a new acquaintance. During the course of our conversation, we asked about his family. He shared with us that he had five married children. He went on to say that three of them will not speak to him. We soon realized we were talking to a hurting father.

Psalm 81:11 and 12 are the words of a hurting Father as He speaks of His children in words like these, "They wouldn't listen to Me; they want nothing to do with Me. They have made their bed; now they will have to sleep in it." Our Heavenly Father doesn't share His heart in disgust, but in regret. "Oh that my people had hearkened unto me, and Israel had walked in my ways!" (v. 13). God had such good things planned for His people, but they wanted to do their own thing. The Jews didn't want God's divinely prescribed way. As a result their prosperity and peace were gone. As much as God wanted the best for them, He could not give His best without their obedience.

Many parents live with regrets as they think of what might have been if their children had just listened to them. Many adult children are now living with the regrets of their rebellious lifestyles. Don't live your life dwelling on the past failures of others or yourself. If you need to ask forgiveness for your failures, do it today and start over again.

Instead of living the rest of your life with "the things that might have been," start experiencing some of "the things that might have been."

"How long will ye judge unjustly, and accept the persons of the wicked?" (Psalm 82:2).

THIS PSALM is addressed to wicked magistrates or judges. The word "gods" in verse 1 is more literally translated "mighty ones" or "judges." The name "god" was used of the judges as representing God, as judging in His name or authority. The judges were abusing the poor and needy and judging unfairly. Bribery and corruption were continual. The psalmist asked, "How long will ye judge unjustly, and accept the persons of the wicked?" (v. 2).

As we read today's newspapers and listen to the news commentators, we echo the psalmist's words, "How long will ye judge unjustly?" It seems the wicked are winning and the good guys are losing. Regardless of how bad things look, God is still in control, and He is the judge of the rulers of our land. "God standeth in the congregation of the mighty; he judgeth among the gods [judges]" (v. 1).

What about us? Have we been guilty of judging unjustly?

"Pray don't find fault with the man who
    limps
Or stumbles along the road,
Unless you have worn the shoes that he
    wears
Or struggled beneath his load.
There may be tacks in his shoes that hurt,
Though hidden away from view;
Or burdens he bears placed on your back
Might cause you to stumble, too.
Don't sneer at the man who is down today
Unless you have felt the blow
That caused his fall, or felt the same
That only the fallen know."

Do you need to be more careful in your judgments?

"They have said, Come, and let us cut them off from being a nation; that the name of Israel may be no more in remembrance" (Psalm 83:4).

THIS IS the last psalm in which we shall hear from the patriotic poet, Asaph. The psalm points to a serious problem. Ten nations had joined together to make war against the Israelites and totally destroy them (vv. 6–11) Their plan was not just to cripple the Israelites as a power, but to totally do away with them as a chosen nation. "They have said, Come, and let us cut them off from being a nation; that the name of Israel may be no more in remembrance" (v. 4).

We know this will never happen. In Jeremiah 31:35 and 36 God said that only if the sun and moon quit shining and the waves cease would Israel cease being a nation.

If Hitler had read the Bible, he would have known you cannot rid the earth of the Jews, as he intended to do. In the 1940s at Auschwitz and in other extermination camps of the Third Reich, his plan almost succeeded. But man cannot thwart God's plan. It is interesting to notice that all the nations that opposed Israel in Psalm 83:6–11 no longer exist. The Third Reich no longer exists; yet the Jewish nation does. God knew what He was doing, but Asaph didn't. He said, "Keep not thou silence, O God: hold not thy peace, and be not still, O God" (v. 1). God had said nothing; it seemed God was doing nothing.

Are you wondering where God is and why He doesn't do something? Many people have asked, "Where was God when Hitler was killing all those Jews?" He was in the same place He was when His Son was dying on the cross!

God knows what He is doing. His plan cannot be thwarted (Job 42:2). You can trust Him!

"How amiable are thy tabernacles, O LORD of hosts! My soul longeth, yea, even fainteth for the courts of the LORD: my heart and my flesh crieth out for the living God" (Psalm 84:1, 2).

THIS PSALM may have been written when David was exiled from the sanctuary, the tabernacle. He was compelled to flee from Jerusalem because of the rebellion of his son Absolom (2 Samuel 15:13, 14). Can you imagine the heartbreak this honored king endured in being driven from his homeland in his old age—perhaps never to return again? David had experienced some crushing blows in his lifetime, but this one must have been one of the most painful.

When David left the holy city, he did not try to hide his feelings of anguish and distress. Second Samuel 15:30 gives us a picture of the hurting king. "And David . . . wept as he went up, and had his head covered, and he went barefoot." During this time of exile, one of his greatest griefs was not being able to worship in the tabernacle of God, for it was there he met with the living God. "My soul longeth, yea, even fainteth for the courts of the LORD: my heart and my flesh crieth out for the living God" (v. 2).

Because they were reared in a pastor's home, our sons never missed a church service. Occasionally they would ask, "Dad, do we have to go to church?" His answer was always the same: "No, you don't *have* to go, you *get* to go."

How much do you appreciate your church? If you were told you could never go again, would you count it as a great loss? Do you look at your church attendance as a duty or a privilege? Why not write a note to your pastor, expressing your appreciation to him for his faithfulness to you and to the Word of God. You'll never know what those kind of notes do for a pastor.

"For a day in thy courts is better than a thousand. I had rather be a doorkeeper in the house of my God, than to dwell in the tents of wickedness" (Psalm 84:10).

PART OF old age is reminiscing. David—if indeed he wrote Psalm 84—was old and had been exiled from his kingdom and abandoned by his son. All he had were his memories. His most precious memories were of times in the house of his God. He said, "For a day in thy courts is better than a thousand" (v. 10).

A thousand what? A thousand days, a thousand dollars, a thousand kingdoms? Just one day of serving the Lord is better than a thousand of anything else. David had no regrets that he had lived his life in service to God.

Living for Christ may not seem like the most exciting life, but it sure is a satisfying life. I have no regrets that I have lived my life to serve God and others. I can't imagine being anything else but a pastor's wife. However, if I had done what I wanted to do, I would never have been a pastor's wife. When my husband told me God was calling him to be a preacher, I said, "You'll be a preacher over my dead body. I will never be a preacher's wife!" God had to almost kill me twice to get me to change my mind, but I am so glad He was patient with me. I will never forget the day I fell to my knees and said, "God, You win. I lose." I really would have been a loser if I had continued on in my sin and rebellion. I lost nothing but gained everything I would ever need to be happy and satisfied.

When you look back over your life, can you say, "I have no regrets that I have turned my back on the wicked world and have chosen to live my life to please God"? If you haven't made that choice, will you do it today?

"For the LORD God is a sun and shield: the LORD will give grace and glory: no good thing will he withhold from them that walk uprightly" (Psalm 84:11).

NO GOOD thing will he withhold from them that walk uprightly" (v. 11). The psalmist said God doesn't withhold anything that is good from them who walk right before Him. Yet David had lost everything meaningful to him. The king of Israel had been driven from the palace by his own son and forced to wander in the wilderness.

It seems sometimes that the wicked prosper even more than those who live right. What "good thing" do the righteous have that the unrighteous don't have? They have things that money cannot buy! They have joy, peace, and contentment. David knew he had Someone in his life Who could give him light in the darkest night—"a sun" (v. 11). He had Someone Who could protect him against his enemies—his "shield." His "sun and shield" gave him grace to handle every situation. David's enemies could withhold the kingdom from David, but they could not withhold the things that really count in life.

What things count most in your life? A new house? furniture? more clothes? a big bank account? There is nothing wrong with these things, but they are just "things"! If all your "things" were snatched away from you, do you have the "good things" that no one can take from you?

"Wilt thou not revive us again: that thy people may rejoice in thee?" (Psalm 85:6).

THIS PSALM may have been written after the return of the exiles from the Babylonian Captivity. Some scholars feel David wrote it; others are not sure. We can be sure of one thing: it is a prayer for revival. The Israelites had sinned, and now they were praying that God would give them a repentant heart and turn them from their sin. "Wilt thou not revive us again?" (v. 6).

The people knew they did not deserve God's mercy, but they were pleading for it so they might be delivered from their calamities. They were tired of the consequences of sin; they wanted some joy in their lives again. They prayed that God would show mercy to them (v. 7) so that "thy people may rejoice in thee" (v. 6). They had found no joy in sin. They knew only God's favor on their lives could restore their joy.

Do you need revival in your life? Have you lost your joy? Are you just going through the "motions of devotions"? If you really want to be revived, I have a challenge for you. Make a new commitment before God to read your Bible and keep a journal for the next thirty days. Why keep a journal? I once read, "There is no impression without expression." We need to write down each day what God has impressed on our hearts as a result of reading His Word. This will help make daily Bible reading a vital experience.

Nothing can revive you and restore your joy more quickly than the Word of God. God will do His part if you will do your part. Will you accept my challenge?

"Be merciful unto me, O Lord: for I cry unto thee daily" (Psalm 86:3).

W E DO NOT know when David wrote this prayer. He prayed it himself, and I am sure he would recommend it to others in times of affliction. "In the day of my trouble I will call upon thee" (v. 7). The psalm seems clearly to be a prayer because the words "Lord," "God," "thee," and "thy" are used in each of the seventeen verses. Verse 3 seems to indicate that daily prayer was a habit of David's life: "Be merciful unto me, O Lord: for I cry unto thee *daily.*"

Some people use the acronym ACTS as a guide for prayer. Notice how David included each element in his Psalm 86 prayer:

A - doration (vv. 5, 8, 10, 15)
C - onfession (v. 1)
T - hanks (vv. 7, 9, 12–14)
S - upplication (vv. 1–4, 6, 11, 16, 17)

Has your prayer life become dull? If you have never tried ACTS, try it for a while. Here is another suggestion to broaden your praying:

Monday—Missions (foreign)
Tuesday—Thanksgiving (count your
   blessings)
Wednesday—Workers (home missions
   and Christian servants)
Thursday—Tasks (jobs I have to do)
Friday—Families (my own and others)
Saturday—Saints (fellow believers)
Sunday—Sinners (people who need to
   be saved)

Aren't you glad God doesn't keep office hours, has no answering machines, and never puts us on hold?

"In the day of my trouble I will call upon thee: for thou wilt answer me" (Psalm 86:7).

EVERY PERSON has some burden he must bear, some trouble he must endure. The Bible reminds us of this in Galatians 6:5: "Every man shall bear his own burden." David seemed to have more than his share of burdens. He could easily have said, "In my days of trouble," or "in my times of trouble"; but he didn't. He said, "In the day of my trouble" (v. 7).

Even though it may not seem this way at first, most of our troubles are short-lived. Very few people have lives of continual hardship and suffering. But if they do, how do they survive? The same way David did. "I will call upon thee: for thou wilt answer me" (v. 7). David knew the Lord was a very present help in the time of trouble (Psalm 46:1).

I once read that people who have to experience long periods of suffering handle it in one of three ways: they commit suicide, go insane, or just learn to endure. I know a family who endured twenty years of heartache and turmoil. People who don't know what they have gone through look at their lives and say, "Do they have it made! A beautiful big home on a lake, two boats, two cars, and all the luxuries that money can buy." But I don't think anyone would want to exchange places with them if they knew the whole story. How have they survived? They never turned away from God. When the trials started, they took God at His Word when He said He would be their refuge and strength and a very present help in trouble.

Are you calling on the right person in your time of trouble?

"The LORD shall count, when he writeth up the people, that this man was born there"
(Psalm 87:6).

THIS SONG is dedicated to the sons of Korah who kept the doors of the house of the Lord, probably the temple. The psalm is in honor of Zion, better known to us as Jerusalem. Zion was the dwelling place of God on earth in the Old Testament. "The LORD loveth the gates of Zion more than all the dwellings of Jacob. Glorious things are spoken of thee, O city of God" (vv. 2, 3). It was an honor to be a native of Jerusalem. "The LORD shall count, when he writeth up the people, that this man was born there" (v. 6). Later in Israel's history, the city was untouched by the Assyrian king Sennacherib, as a result of Hezekiah's prayer for deliverance (2 Kings 19:15–19, 32–34).

Today believers are the dwelling place of God on earth (John 14:17; 1 Corinthians 6:19). When God opens the Book of Life (Revelation 20:12; 21:27), it will be the highest honor to be a native of spiritual Zion, the heavenly city of God.

God keeps the register of all of those who are born-again citizens of the city "whose builder and maker is God" (Hebrews 11:10).

Are you a citizen of spiritual Zion? Is your name written in the Book of Life? Registration on church rolls on earth will avail us nothing unless our names are in the Book of Life. "And whosoever was not found written in the book of life was cast into the lake of fire" (Revelation 20:15).

When the roll is called up yonder, I'll be there! Will you?

"For my soul is full of troubles: and my life draweth nigh unto the grave" (Psalm 88:3).

THIS IS A psalm of sadness and sorrow, believed to be written by Heman, one of the chief singers, who was called the king's seer (1 Chronicles 25:5). The psalmist may have been suffering from some painful disease or illness. He was seemingly so close to death he thought surely it would come soon; "my life draweth nigh unto the grave" (v. 3). His body was afflicted, but even worse was the mental distress and affliction he was enduring. "My soul is full of troubles" (v. 3); "Thou hast laid me in the lowest pit, in darkness, in the deeps" (v. 6).

In the last few years I have often longed for days when life was simpler, when the physical and mental stress was much less. One time in particular I was so distressed I thought surely I would never be happy again on the earth. I felt like Humpty Dumpty. Remember what happened to him?

"Humpty Dumpty sat on the wall;
Humpty Dumpty had a great fall;
All the king's horses and all the king's men
Couldn't put Humpty together again."

Have you ever wondered if your life could be put back together again? Praise God, it can! "Blessed be God, even the Father of our Lord Jesus Christ, the Father of mercies, and the God of all comfort; Who comforteth us in all our tribulation, that we may be able to comfort them which are in any trouble, by the comfort wherewith we ourselves are comforted of God" (2 Corinthians 1:3, 4). All the king's horses and men couldn't fix Humpty Dumpty, but the King of Kings, Jesus Christ, can fix our lives if we give Him all the pieces! He did it for me, and He'll do it for you!

If it seems like your life is in pieces, ask the King to put it back together again.

"I am afflicted and ready to die from my youth up: while I suffer thy terrors I am distracted"
(Psalm 88:15).

PROLONGED bodily afflictions or mental anguish tends to wear us down to the point that death seems a welcome relief. The psalmist felt he had been at death's door since his youth. "I am afflicted and ready to die from my youth up" (v. 15). This is either the exaggeration of a depressed spirit or the expression of how it feels to live with a chronic illness since birth or for many years. Whichever it was, the monotony of the constant weariness of his body had brought the psalmist to the place where he felt he couldn't endure anymore; his strength was gone. "I am as a man that hath no strength" (v. 4).

One writer expressed how he thought the psalmist might have felt: "My heart is too tired to hope; I dare not look forward to the future; I expect nothing from the days to come, and yet my heart sinks at the thought of the grey waste of years before me; and I wonder how I can endure, whether I shall faint by the way, before I reach my far-off home."

You may feel your trials and pains will never end, but that's not so for the believer. All the miseries of life will end in Heaven, never to be remembered again (Revelation 21:4). Better days are ahead!

"It will be worth it all when we see Jesus,
Life's trials will seem so small when we
    see Christ;
One glimpse of His dear face all sorrow
    will erase,
So bravely run the race till we see Christ."

Are you looking forward to Heaven? I am!

"Lover and friend hast thou put far from me, and mine acquaintance into darkness"
(Psalm 88:18).

NO ONE cares whether I live or die," moaned the psalmist. "Where are your friends and loved ones when you need them?" his complaint continued. "I am crying alone in the darkness." Whether real or imagined, the psalmist felt he had been forsaken and abandoned by his loved ones, friends, and acquaintances. "Lover and friend hast thou put far from me, and mine acquaintance into darkness" (v. 18).

He referred to his loneliness in verse 8 as well: "Thou hast put away mine acquaintance far from me." To complete the cycle of his feeling of abandonment, he felt the Lord had also forsaken him. "Lord, . . . why hidest thou thy face from me?" (v. 14).

Have you ever felt the Lord had hidden His face from you? Have you ever felt your friends and loved ones had forsaken you? Friends and loved ones are divided into two groups when a crisis comes crashing into your life: those who will stand with you through the crisis and those who either do not know how or do not want to cope with it. Peter told the Lord he would never forsake Him, but he did (Matthew 26:35, 75). People may forsake us, but our Friend, the Lord Jesus, never will. He is "a friend that sticketh closer than a brother" (Proverbs 18:24).

❖

You may feel alone, but you are not alone if Jesus Christ is your closest friend!

"I will sing of the mercies of the LORD for ever: with my mouth will I make known thy faithfulness to all generations" (Psalm 89:1).

THIS PSALM was written by Ethan, the Ezrahite, one of the head musicians in the temple during David's reign (1 Chronicles 15:17, 19). Ethan, who probably wrote this in his old age, mourned the troubles coming upon David's dynasty and the land of Judah. He started the psalm singing of the Israelites' glorious past and God's faithfulness to them. "I will sing of the mercies of the LORD for ever: with my mouth will I make known thy faithfulness to all generations" (v. 1). The psalmist's only hope for rising above the grief and discouragement of the present was to remember God's faithfulness in the past.

Remembering past blessings has a healing effect on our soul, especially in old age. My husband and I have mothers whose mates have gone on to Glory. When we visit them, they spend a great deal of their time talking about the past and remembering "the good old days." They both lived through the Depression, but they never went without a meal.

God's faithfulness to these women through the years gives me hope for the present and the future. As they pass on to this generation the stories of God's faithfulness, we want to pass it on to the next generation.

What legacy will you leave? Will you have stories of God's faithfulness to pass on to the next generation?

"Justice and judgment are the habitation of thy throne: mercy and truth shall go before thy face" (Psalm 89:14).

THIS SONG continues the message of God's faithfulness that was started in verse 1. Here we see God as an impartial judge and a merciful father. "Justice and judgment are the habitation of thy throne: mercy and truth shall go before thy face" (v. 14).

God, the impartial judge, in His justice always does what is right, and His judgment always decides what is right. Only God always *does* what is right because only He always *knows* what is right. God will always act as a merciful father, holding truth in one hand and mercy in the other. As a merciful father, He will always do what He promised whether it is blessing or punishment. He always does it in mercy with a heart full of compassion.

I have gained much from a book written by Joel Freeman, *God Is Not Fair*. His analysis is that life isn't fair and that God never said He would be fair; He said He is just (Deuteronomy 32:4). Therefore, He will always do what is right and do it in mercy. We must be reminded every now and then that mercy and judgment both come from God—just like honey and the sting both come from the bee.

Have you thanked God for His justice and mercy? I want to praise Him for both.

"My covenant will I not break, nor alter the thing that is gone out of my lips"
(Psalm 89:34).

WE LIVE in a land of covenant-breaking people. Many people, including Christians, do not think twice about lying. Every covenant or promise God made to His people He carried out. He cannot, nor would not, lie to those He loves. "My covenant will I not break, nor alter the thing that is gone out of my lips" (v. 34). The Israelites broke the promises they made to God. In Exodus 19:8 they promised to obey and keep the Lord's covenant with them: "All that the LORD hath spoken we will do." Yet only a few weeks later they made and worshiped a golden calf (Exodus 32) in direct violation of the first two commandments: "Thou shalt have no other gods before me. Thou shalt not make unto thee any graven image" (Exodus 20:3, 4).

As I was sitting at a twenty-fifth wedding anniversary celebration, the thought crossed my mind, "Will silver and golden wedding anniversaries be a thing of the past in years to come?" Young couples take sacred vows before God, and yet they break them so easily. Couples married twenty, thirty, or even forty years are breaking their vows.

Think on these challenging words from Charles Spurgeon: "A word once given is sacred; once let a promise pass our lips and honesty forbids that we should recall it—unless indeed the thing promised be impossible, or wicked."

Is your promise to others, whether in marriage or other dealings, as good as gold? God's is!

"How long, LORD? wilt thou hide thyself for ever? shall thy wrath burn like fire?"
(Psalm 89:46).

UP TO THIS point in Psalm 89, Ethan had been able to keep up his spirits by remembering God's faithfulness in the past. But when he started to dwell on the present circumstances in David's kingdom, his mood changed. His spirits drooped, and his mouth was full of complaints. That which seemed to grieve him most was that God did not appear to him. Why did He keep him in the dark? "How long, LORD? wilt thou hide thyself for ever? shall thy wrath burn like fire?" (v. 46).

John Howe wrote these words to describe a person who is overwhelmed with his circumstances: "An eye bleared with present sorrow sees not far, nor comprehends so much at one view." How true! Our circumstances often make us shortsighted.

Have your present circumstances made you so shortsighted that you have forgotten your past blessings? Do you feel God has hidden Himself from you? Try singing of the mercies of the Lord (Psalm 89:1), and ask God to restore your vision to a correct view of Himself and your circumstances.

"Before the mountains were brought forth, or ever thou hadst formed the earth and the world, even from everlasting to everlasting, thou art God" (Psalm 90:2).

THIS IS probably the oldest psalm, one written by Moses. It is a prayer with two parts: verses 1–11 are meditations on the past; verses 12–17 are a prayer for the future. It was probably written in the wilderness, near the end of the forty years of wandering (vv. 9, 10).

Moses started his prayer with his affirmation of God as the eternal creator: "Before the mountains were brought forth, or ever thou hadst formed the earth and the world, even from everlasting to everlasting, thou art God" (v. 2). Moses was not an evolutionist; he believed God created man and everything else in this world. How could a mountain evolve from nothing? God brought them forth (v. 2); He spoke them into being (Genesis 1:9, 10), and they are still standing.

Genesis 1:27 tells us God created man in His image, but man has created God in his imagination. A lady once told me, "I like the God of the New Testament but not the God of the Old Testament. It can't be the same God." She had created God as she imagined He should be, just a God of love. However, I think she must have not read the last book of the New Testament. Because God is full of love and kindness, He must always tell the truth. He tells us in His Word He will punish sin (Revelation 20). In order to be truthful and just, He must do what He said He would do. A person who really loves us would never lie to us.

Have you thanked God that He created you and that He controls all of His creation?

"The days of our years are threescore years and ten; and if by reason of strength they be fourscore years, yet is their strength labour and sorrow; for it is soon cut off, and we fly away" (Psalm 90:10).

WHEN MOSES wrote those words, it was not uncommon for men to live 100 to 150 years. But 70 to 80 years is God's appointed life span for man. "The days of our years are threescore years and ten; and if by reason of strength they be fourscore years . . ." (v. 10).

Not many people exceed age 80, although life expectancy continues to increase. Living beyond 80 for many older people is, as Moses said, "labour and sorrow" (v. 10). Many labor to breathe, to walk, or even to think clearly. Such is old age! But old age can be a glorious time, for soon the toiling of life will be over. The sun will set, the heat of the day will be over, and a perfect, unclouded, eternal day will begin.

I wonder how many people are really satisfied with their age? Twelve-year-old girls want to dress and act like sixteen-year-olds. Seventy-year-olds wish they were 50 again; fifty-year-olds wish they were 30 again. Thomas Fuller said, "Life is to be measured by action, not by time; a man may die old at thirty, and young at eighty; nay, the one lives after death, and the other perished before he died."

How can we keep from becoming old and grumpy? I think Paul gave us the secret in Philippians 4:11, "I have learned, in whatsoever state I am, therewith to be content." No one likes to be around an old grump.

Stay content, and you'll be happy and young at 80! Are you contented or contentious?

"So teach us to number our days, that we may apply our hearts unto wisdom"
(Psalm 90:12).

MOSES may have been reflecting on the events recorded in Numbers 14 when he wrote this psalm. God had told His people to go in and possess the Promised Land, but they would not. They doubted God and did not believe He could enable them to conquer the land. As a result, God told them that everybody twenty years and older was going to die within the next forty years in the wilderness. The next generation would conquer the land (Numbers 14:29, 30). Moses may have been challenging the people to make wiser choices with the years they had left since they had not done so well up to that point. "So teach us to number our days, that we may apply our hearts unto wisdom" (v. 12).

Considering that life is brief and none of us has any promise of tomorrow, we need to live every day as wisely as we can. I'm sure each of us can look at some segment of life and say, "I wish I could live that part of my life over again. If I'd had the wisdom then that I've gained through years of living, I'm sure I would have made better choices."

We can't live even one moment of life over again, but we can make wiser choices in the future. God's wisdom is offered to all who will ask for it. "If any of you lack wisdom, let him ask of God, that giveth to all men liberally." (James 1:5).

Have you asked for wisdom so that you can make good choices each day?

"He that dwelleth in the secret place of the most High shall abide under the shadow of the Almighty" (Psalm 91:1).

WE DO NOT know who wrote this psalm or the occasion when it was written. One thing we know for sure, this psalm has been a "security blanket" for the saints of God all through the centuries. Verse 1 summarizes the whole psalm: "He that dwelleth in the secret place of the most High shall abide under the shadow of the Almighty."

Imagine yourself in a desert with the sun beating down. No matter where you look, as far as your eyes can see, there is no shelter or trees, no place of refuge from the intense heat of the sun. As you continue to walk, you come upon a hidden spot. There, protected from the noonday sun, you find relief—shade and shelter. Spending time in God's presence is like finding that place of refuge—a place of shade and shelter "under the shadow of the Almighty."

All through the Bible we see God's care for His children and even His creatures. One day a group of people stood on the great Matterhorn in the Swiss Alps. A man in the group caught a fly and pulled a small microscope from his pocket. He told the group that the legs of the household fly in England were naked; then he asked those around him to look at the legs of the fly he had caught. To their amazement, the legs were thickly covered with hair. The God Who made the mountains even made socks and mittens for the little flies who live in the mountains.

What a privilege to dwell "under the shadow of the Almighty," Who takes care of stumbling saints and crawling creatures. Are you dwelling in the hot heat or the soothing shadows?

"For he shall give his angels charge over thee, to keep thee in all thy ways" (Psalm 91:11).

NO ONE is more secure and has less reason to be fearful than the believer who is walking in God's ways. The Holy Spirit indwells us (John 14:16, 17), and angels watch over us. "For he shall give his angels charge over thee, to keep thee in all thy ways" (v. 11).

The "ways" spoken of here are the ways of obedience. As long as we walk in God's ways, we are sure of His divine help and protection. God has commanded His angels to watch over us. Only when we get to Heaven will we know all that angels did for us besides divert demons, ward off disease, and keep us from besetting temptations.

However, if we are disobedient and walk in our ways, we are exposed to dangers from every side. God never promised to protect us and bless us when we're walking in sin. On the contrary, He promised to chasten us (Hebrews 12:5, 6). How unwise we would be to forfeit the help of ministering angels by living in disobedience.

I once read of a dying saint who asked that only one word be on his tombstone besides his name and dates of birth and death. The only word was "KEPT." "For he shall give his angels charge over thee, to keep thee in all thy ways" (v. 11).

No one in her right mind would want to walk in enemy territory when she could enjoy divine protection. Where are you walking?

"To shew forth thy lovingkindness in the morning, and thy faithfulness every night"
(*Psalm 92:2*).

THIS PSALM was probably written to sing on the Sabbath Day. The Sabbath was set apart for honoring the Lord for His finished work of creation (Exodus 20:8–11). Today Sunday is set apart to worship Christ for His finished work of redemption as evidenced by the Resurrection (Luke 24:1–3). We set apart one day for public worship, but every day should be a thanksgiving day for believers. "To shew forth thy lovingkindness in the morning, and thy faithfulness every night" (v. 2).

Zig Ziglar says we should start each day like this: Before we put our feet on the floor, we should sit on the side of the bed, clap our hands, and say, "It's going to be a great day!" He has determined that our attitude determines our altitude for the day. How high or how low we feel is determined by our attitude.

I agree! I do not sit on the side of the bed and clap my hands, but I do try to start each day with a positive attitude. My attitude cannot change my aches and pains or my problems, but it can help me handle them without grumbling and complaining.

Try focusing on God's love in the morning and His faithfulness in the evening. It will work wonders for your attitude!

"The righteous shall flourish like the palm tree: he shall grow like a cedar in Lebanon"
(Psalm 92:12).

GOD'S PEOPLE, the righteous ones, are compared to the palm and cedar trees in this psalm. "The righteous shall flourish like the palm tree: he shall grow like a cedar in Lebanon" (v. 12).

Palm and cedar trees have something in common: they are evergreens. In winter and summer they stay green, beautiful, and productive. They can survive extreme heat and the cold because their roots go deep. The palm endures the intense heat of the desert and the hurricane winds. The cedar endures the extreme cold of the northlands and the winter gales.

Are you like the palm and the cedar? Are your roots going deeper and deeper so you can survive the storms of life? When those dry, lonesome, desert times come, we can make it through the drought if we're deeply rooted in the Word of God. When cold, bitter blasts hit us in the face, we can make it through the storms if we're deeply rooted in the Word of God.

I appreciate this thought from *Streams in the Desert:* "When first affliction comes upon us, how everything gives way! Our clinging, tendril hopes are snapped, and our heart lies prostrate like a vine that the storm has torn from its trellis; but when the first shock is past, and we are able to look up, and say, 'It is the Lord,' faith lifts the shattered hopes once more, and binds them fast to the feet of God. Thus the end is confidence, safety, and peace."

Are your roots deep enough to survive the storms of life?

"The LORD reigneth, he is clothed with majesty; the LORD is clothed with strength, wherewith he hath girded himself: the world also is stablished, that it cannot be moved"
(Psalm 93:1).

THE WRITER of this short psalm is unknown, as is the time of the writing. The subject of the psalm is the majestic, sovereign God. It could have been that Israel was in danger from enemies when this was written. The people's hope for the future was encouraged by remembering the majesty and strength of their God. "The LORD reigneth, he is clothed with majesty; the LORD is clothed with strength" (v. 1).

We are encouraged, as well, when we remember that God is in control. When faced with chaotic situations, we sometimes cheer one another with these words, "Praise the Lord, God is still on the throne!" God is not caught by surprise when adversity strikes our lives because He is in control of the adversity. "I form the light, and create darkness: I make peace, and create evil [calamity]: I the LORD do all these things" (Isaiah 45:7). "The LORD reigneth." God is still on the throne, doing as He pleases for our spiritual good and His glory (Romans 8:28, 29).

Consider these challenging words by Peter Marshall: "God will never permit any troubles to come upon us unless He has a specific plan by which great blessing can come out of the difficulty."

I'm trying to always believe that. What about you?

"He that planted the ear, shall he not hear? he that formed the eye, shall he not see?"
(Psalm 94:9).

THIS IS another anonymous hymn that could have been written in a night of weeping. It sounds something like Asaph's words in Psalm 73. The psalmist was perplexed by the prosperity of the ungodly, but he cheered his heart by remembering that the King of Kings is still ruling and overruling the affairs of men.

Verse 7 speaks to the practical atheist who believes in the God of creation but doesn't believe He controls the lives and affairs of mankind. "Yet they say, the LORD shall not see." How foolish to think that the God Who created us should not Himself have eyes and ears! "He that planted the ear, shall he not hear? he that formed the eye, shall he not see?" (v. 9).

How often have we acted like practical atheists, thinking God won't see or hear what we're doing? How foolish! He not only sees and hears our words and deeds, He even knows every good and evil thought that passes through our minds. "The LORD knoweth the thoughts of man" (v. 11).

Here is wise counsel as a safeguard against sin: "There is an ear which hears everything; . . . there is an eye which sees everything; . . . there is a hand which writes everything in the Book of Knowledge, which shall be opened at the Judgment."

"Lord, help us remember You see and hear everything, and You know our thoughts."

"Blessed is the man whom thou chastenest, O Lord, and teachest him out of thy law"
(Psalm 94:12).

IN VERSES 1–11 the psalmist reflected on the just judgment that, in due time, would fall upon his enemies. However, the fact that God would chasten the enemy was not much comfort to him right then. What relief could that bring?

Evidently the psalmist changed his thinking in verse 12 because the rest of the psalm has a different tone. He changed his thinking from his miserable enemies and his miserable circumstances to his blessings. He switched from negative to positive thinking. He decided he was a blessed person. "Blessed is the man whom thou chastenest, O LORD, and teachest him out of thy law" (v. 12).

The psalmist didn't have the book of Hebrews, but somewhere in the teachings of the Law (God's Word) he had learned the principle of Hebrews 12:6: "For whom the Lord loveth he chasteneth."

You may not feel God loves you when He chastens you, but He does! God's chastening is always done in love to teach us to hate sin, love the world less and Heaven more, and walk faithfully with God each day. Don't waste your chastening; learn the valuable lessons God wants to teach you.

Back in the 1600s Thomas Brooks wrote some wise words regarding verse 12: "All the chastening in world, without divine teaching, will never make a man blessed; that man that finds correction attended with instruction, and lashing with lessoning, is a happy man."

Isn't it comforting to know God loves us so much He will not allow us to continue in our sin but will do whatever needs be done to stop us? What lessons have you learned from chastening?

"For he is our God; and we are the people of his pasture, and the sheep of his hand . . ."
(Psalm 95:7).

THIS PSALM was probably written to be sung as a call to worship. It is a song with two stanzas, one happy and one sad. Verses 1–7 ring out an invitation for us to sing a joyful song to the Lord. From the end of verse 7 through the rest of the psalm we hear a somber tone, a solemn warning.

We see five descriptions of God in this psalm: "the rock of our salvation" (v. 1); "a great God" and "a great King" (v. 3); "the LORD our maker" (v. 6); and "our God" (v. 7). This great God and King is also our shepherd. "For he is our God; and we are the people of his pasture, and the sheep of his hand" (v. 7). In "his pastures" He feeds us, and by "his hand" He leads us.

Aren't you glad you have a Shepherd to feed and lead you? I sure am! I can feed my body, but only He can feed my soul. "Man shall not live by bread alone, but by every word that proceedeth out of the mouth of God" (Matthew 4:4). However, God will not spoon-feed me. I must daily feed my soul by reading His Word; no one else can do it for me.

I can make my plans, but only He can lead me in the right paths. "He leadeth me in the paths of righteousness" (Psalm 23:3).

Are you being fed and led by the Shepherd each day?

"To day if ye will hear his voice, Harden not your heart, as in the provocation, and as in the day of temptation in the wilderness" (Psalm 95:7, 8).

GOD EXPECTS "the people of his pasture" and "the sheep of his hand" (v. 7), His children, to hear and heed His voice. "To day if ye will hear his voice, Harden not your heart, as in the provocation, and as in the day of temptation in the wilderness" (vv. 7, 8).

God was about to give His children a history lesson, with a solemn warning to remember the past. "Remember how your fathers repeatedly and willfully rebelled against My voice, provoking Me to anger? Remember how they continued to resist My will for them until they became so hardened they could no longer even hear My voice? I could not allow them to enter the land of promise. Don't repeat the sins of your fathers!"

A pirate named Gibbs was, for many years, a terror on the seas. He told this story before his execution: "When I committed the first murder, my soul was a hell within my bosom; but, after I had sailed for years under the black flag, my conscience became so hardened, I could rob a vessel, murder all its crew, and then lie down to rest as peaceful as an infant in a crib."

Do you know people who once were joyfully living for Christ but today are hard and cynical? They want no part of the church or Christ. What happened? Such a change is usually the result of a series of choices to disregard God's will.

Are you resisting God's work in your life? Determine today to heed God's voice before your heart is hardened and you experience God's chastening.

"O sing unto the LORD a new song: sing unto the LORD, all the earth" (Psalm 96:1).

IN 1 CHRONICLES 15 and 16 we read the account of David's moving the ark of the covenant back to Jerusalem. Verses 23–32 of chapter 16 are the much the same as Psalm 96, which leads us to believe that David wrote Psalm 96. It is a song of worship and praise to declare the glory of God. The psalmist encouraged the congregation to sing along with him: "O sing unto the LORD a new song: sing unto the LORD, all the earth" (v. 1).

Did David have in mind the "new song" the whole earth will sing when the King enters His millennial Kingdom? In that marvelous age all people, as well as all creation, will give glory to the King of Kings. "Let the heavens rejoice, and let the earth be glad; let the sea roar, . . . Let the field be joyful, . . . then shall all the trees of the wood rejoice" (vv. 11, 12).

What will our song be when we bow before the King on that grand coronation day? Revelation 5:9–13 tells us: "And they sung a new song, saying, Thou art worthy to take the book, and to open the seals thereof: for thou wast slain, and hast redeemed us to God by thy blood. . . . Worthy is the Lamb that was slain to receive power, and riches, and wisdom, and strength, and honour, and glory, and blessing."

We will never run out of words to express the honor and glory due to our Savior, Who was slain for us. Is it any wonder that people around the world, saved or unsaved, still stand when the "Hallelujah Chorus" is sung? One day we'll all bow when we sing the new "Hallelujah Chorus."

I can hardly wait to learn to sing that "new song!" What about you?

*"Give unto the LORD the glory due unto his name: bring an offering,
and come into his courts" (Psalm 96:8).*

THE PSALMIST was overwhelmed by all God had done and shall do in the future, so he sang praises to God. He invited his listeners to join him in coming before the Lord with an offering to express their praise and thanks. "Give unto the LORD the glory due unto his name: bring an offering, and come into his courts" (v. 8).

The Hebrew word for "offering" was commonly used to mean "bring presents." It alluded to the oriental custom that required anyone who wanted to be admitted into the presence of a king to bring gifts.

How often do we bring an offering of praise when we come into the presence of the King of Kings, the Lord Jesus Christ, our Savior? Hebrews 13:15 tells us to offer "the sacrifice of praise to God continually."

It is not easy to praise the Lord when circumstances in our lives are burdensome. But even when we don't feel like praising the Lord, we need to lay our feelings on the altar and praise the Lord through our tears. We can't always praise the Lord for what He is allowing in our lives, but we can always praise Him for Who He is, the sovereign God Who has everything under control—even when it seems like things are out of control!

Forget your feelings and remember the facts. "Our God is in the heavens: he hath done whatsoever he hath pleased" (Psalm 115:3).

"Ye that love the LORD, hate evil: he preserveth the souls of his saints; he delivereth them out of the hand of the wicked" (Psalm 97:10).

THIS PSALM deals with the same subject as Psalm 96 and might have been a continuation of that song. In the first nine verses the psalmist seemed to imagine that the kingdoms of the world have already become the Kingdom of Jehovah. Verses 10–12 are an encouragement to the saints to stay steadfast in spite of the wicked persecution that will follow.

We know wicked men will continue until the Lord returns, but we must hate the evil they devise and stand against it. "Ye that love the LORD, hate evil" (v. 10). With the same intensity that we love God we must hate evil.

The story is told of a lady who was strolling through her rose garden and noticed one bush loaded with flowers. She stooped to admire the beautiful roses; one rose near the ground especially caught her eye. As she reached down to pick it, a black snake wrapped itself around her arm. She was almost to the point of hysteria as she ran screaming from the garden. It took her many hours to calm down. The snake was not poisonous, and she was not hurt. But her fear and hatred for snakes was so great that she could never even look at a snake again; nor could anyone convince her to go into the rose garden.

This is the way we should hate evil. We should hate the places where evil dwells. We should fear and hate evil as much as we would fear walking into a pit filled with rattlesnakes.

Do you hate evil as much as you love God?

"O sing unto the LORD a new song; for he hath done marvellous things" (Psalm 98:1).

THIS IS another hymn of praise to God, looking forward to the coming of the Lord to rule His people. This song has three stanzas: verses 1–3: *why* God should be praised; verses 4–6: *how* God should be praised; verses 7–9: *who* should praise Him.

Why should God be praised? Because of all the marvellous things He has done for us, is doing for us, and shall do for us. "O sing unto the LORD a new song; for he hath done marvellous things" (v. 1). *How* should God be praised? Daily. Because God's mercies are new every morning, we need to have a new song of praise to Him each day (Lamentations 3:22, 23). *Who* should praise Him? We should (v. 4)!

Have you lost your song? If you have, you lost something else first; you lost your confident trust in God. When we lose our trust, we lose our song.

> "I know not, but God knows;
> Oh, blessed rest from fear!
> All my unfolding days
> To Him are plain and clear.
> Each anxious, puzzled 'why?'
> From doubt or dread that grows,
> Finds answer in this thought:
> I know not, but He knows"
>
> (ANNIE JOHNSON FLINT).

Can you trust God with all the uncertainties in your life? Your life is plain and clear to Him. Start trusting today, and you'll be singing a new song tomorrow.

"Thou answeredst them, O LORD our God: thou wast a God that forgavest them,
though thou tookest vengeance of their inventions" (Psalm 99:8).

CHARLES Spurgeon wrote a vivid description of this psalm. "It is a hymn fitted for the cherubim who surround the throne, who are mentioned in verse 1; it is a Psalm most fitting for saints who dwell in Zion, the holy city, and especially worthy to be reverently sung by all who, like David the king, Moses the lawgiver, Aaron the priest, or Samuel the seer, are honoured to lead the church of God, and plead for her with her Lord."

Moses, Aaron, and Samuel are named in verse 6 as men who called upon God in prayer. Verse 8 indicates their prayers were for forgiveness. "Thou answeredst them, O LORD our God: thou wast a God that forgavest them, though thou tookest vengeance of their inventions." Yes, God forgave, but they paid the consequences for their own schemes and plans. Moses and Aaron's sin kept them from entering the Promised Land (Numbers

20:24; Deuteronomy 32:48–51). Samuel's sin caused the people to want a king, who eventually caused the prophet and the people much sorrow (1 Samuel 8:1–9).

Have you ever devised your own plan or invention and had to pay the consequences for it? I have! I have a physical problem that requires daily medication. Once when I wasn't feeling up to par, I decided to alter the dosage to see if that would help me. I felt a little better at first; then all of a sudden I ran out of gas. When I went to the doctor, I found out I was doing just the opposite of what needed to be done. The doctor forgave me, but I paid the consequences.

When you think your invention is better than God's, you'd better be careful. You may be going in the opposite direction. Where will your plans lead you?

"Make a joyful noise unto the LORD, all ye lands" (Psalm 100:1).

PSALM 100 is the grand finale of the wonderful series of praise psalms that began in Psalm 94. Psalm 100 could be called a doxology.

Do you sing the Doxology in your church? Some churches sing it each week; others, like ours, sing it when something really special happens and we want to express our praise to God. If you're not familiar with the words, you will find them in a hymnal under the title "Praise God, from Whom All Blessings Flow" or "Doxology" or "Old Hundredth."

> "Praise God, from whom all blessings flow;
> Praise Him, all creatures here below;
> Praise Him above, ye heav'nly host;
> Praise Father, Son, and Holy Ghost.
>   Amen."

Many bars advertise an assigned time as the "Happy Hour." Maybe we should put on our church signs "11:00 A.M.–Noon—HAPPY HOUR" instead of "Morning Worship Service." That's what it should be: an hour of joyful praise and thanksgiving to God. "Make a joyful noise unto the LORD" (v. 1). Billy Sunday said, "If you have no joy in your religion, there's a leak in your Christianity somewhere."

Is your worship service a joyful hour or a dreary hour? Do you help make it a joyful hour by coming with a heart full of joy, ready to praise the Lord? If not, maybe you need to check for a leak!

"Serve the LORD with gladness: come before his presence with singing" (Psalm 100:2).

NO DOUBT about it! God wants His people to be "happy holy ones!" If we can't sing, then we at least can make "a joyful noise" (v. 1). When we serve, He wants us to do it with gladness. "Serve the LORD with gladness" (v. 2). We are to come into His presence with singing, not complaining and growling. "Come before his presence with singing" (v. 2). No, the Lord doesn't want us to be "sober saints," just grinning and bearing it; He wants us to be happy and full of joy.

How many really happy Christians do you know? Stop and reflect a few minutes; let their smiling faces dwell in your mind. We're commanded to serve the Lord with gladness, but how many of us obey that command? Here are a few people who don't: Sally serves with complaining—nothing or no one is ever quite right; she is always criticizing something. Sam serves with bitterness—he is cantankerous, negative, and discouraging to be around. Sarah serves with halfheartedness—she is always late and forgets to call if she can't be there; she is only serving because no one else would do it. Is the Lord pleased with this kind of service when He clearly says, "Serve Me with gladness"?

❖

The Lord knows if your service to Him is a drudgery or a delight. Are you a "happy holy one" or a "sober saint"?

"Know ye that the LORD he is God: it is he that hath made us, and not we ourselves; we are his people, and the sheep of his pasture" (Psalm 100:3).

PSALM 100 is a psalm of praise, so let's think about a few reasons why we should praise the Lord. Look at verse 3: "Know ye that the LORD he is God: it is he that hath made us, and not we ourselves; we are his people, and the sheep of his pasture."

Here are three reasons for praising the Lord: (1) *The Lord is God.* He is not human like us with limited power and knowledge. He is the all-powerful, all-sufficient, self-existent, eternal God. (2) *He made us.* We had nothing to do with who we are. God created us with a plan and a purpose for our lives. (3) *He is our shepherd, our caretaker.* He didn't create us and then leave us to wing it on our own.

If you have been to Israel, you may remember seeing a donkey out in the field alone as you rode from town to town. Occa-sionally, you will see a camel alone in the field. But you never see a sheep alone. Sheep cannot survive alone; they need a shepherd. So do we! We are weak, helpless, and dumb. That's why the Lord calls us sheep.

I'm embarrassed to tell you how often I show how dumb I am. You know what I do? I try to run my life by my schemes, manipulating people and circumstances. After I mess everything up and realize I've been trying to run things on my own, I turn to God to straighten out my mess. (I'm sure you have never done that, have you?) Who better can care for me and understand me than the One Who made me? I'm so glad I'm learning to walk with the Shepherd.

Are you walking with the Shepherd or trying to make it on your own?

"For the LORD is good; his mercy is everlasting; and his truth endureth to all generations"
(Psalm 100:5).

D ID YOU ever sing this little tune, "When you're down and out, lift up your head and shout, 'It's going to be a great day' "? Here's my version of that tune, "When you're down and out, lift up your head and shout Psalm 100." When your circumstances seem to be overwhelming you and you're having a hard time finding anything for which to praise the Lord, meditate on Psalm 100:3 and 5.

Yesterday we looked at three reasons for praise from verse 3; there are three more in verse 5: "For the LORD is good; his mercy is everlasting; and his truth endureth to all generations."

The Lord is good. Your circumstances may not be good, but God is good. God is taking all the experiences of your life and fitting them into a plan for your spiritual good (Romans 8:28, 29).

God is merciful. Mercy is kindness in excess of what is expected or deserved. Would you stop for a minute and get a piece of paper? On one side of the paper, write, "What I Deserve." At the top of the other side, write, "What I Have That I Don't Deserve." Now make your lists. You will find that you have so much more than you deserve.

If that isn't reason enough to praise the Lord, there is one more reason. *His Word endures;* what He has promised will come to pass.

If you are hanging on to one of the promises of God, don't turn loose. God is good; God is full of mercy; and God always keeps His Word. When you breathe your last breath, you will be able to say, "He never failed me once!" Are you hanging on to the promises?

"I will behave myself wisely in a perfect way. O when wilt thou come unto me? I will walk within my house with a perfect heart" (Psalm 101:2).

MATTHEW Henry calls this the "Household Psalm." David wanted to walk in a perfect (blameless) way with a perfect (blameless) heart in his home. "I will behave wisely in a perfect way. . . . I will walk within my house with a perfect heart" (v. 2).

This should be the goal of every husband and wife or single person. How can we accomplish this goal? If we want to behave, or walk, in a perfect, or blameless, way, we must walk in God's way. "As for God, his way is perfect" (Psalm 18:30). To have a blameless, sincere heart requires that we get rid of those hidden areas of hypocrisy. Sincerity and hypocrisy just don't mix.

In no place is it more vital that we walk and talk right than in the home. Yet that's where most Christians fail the most misera-

bly. If you want to know what a person is like, don't ask the pastor; ask his or her mate, children, or closest friend. What we are at home is what we really are. We can sing in the choir and sin in our relationships. We may be saints at church and devils at home. Our outbursts of temper at home can put the whole house in turmoil. Hypocrisy deceives!

Let's quit deceiving ourselves and others. The best way to have a blameless heart is to start hiding God's Word in our hearts. "Thy word have I hid in mine heart, that I might not sin against thee" (Psalm 119:11).

Are you seeking to be as saintly at home during the week as you are on Sunday in church? Ask God to help you live in your home "with a perfect heart."

"Mine eyes shall be upon the faithful of the land, that they may dwell with me: he that walketh in a perfect way, he shall serve me" (Psalm 101:6).

DAVID wanted to be blameless outwardly and inwardly. He wanted his walk and his heart to be perfect, or blameless (v. 2). Who could model this kind of life for him? He would model his life after God and other faithful men who walked in a blameless way. "Mine eyes shall be upon the faithful of the land, that they may dwell with me: he that walketh in a perfect [blameless] way, he shall serve [minister to] me" (v. 6).

Sometimes we minister to others just by giving them a godly example to follow. Amy Carmichael has ministered to me time after time, not only in her writing, but also by the blameless life she lived. When you read her life story in *A Chance to Die*, you know she will surely be listed in God's "Hall of Faith" someday.

Do you have a spiritual model? Your first answer is probably "Jesus Christ." But do you have an earthly model who inspires you on toward godliness? In this age of selfishness and unfaithfulness, it is not easy to find Spirit-filled role models who are totally sold out to Jesus Christ.

Are you such a model? Are you leaving behind a godly example for others to follow?

"Hide not thy face from me in the day when I am in trouble; incline thine ear unto me: in the day when I call answer me speedily" (Psalm 102:2).

SOME people believe David wrote this psalm at the time of his son Absalom's rebellion. Whether it was written by David or someone else is not clear, but the state of mind of the writer is clear. The psalmist was in great distress; his troubles had totally consumed him. Every inch of his body felt the agony he was enduring: his voice (vv. 1, 5); his emotions and feelings (vv. 1, 2, 5–9); his bones (vv. 3, 5); his heart, appetite, and memory (v. 4); his skin (v. 5); his tear ducts (v. 9); his strength (v. 23). Listen to the prayer of this overwhelmed saint: "Hide not thy face from me in the day when I am in trouble; incline thine ear unto me: in the day when I call answer me speedily" (v. 2).

Everyone has troubles. Some people have more, some less, but everyone has them. Some troubles are nitty-gritty little ones, and some are super-duper whopper ones. When something comes along that knocks you down, turns you upside down, gives you a good shaking, and then drops you, you know you're having a super-duper whopper trouble.

People in general do not handle these huge troubles very well. They find it very difficult to accept them and carry on. Some Christians don't handle huge troubles well either. They want a quick fix: "answer me speedily."

A few years ago I read a statement by Amy Carmichael that has helped me so much when huge troubles make a sudden interruption into my life. She said, "In acceptance lieth peace." God may not answer speedily, so we must wait and accept His time and plan. The sooner we accept, the sooner we have peace.

Are you accepting or asking for answers?

"But thou art the same, and thy years shall have no end" (Psalm 102:27).

DAVID'S son Absalom had changed. The sweet little boy had grown into an angry young man. Everything and everyone in David's life had changed, except one Person. The Lord had not changed, nor would He ever change. David could cling to this truth: "But thou art the same, and thy years shall have no end" (v. 27).

Everything we see in this world is changing. Everyone we know is changing. Nothing or no one is exactly the same as it was ten years ago. The heavens and the earth are eternal, but even they will be totally changed one day (2 Peter 3:12, 13). The only thing that never changes is our God. In this restless, changing world it is so good to know there is Someone Who will never change. You can depend on Him until the end.

While God does not change, we need to change, develop, mature. Are you the same as you were ten years ago? What about your knowledge? Hopefully, you have increased in knowledge, and this has led to some profitable changes in your life. Have your enjoyments changed? Do you have new interests? What about your affection? Has your love deepened for those who are close to you? What about your love for Christ? Has it deepened? Have you changed spiritually these past ten years? Have you moved forward or backward?

Are you pleased with the changes you have made in your life? Even more important, is the Lord pleased with the changes in your life?

"Bless the LORD, O my soul: and all that is within me, bless his holy name" (Psalm 103:1).

PSALM 103 is a psalm of praise. Not even once does David make a request. David may have written this psalm in his declining years when he had a keener sense of sin and a higher sense of the value of pardon than he had in his younger years. David didn't just praise God with his lips, but with every part of his being. His intellect, emotions, and will were all involved. "Bless the LORD, O my soul: and *all* that is within me, bless his holy name" (v. 1). As you read this psalm for the next week, see how many treasures you can find in it.

Some days praising the Lord is so easy; it just flows out of me. Other days, I feel someone would have to pump it out of me. Why is this? Spiritually, I may feel like praising the Lord, but physically and emotionally I feel drowsy, half empty. I guess I'm like my grandpa's old well. Very seldom was the well so full that the water started flowing on one pump; usually it took two or three.

I guess God isn't as concerned about how fast the praise starts flowing as He is about the fact that it flows. Am I daily filled with the Spirit so that out of me can flow rivers of living water (John 7:38)? Or am I so dried up spiritually that no amount of pumping will bring forth praise?

How about you? Is this a day when praise comes easily, or do you need some pumping to get going?

"Bless the LORD, O my soul, and forget not all his benefits" (Psalm 103:2).

BEFORE you make your requests to God each day, do you take time to thank Him for all the good things He has done for you? David rehearsed some of his blessings in this psalm. "Bless the LORD, O my soul, and forget not all his benefits" (v. 2).

Why don't you take a few minutes and jot down David's blessings in this psalm. After you list all his blessings, put a check mark by the blessings that you also enjoy as a child of God. Remembering the blessings in our lives will help us when we think we have nothing for which to be thankful.

I once read of a lady who had many troubles. In spite of all her troubles she kept a happy smile on her face and she had a cheerful heart. When asked the secret for her happy disposition, she said that for many years she had been keeping a "Pleasure Book." Every evening she would write down some pleasant thing that had happened that day. Sometimes it was a flower that bloomed in the garden or an enjoyable walk. On other occasions it was a visit with a friend or a note she received.

I decided to start a Pleasure Book and to include in it pleasant things I did for others as well as pleasant things in my own life. ("It is more blessed to give than to receive" [Acts 20:35].)

Why not start a Pleasure Book today? Thank God for the pleasant thing you are able to record for this day.

"Who satisfieth thy mouth with good things; so that thy youth is renewed like the eagle's"
(Psalm 103:5).

IF DAVID wrote Psalm 102, he was moping in that psalm. But in Psalm 103 he was soaring with eagles. His mouth was filled with praises to God. "Who satisfieth thy mouth with good things" (v. 5). If our mouths are filled with praise, it is because our hearts are also filled with praise, "for out of the abundance of the heart the mouth speaketh" (Matthew 12:34).

We have every reason to praise the Lord, for He surely does give good things to His children. His blessings are not just trinkets and toys that will break and become useless, but valuable things like peace, contentment, and comfort. These gifts keep giving us a new lease on life, just like the eagle who loses his old feathers and gets new ones during the molting season. "So that thy youth is renewed like the eagle's" (v. 5).

Oh, to be young again and have the energy of youth! Do you feel too tired to go on? Do you need a new lease on life? Try the formula found in Isaiah 40:31: exchange your strength for God's strength. "But they that wait upon the LORD shall renew their strength." (The word "renew" means "exchange.")

Why not exchange your pocket battery for God's 220 electric current? Let Him charge you up and keep you running.

"The LORD is merciful and gracious, slow to anger, and plenteous in mercy"
(Psalm 103:8).

MERCY pardons the sinner, and grace bestows favor on the sinner. And what does the sinner deserve? Nothing but the wrath of God. God holds back the deserved wrath not just because He is merciful, but because He is "plenteous" in mercy. "The LORD is merciful and gracious, slow to anger, and plenteous in mercy" (v. 8). David knew he was a sinner and deserved punishment, but God gave undeserved mercy. God was gracious and patient with David—just like He is with each of us.

Not many of us are patient with people who fail us. We usually end up getting angry and then we want to get even. We want to let the other person know how we feel. We are not usually "slow to anger" and "plenteous in mercy."

I'm still feeling the hurt in my heart over a broken friendship. My friend asked my advice, and I gave her what I felt was a Biblical answer on how to resolve her problem. She did not like my answer and told me so. Now both of us are hurt, and our friendship has been injured. It may be healed, and it may not. I have tried, but to no avail.

When I thought of this situation, I was reminded again that the Lord is the only friend I have who will *always* be merciful and gracious and slow to anger.

Have you thanked the Lord recently for His mercy, His *"plenteous"* mercy?

"As far as the east is from the west, so far hath he removed our transgressions from us"
(Psalm 103:12).

DID YOU know you cannot measure the distance between east and west? East just keeps going east, and west just keeps going west. There are no east and west poles, only north and south poles. The distance between the north and south poles is said to be twelve thousand miles. If the psalmist had said, "As far as the north is from the south," then God's forgiveness of our sin would be limited. But when God forgives our sin, it is so far removed from Him there is no way He can remember it again. "As far as the east is from the west, so far hath he removed our transgressions from us" (v. 12).

When we confess our sin (1 John 1:9), God forgives and forgets. We should do the same! If we still feel weighed down with guilt, it is of our own making. God has already forgotten. We tend to dig up the past when God has already wiped our record clean. We do not need to wallow in past miseries.

If we want to be Christlike, we need to follow His example in forgiveness. When we forgive another person, we must make sure we don't dredge up the past and throw it in the person's face again. If we do, we haven't really forgiven.

Are you living in the joy of sins forgiven —yours and others? Or do you keep bringing up what God has forgotten?

"Like as a father pitieth his children, so the LORD pitieth them that fear him"
(Psalm 103:13).

A LOVING father feels for his children. Could David have been thinking of rebellious Absalom when he wrote these words? "Like as a father pitieth his children, so the LORD pitieth them that fear him" (v. 13).

Oh, how David must have grieved for and even felt sorry for his son. As much pain and agony as David was in, he knew his son must be hurting as well. But what may have hurt David the most was the fact that Absalom didn't fear God.

As a father "pitieth," or shows compassion to, his children, so our Heavenly Father cares for us. When the son needs instruction, the father teaches him; when he is sick, the father comforts him; when he falls down, the father helps him back up; when he fails to do right, the father forgives him. In the same way our Heavenly Father expresses His compassion to us.

"Does Jesus care when my heart is pained
Too deeply for mirth and song;
As the burdens press, and the cares distress,
And the way grows weary and long?
O yes, He cares, I know He cares!
His heart is touched with my grief;
When the days are weary, the long nights dreary,
I know my Savior cares" (FRANK E. GRAEFF).

Is your heart hurting? Dwell on your Father's compassion. He cares that you are hurting.

"For he knoweth our frame; he remembereth that we are dust" (Psalm 103:14).

DAVID knew that God understood his temperament; He created it. God knew David's frame and makeup physically; He built him and knew his limitations. David had many down times in his life, but he tried to not get down on himself. He realized he had weaknesses, but he knew God knew his weaknesses and still loved him. "For he knoweth our frame; he remembereth that we are dust" (v. 14).

One person on this earth knows me better than anyone else: my husband. I've lived with him the longest, and he knows me inside and out. But he doesn't know me as well as the One Who created me and knows my limitations. Sometimes I forget my limitations. I forget I am dust, and I try to push my body and mind as if I were made of iron. God knows I can't handle this, and He has His way of slowing me down.

By God's divine appointment, I have a physical problem that occasionally drains my energy and leaves me feeling useless and unproductive. When these down days come, all I can do is say, "God, You know my heart."

"When obstacles and trials seem
Like prison walls to be,
I do the little I can do
And leave the rest to Thee.
And when there seems no chance, no change,
From grief can set me free,
Hope finds its strength in helplessness,
And calmly waits for Thee."

Aren't you glad God knows you better than anyone else? You can trust Him to always do what is best for you.

"Who laid the foundations of the earth, that it should not be removed for ever"
(Psalm 104:5).

THIS psalm is a summary of God's creation of the world as found in the first chapter of Genesis. "In the beginning God created the heaven and the earth" (Genesis 1:1). He "laid the foundations of the earth, that it should not be removed for ever" (Psalm 104:5).

The psalmist praises God for each aspect of creation. God created light on the first day (Genesis 1:3–5; Psalm 104:20); the heavens and earth on the second day (Genesis 1:6–8; Psalm 104:2, 3); land and vegetation on the third day (Genesis 1:9–13; Psalm 104:6–18); the sun, moon, and stars on the fourth day (Genesis 1:14–19; Psalm 104:19–23); fish and birds on the fifth day (Genesis 1:20–23;

Psalm 104:25, 26); animals and man on the sixth day (Genesis 1:24–31; Psalm 104:21–24, 27–30).

Have you ever wondered what God laid the foundation of the earth upon? Job 26:7 gives us the answer: "He . . . hangeth the earth upon nothing." The earth is balanced in space by its own weight, yet it is as immovable as if it were laid on the most solid foundation. "It should not be removed for ever" (v. 5). What a mighty God is He!

Are you trusting our mighty God to care for the details of your life? If you're not, is it because you think you are wiser than He is?

"Thou hast set a bound that they may not pass over; that they turn not again to cover the earth" (Psalm 104:9).

HAVE you ever considered the fact that the ocean waters would cover the earth if God did not keep them in their bounds? This is just another one of the marvels of God's creation that we often take for granted. "Thou hast set a bound that they [the waters of verse 6] may not pass over; that they turn not again to cover the earth" (v. 9).

Only once did God allow water to completely flood the earth: the great Flood of Noah's day. After the waters receded, God said He would never allow such a flood to happen again. He gave us the rainbow as a reminder of His promise (Genesis 9:9–17). Every time you see a rainbow, you should remember God's promise and Psalm 104:9.

Just as God has set bounds for the oceans and seas, so He has set bounds for our lives as well. He has promised we will never have more trials than we can bear; He will set a boundary on them. "God is faithful, who will not suffer [permit] you to be tempted [tested] above that ye are able" (1 Corinthians 10:13). "God will either keep His saints *from* temptations by His preventing mercy, or *in* temptations by His supporting mercy, or find a way for their escape by His delivering mercy" (Mason).

Aren't you glad God has set the limit on how many trials He will allow in our lives?

"He causeth the grass to grow for the cattle, and herb for the service of man: that he may bring forth food out of the earth" (Psalm 104:14).

WHY DID God cover the land with grass? It's not just so we can have pretty lawns to make our houses look nicer. God made the grass so the cattle would have food to eat, just as He made plants for man to cultivate to have his food to eat. "He causeth the grass to grow for the cattle, and herb for the service of man: that he may bring forth food out of the earth" (v. 14).

God is concerned about every part of His creation. He is as concerned about the beast of the field and the birds in the sky as He is about the nurturing of men and women. God is so concerned about His creation that not even a sparrow falls from the sky without His knowledge of it (Matthew 10:29).

Have you ever considered how God feeds His creation? Birds eat worms and bugs; ants eat the food we drop on the ground; spiders and lizards eat the ants. If God can take care of birds and insects, don't you think He can take care of us? We know He can, and we know does, but we often forget His promise in Philippians 4:19: "My God shall supply all your need according to his riches in glory by Christ Jesus." I can be content with His provision unless I want more than I need.

The Children of Israel had all their needs met each day, but they got tired of the necessities; they wanted more and became discontent and started grumbling. Someone has estimated that it would have taken fifteen hundred tons of food each day for God to feed the Children of Israel in the desert. God did this for 14,600 days!

What is your need? Do you think He can meet it?

"He appointed the moon for seasons: the sun knoweth his going down" (Psalm 104:19).

WHY IS the moon used as a gauge to divide the year into months and weeks? Why does the moon determine the date of Easter Sunday each year? Because that is the way God determined it should be. "He appointed the moon for seasons" (v. 19). It was God's plan, not man's. The sun comes up and goes down right on schedule each day because it, too, is controlled by God. "The sun knoweth his going down" (v. 19).

God never created anything and then walked away from it. He keeps our world in perfect order. "By him all things consist [hold together]" (Colossians 1:17). We know each night where the moon will be in the sky and what its phase will be. We know exactly what time the sun will rise and set each day, right down to the very minute.

God made us, and we need to let Him control us just as He does other aspects of His creation. Who better knows how to manage us than the One Who created us? Would you try to perform brain surgery or fly a jet? I wouldn't! Would you try to walk a tightrope or cut a diamond? I wouldn't! We would be foolish to attempt any of those things unless we were qualified. Why, then, do we try to run our own lives when only God has the credentials for such a complicated job?

Will you let the One Who made you control you?

"Thou hidest thy face, they are troubled: thou takest away their breath, they die, and return to their dust" (Psalm 104:29).

GOD creates life; He preserves life; He governs life; and He ends life. "Thou takest away their breath, they die, and return to their dust" (v. 29). Every man, creature, and beast is dependent upon the will of the eternal God and Creator. Why is it that some people survive a disease and others die from it? We do not know. Only God knows; He is the controller of life and death.

We may think we have many years of life left, but God knows when our life on earth will end. The Roman poet Horace said death "knocks with impartial steps at the door of the cottage and the palace of the prince."

The wealthy person cannot bribe God to lengthen life, and the pauper cannot shorten his days by begging God to end it all. God has set our appointment with death. Recently one of my friends found out her husband is filled with cancer. Just the word "cancer" strikes fear in our souls. Will it be a slow death, dying inch by inch, or will it be swift and ruthless? The doctors can *predict* how long we will live, but only God *knows*. He has the date already set.

I once heard of a preacher who was speaking on Heaven. He asked his listeners to raise their hands if they were ready to go to Heaven. One of the deacons did not raise his hand. Later, when asked why he didn't raise his hand, he said, "I thought you were getting up a load right now."

Are you ready to go today? I sure am!

"My meditation of him shall be sweet: I will be glad in the LORD" (Psalm 104:34).

WHEN your meditations are confusing and troubling and you don't know what to do, change your meditations to something you know is sure, true, and dependable. If you want sweet and peaceable meditations instead of sour and distressing ones, think about the Lord. "My meditation of him shall be sweet: I will be glad in the LORD" (v. 34). Start thinking about everything you know about God, and you'll be glad instead of sad.

Take a minute right now and meditate on three things you know about God. What three words came to your mind? When I start thinking about my God, I know He is trustworthy, patient, faithful, loving, all-powerful, good, forgiving, tenderhearted—and the list could go on and on.

When a hound dog is tracking something and loses its scent, the dog hunts backwards until he finds the scent again. When he finds the scent, he pursues his game with an even louder bark than before. When life seems confusing and you're losing your sense of direction, back up and go with what you know about God. Rehearse the attributes of God. Men may change, but we know our God will never change. He is our rock, our fortress, our deliverer, our strength, our high tower (Psalm 18:2).

Do you need to change your meditations to the One Who is sure, true, and dependable?

269

"Seek the LORD, and his strength: seek his face evermore" (Psalm 105:4).

PSALM 104 deals with the creation account in the opening chapters of Genesis; Psalm 105 covers events at the end of Genesis as well as the books of Exodus and Numbers.

The first fifteen verses of Psalm 105 are also found in 1 Chronicles 16:8–22. Those verses were sung as part of the celebration when David brought the ark of the covenant to Jerusalem. The people were admonished to worship regularly. They were to do this in order to seek the Lord and gain His strength in their lives. "Seek the LORD, and his strength: seek his face evermore" (v. 4).

Have you come to the realization that you must seek the Lord daily for His strength if you want to live a victorious life? Some people need to check their blood pressure daily; other people test their blood sugar daily. Maybe we all need to take a spiritual "reading" each evening. We might ask ourselves these questions: What did I do today that I needed God's strength to accomplish? Did I say no to a sin because I drew upon God's strengthening power? Was I kind to someone who was unkind because I exchanged my strength for God's strength? I am challenged by these words from Phillips Brooks: "Do not pray for easy times. Pray to be stronger men [and women]! Do not pray for tasks equal to your powers. Pray for powers equal to your tasks."

Are you growing in spiritual strength and dependency upon Christ?

"Touch not mine anointed, and do my prophets no harm" (Psalm 105:15).

IN THE context of Psalm 105, the words of verse 15 apply to Isaac: "Touch not mine anointed, and do my prophets no harm." When Isaac went to Gerar and lied about his wife (as Abraham had done earlier in Egypt), Abimelech, king of the Philistines, gave the order that no one was to touch Isaac or his wife (Genesis 26:6–11). Isaac was one of God's anointed, or chosen, ones.

In a sense all believers are "anointed" ones because we have been placed into the body of Christ by divine appointment. "Ye have not chosen me, but I have chosen you" (John 15:16). "According as he hath chosen us in him before the foundation of the world" (Ephesians 1:4).

We are God's anointed ones, commissioned to be spokesmen (Acts 1:8), in a world that is really not too interested in what we have to say. However, if we are in touch with God, our hearts will be so full of the love of God it will be impossible to keep our lips shut. If our hearts are full, we will overflow onto those around us.

God said, "Touch not mine anointed, and do my prophets no harm." God has a job for each of His anointed ones to do, and neither the meanest nor the mightiest can stop us until our job is done.

Isn't it exciting to realize we are under divine protection?

"He sent a man before them, even Joseph, who was sold for a servant. . . . Until the time that his word came: the word of the LORD tried him" (Psalm 105:17, 19).

WHEN Joseph was a young man, God revealed to him in a dream that honor would come to him. Joseph had to wait a long time for this promise to be fulfilled: "Until the time that his word came: the word of the LORD tried him" (v. 19).

While Joseph waited, God allowed many long years of testing and trials. Before honor he had to experience dishonor. His trials started with rejection by his brothers, who threw him into a pit to die. From the pit he became a slave, from slavery to prison, and finally from prison to a place of honor (Genesis 37:20–36; 39—50).

Samuel Lee expressed how Joseph's trials worked together for his good (Romans 8:28): "Joseph's feet were hurt in irons, to fit him to tread more delicately in the King's Palace at Zoan; and when the Lord's time was come, by the same stairs which winded him into the dungeon he climbs up into the next chariot to Pharaoh's. Few can bear great and sudden mercies without pride and wantonness, till they are hampered and humbled to carry it moderately."

Joseph endured many trials, but he could look back on them as good. Years later, when confronted by his brothers who threw him into the pit, he said, "But as for you, ye thought evil against me; but God meant it unto good" (Genesis 50:20).

Are you having a hard time waiting to see the promise of God fulfilled in your life? Remember that God's way is the best way, the wisest way, and sometimes the shortest way. If you get tired of waiting and decide to do things your way, then you have to wait for God to straighten out your mess before He can do it His way.

Are you being tried? Keep waiting and trusting!

272

"And he increased his people greatly; and made them stronger than their enemies"
(Psalm 105:24).

THE MORE Pharaoh oppressed God's people, the more they multiplied (Exodus 1:8–22). "And he increased his people greatly; and made them stronger than their enemies" (v. 24). The Children of Israel multiplied, just as God had promised Abraham they would (Genesis 22:17).

What God has promised man cannot change. "For the LORD of hosts hath purposed, and who shall disannul it?" (Isaiah 14:27). God's plan may be slowed down by the free will of man, but even the worst of men's sins are not outside His plan. God is not the author of sin, but He allows it for His purpose to be accomplished. God so ordered events that the Egyptians hated God's people and wanted them out of their land. God was going to take them to a better land, a land flowing with milk and honey (Exodus 3:8).

Is God in everything? Yes! Hannah Whitall Smith wrote a book in the 1800s called *The Christian's Secret of a Happy Life*. She made this interesting comment: "To the children of God, everything comes directly from their Father's hand. . . . It may be the sin of man that originates the action, and therefore the thing itself cannot be said to be the will of God; but by the time it reaches us it has become God's will for us, and must be accepted as directly from His hands. . . . If God be for us, it matters not who may be against us; nothing can disturb or harm us, except He shall see that it is best for us, and shall stand aside to let it pass."

God's promises, though they sometimes work slowly, work surely. Be patient; God may not be finished yet!

"Then believed they his words; they sang his praise. They soon forgat his works; they waited not for his counsel" (Psalm 106:12, 13).

PSALM 105 is a summary of God's faithfulness; in stark contrast, Psalm 106 is a summary of man's sinfulness. Notice the contrast between verses 12 and 13 of Psalm 106: "Then believed they his words; they sang his praise. They soon forgat his works; they waited not for his counsel."

The psalm rehearses events from the Israelites' exodus from Egypt to the Babylonian captivity (2 Kings 25). One would think the Israelites would never forget what God did at the Red Sea. He parted the water so they could walk through on dry ground; then He brought the water back together when the Egyptians started across (Exodus 14). How long did the people sing God's praises and remember the miracle? About three days! Three days after the Red Sea, the Israelites were complaining rather than waiting for God (Exodus 15:22–24). "They waited not for his counsel" (v. 13).

I have read that memory is one of the first things we lose. The older I get, the more I agree with that statement. I think I am developing a new disease: "Half-heimer's." It's not Alzheimer's yet, just "Half-heimer's." It is humiliating to go to the refrigerator and wonder what I want, or dial a phone number and forget who I'm calling. However, it is far worse to forget what God has done. He has always met my needs; He has never failed me.

Too often we are like the Israelites. When things go wrong, we so easily forget all the years of blessings from God's hand.

Why do we forget what we should remember and remember what we should forget?

"And he gave them their request; but sent leanness into their soul" (Psalm 106:15).

HOW WOULD you like to fix the same food every day? That's what the Israelite women had to do. The daily diet was manna. God fed the people with angel food, manna from heaven. All they had to do was step outside each morning and pick it up. But the people got tired of God's provision; they wanted meat. (Maybe it was the men who weren't satisfied with angel food!)

God gave the people the meat they wanted, but look at the price they paid for it: "And he gave them their request; but sent leanness into their soul" (v. 15). While they were still eating, many of them died (Numbers 11:18–33).

Do you have a demanding spirit or submissive spirit when you pray? A demanding spirit says, "Lord, I have to have this. You must answer this prayer. I can't live without it." A submissive spirit says, "Lord, if it is Your will, would You please. . . ." In love the Lord denied Paul's prayer for the removal of his "thorn in the flesh" (2 Corinthians 12:7–9). The tormenting thorn may have kept Paul from spiritual pride, which could have destroyed him.

Even Shakespeare knew it is best that God doesn't answer all our prayers.

> "We, ignorant of ourselves,
> Beg often our own harms, which the
>   wise powers
> Deny us for our good; so find we profit
> By losing of our prayers."

The way we pray will depend on which means the most to us: comfort or character. For what are you praying?

"They angered him also at the waters of strife, so that it went ill with Moses for their sakes:
Because they provoked his spirit, so that he spake unadvisedly with his lips"
(Psalm 106:32, 33).

ABRAHAM is remembered for his faith, Job for his patience, Moses for his meekness (Numbers 12:3). Perhaps Moses, by nature, was prone to sensitiveness and hastiness of temper. In anger he slew an Egyptian (Exodus 2:12). God took Moses to the backside of the desert for forty years to teach him many lessons. Maybe one of them was to rule his own spirit before God called him to rule an unruly, murmuring, and complaining mass of people.

Moses led the rebellious Children of Israel through the desert for forty years. He was close to 120 years of age. No doubt he was tired and worn down from carrying the burden of these stubborn people. For forty years he demonstrated meekness before them and presented himself as a man of dignity. But he lost his cool when the people provoked him to anger. "They angered him also at the waters of strife, so that it went ill with Moses for their sakes: Because they provoked his spirit, so that he spake unadvisedly with his lips" (vv. 32, 33).

Does it seem unfair that God would not let Moses go into the Promised Land because he smote the rock instead of speaking to it (Numbers 20:7–13)? Our tendency would be to say it was the people's fault; they caused him to sin. But we can't blame our sin on someone else. We sin when we choose to obey the lusts of the flesh rather than listen to the voice of God.

Are you willing to take responsibility for your sin, or are you blaming someone else?

"They sacrificed their sons and their daughters unto devils" (Psalm 106:37).

WHEN YOU read about the Israelites, do you see their inconsistency and ungratefulness? They frequently turned their backs on God. After all the great miracles they had seen, how could they turn from God and serve the Canaanite idols? How could they stoop that low?

It was a downward progression. First, they "mingled among the heathen" instead of destroying them as God had commanded (v. 35; see also Deuteronomy 7:2; 12:2; 20:17). Next, the Israelites got involved with the Canaanites; they "learned their works" (v. 35). The final step downward was to make sacrifices to the heathen gods (v. 36). What did they give as living sacrifices to these dead gods? Their children. "They sacrificed their sons and their daughters unto devils" (v. 37).

It's hard to imagine people sacrificing their own children, but it happens even today. No, not sacrificing in the sense of killing, but in the sense of offering children to the god of the this world, the Devil. When parents are so consumed with their problems that they have no time for their children, the Devil works havoc in children's lives, filling them with doubts and fears. Some parents offer their children to the god of this world by encouraging them to bow to materialism, following the lifestyle of their parents. Some parents push their children into the sports arena until their lives become consumed with athletics, and the children end up serving the god of this world.

Whether we are parents, grandparents, or singles, we all touch children's lives in one way or another. We need to be doing all we can to encourage them toward godliness rather than toward the god of this world, the Devil.

"Let the redeemed of the LORD say so, whom he hath redeemed from the hand of the enemy"
(*Psalm 107:2*).

THE message of this psalm is clear (even though who wrote it is unclear): God's goodness and wonderful works to the children of men (vv. 8, 15, 21, 31). Who has the most credibility in talking about God's goodness? One of His own children. "Let the redeemed of the LORD say so, whom he hath redeemed from the hand of the enemy" (v. 2).

Do you take time every now and then to remember what you were redeemed *from?* In an earlier psalm David wrote, "He brought me up also out of an horrible pit, out of the miry clay" (40:2). Perhaps God saved you *out of* a life of sinful habits and wicked lifestyles. If you were saved as a child, He saved you *from* those things; you never had to experience them. Whatever your background and

whenever you were saved, take time to thank God that He has redeemed you.

The command is clear: redeemed ones are supposed to tell others. "Let the redeemed of the Lord say so." We need to tell others how good God is and how much He loves us. "O give thanks unto the LORD, for he is good: for his mercy endureth for ever" (v. 1).

> "Redeemed—how I love to proclaim it!
> Redeemed by the blood of the Lamb;
> Redeemed through His infinite mercy—
> His child, and forever I am"
>
> (FANNY CROSBY).

Do you "love to proclaim" the message of redemption? With whom can you share that message today?

"Then they cried unto the LORD in their trouble, and he delivered them out of their distresses" (Psalm 107:6).

AFTER addressing the psalm to the redeemed (v. 2), the psalmist recounted some of the history of the Children of Israel. What did they do when they got in a tough spot? They prayed. "Then they cried unto the Lord in their trouble, and he delivered them out of their distresses" (v. 6).

Four times in this psalm the writer said God heard the cry of the distressed and delivered them (vv. 6, 13, 19, 28). Surely those who were delivered would be overflowing with praise and thanks to God, but the text seems to indicate otherwise. The psalmist had to encourage the people to praise God: "Oh that men would praise the LORD for his goodness, and for his wonderful words to the children of men" (v. 8; also vv. 15, 21, 31). God seemed to be saying, "Oh, if men would just express some appreciation for My goodness to them."

People in general are an ungrateful lot. Sometimes animals are more grateful to their masters than men and women are to their master, the Lord God.

"Man, O most ungrateful man, can ever
Enjoy Thy gift, but never mind the Giver;
And like the swine, though pampered
    with enough,
His eyes are never higher than the trough!"

(F. QUARLES).

Gratitude should be the habit of the redeemed at all times, not just when they've been delivered from distress. Are you in the habit of daily praise?

"They wandered in the wilderness in a solitary way; they found no city to dwell in"
(Psalm 107:4).

PSALM 107 pictures four groups of people who cried to God in their distress: those who wandered in the wilderness (v. 4); those who were in bondage because of their rebellion (v. 10); those who were deathly ill (v. 18); those who were overwhelmed by the storms of life and at their wit's end (v. 27).

Let's take a closer look at the first group. "They wandered in the wilderness in a solitary way; they found no city to dwell in" (v. 4). The wilderness wanderings of the Children of Israel are a picture of a barren, desolate Christian life.

The songwriter asked the question, "Is this vile world a friend to grace, To help me on to God?" The answer is a resounding no! This world is a dreary and desolate place, empty and lonely. It cannot fill the longings of our souls. It leaves us hungry and thirsty. "Hungry and thirsty, their soul fainted in them" (v. 5). The world cannot offer anything to take the place of the peace and joy we once knew when we walked in obedience to Christ.

What is the solution for one who is wandering in the wilderness? The same solution the Children of Israel used: cry unto the Lord (v. 6). Ask God to draw you back to Himself. You need to return to a life of obedient submission to the will of God.

Are you drifting aimlessly in the wilderness of this world, or are you living above this world on higher ground?

"Such as sit in darkness and in the shadow of death, being bound in affliction and iron; Because they rebelled against the words of God, and contemned the counsel of the most High" (Psalm 107:10, 11).

SINFUL man cries, "I want to be free to do my own thing! I don't want to be bound by God's Word or any man's word. I just want freedom!" When men rebel against God's counsel or plan for their lives, they pay a high price. "Such as sit in darkness and in the shadow of death, being bound in affliction and iron; Because they rebelled against the words of God, and contemned the counsel of the most High" (vv. 10, 11).

When a person says, "I don't want to be bound by God's Word," then he or she will be bound by the shackles of sin and put in Satan's prison house. Satan's tricks are subtle and deceitful. He whispers in the rebel's ear, "Just try drugs this once"; or "everyone is doing it"; or "just one drink won't hurt you";

or "everyone cheats on his or her mate once in a while." Soon Satan has a captive who is chained to his or her sin and can't get free. This person is in a dungeon of defeat and despair. But it is never too late for God's mercy! When he cries out to God for His help, He hears and delivers (v. 13).

You may not be bound to the sins of drugs, alcohol, or infidelity, but other sins are just as disgusting to God. God hates *all* sin!

What sin binds you? Is it worry, fear, gossip, discontentment, anger? God wants to release you from your sin. Have you asked Him to deliver you from the sin that binds you?

"Fools because of their transgression, and because of their iniquities, are afflicted. . . . and they draw near unto the gates of death" (Psalm 107:17, 18).

ALL SICKNESS is not the result of sin, but some is! Some suffering is self-inflicted, we bring it on ourselves. Things such as overwork, gluttony, sexual sins, alcohol, drugs, and smoking can lead to physical suffering, even to the point of death. "Fools because of their transgression, and because of their iniquities, are afflicted. . . . and they draw near unto the gates of death" (vv. 17, 18).

Sin can bring people to death's door, but God can shut the door in answer to prayer. "Then they cry unto the LORD in their trouble, and he saveth them out of their distresses" (v. 19). I wonder how many people have been saved from death in answer to their prayers or the prayers of other people for them?

A person who has been living in sin needs more than prayer and medicine to heal him; he needs God's Word. Only God's Word can heal the soul. "He sent his word, and healed them, and delivered them from their destructions" (v. 20). God's Word is the only medicine that can cure the wounded conscience of a sin-sick person, ridden with guilt and shame.

The Word of God brings healing to sinner and saint alike. "He sent his word, and healed them." Do you have a broken heart? Have you lost hope and given up?

No medicine can heal a broken heart other than the healing medicine of the Bible.

Claim these promises and ask God to heal your broken heart: "Casting all your care upon him; for he careth for you" (1 Peter 5:7); "He healeth the broken in heart, and bindeth up their wounds" (Psalm 147:3).

"They reel to and fro, and stagger like a drunken man, and are at their wit's end"
(Psalm 107:27).

VERSES 23–27 of Psalm 107 give us a picture of men caught in a furious storm at sea. They are tossed about as toys falling off a shelf; they stagger to and fro as they try to walk from place to place. They are terrified! Tempestuous storms and deadly dangers have brought many a man to his knees who would never have bowed to God in the calm.

Some people ignore God when life is smooth and easy; but when the winds are violent and the waves are raging—when they are at their wit's end—then will they call upon God. "They reel to and fro, and stagger like a drunken man, and are at their wit's end" (v. 27). They are at their wit's end, but at least they have enough wits left to do the one thing that can help them: "Then they cry unto the LORD in their trouble, and he bringeth them out of their distresses" (v. 28).

If you are at your wit's end, do the one thing that can help you: cry out to the Lord for help. He can bring you out of your distresses!

"Are you standing at 'Wit's End Corner'?
Then you're just in the very spot
To learn the wondrous resources
Of Him who faileth not;
No doubt to a brighter pathway
Your footsteps will soon be moved,
But only at 'Wit's End Corner'
Is the 'God who is able' proved"

(ANTOINETTE WILSON).

Don't give up; it may be the last key on the ring that opens the door!

"O God, my heart is fixed: I will sing and give praise, even with my glory" (Psalm 108:1).

IF YOU wanted to learn how to sharpen your skills in some area of your life, whom would you ask to teach you? No doubt you would ask someone who had mastered that skill. David was a master in the art of praising God; he has much to teach us. One of the most valuable lessons we can learn from him is that real praise flows from a "fixed" heart: "O God, my heart is fixed: I will sing and give praise, even with my glory" (v. 1).

What is a "fixed" heart? One commentator says it is a heart that is prepared firmly. Psalm 108 has been called the "Warrior's Morning Song." As David started the day, he firmly prepared his heart before he faced the conflicts and challenges of that day. When a tongue is directed by a "fixed" heart, surely glorious praise will flow forth.

Is your heart prepared firmly each morning to face the conflicts and challenges of the day? Just as you may need to take medication to control a physical problem, so you can go to God's "medicine chest," His Word, each morning to find help to prevent serious problems during the day and to strengthen you to face the conflicts that may arise.

Someone has given this prescription from God's Word: For the *blues*, read Psalm 27; for an *empty purse*, read Psalm 37; if you're *discouraged* about work, read Psalm 128; if people seem *unkind* to you, read John 15; if you are losing *confidence* in people, read 1 Corinthians 13; if you cannot have *your own way*, read James 3; if you are *out of sorts*, read Hebrews 12.

Are you using God's medicine chest?

"Give us help from trouble: for vain is the help of man" (Psalm 108:12).

HAVE YOU ever prayed a prayer similar to David's: "Give us help from trouble: for vain is the help of man" (v. 12)? How many times have you been in a spot where human help was vain or worthless? Can people give you peace in your soul, contentment in a less than desirable environment, or joy in the midst of your trials? No, they can't! The help of other people is encouraging and greatly appreciated by all of us, but people can only do so much for us. The real needs in our soul can only be met by God.

The next time you realize human help is vain in meeting your need, you will not seek God's help in vain. He wants to give you help from your trouble. "Through God we shall do valiantly" (v. 13).

Through God we will not only do valiantly, we will be victorous conquerors. God's Word says, "Nay, in all these things we are *more than conquerors* through him that loved us" (Romans 8:37). "In all these things"—the day-to-day things and trials, troubles and distresses—we can be victorious and triumphant time after time. We become more than conquerors when we allow our troubles to serve a good purpose in our lives. Our adversities can be turned around and used for our advantage.

God doesn't want us to be overcome; He wants us to be overcomers! Our past victories should give us confidence for tomorrow. We are not in a battle wondering if we can win; God promises we can excel in winning.

Have you been down in the dumps with the "overcome ones"? It's time to stand up and be counted with the "overcomers."

"As he loved cursing, so let it come unto him: as he delighted not in blessing, so let it be far from him" (Psalm 109:17).

AS YOU read Psalm 109:1–20, it is hard to remember this is a prayer. It sounds like David was revengeful and full of anger. We must remember these were the words of a godly man who was being slandered and persecuted. Why did his enemies hate him? Because he loved them. "And they have rewarded me evil for good, and hatred for my love" (v. 5).

Returning evil for good is one of Satan's tactics, and evil ones on earth (and sometimes even Christians) use the same tactics. This is what brought David to his knees, crying out for justice from God. David knew vengeance was not his to give; that was God's prerogative. So he prayed that God would stop the injustice and give his enemies a taste of their own medicine. "As he loved cursing, so let it come unto him: as he delighted not in blessing, so let it be far from him" (v. 17). Do you detect a bit of vengeance in those words? Maybe so! David was just like us; he wasn't perfect.

In September 1854 at the battle of Alma in the Crimean War, a wounded Russian soldier called for someone to give him a drink. Captain Eddinton, who had a kind and loving heart, gave him a drink. The wounded man revived. As the captain was leaving to join his regiment, the man whom he had just helped raised his gun and shot him in the back.

Can you relate to this story? When someone you thought was your friend stabs you in the back, how can you keep from retaliating in hate and anger? Only God's love will allow you to absorb that kind of hurt without striking back.

Are you striking back or praying for grace to demonstrate unconditional love?

"For I am poor and needy, and my heart is wounded within me. I am gone like the shadow when it declineth: I am tossed up and down as the locust" (Psalm 109:22, 23).

DAVID had been slandered, and he felt terrible. The mighty warrior was weak and helpless. "For I am poor and needy, and my heart is wounded within me" (v. 22). David was not only broken because of his outward troubles, but he was grieving inwardly; he was broken-hearted. He felt as if he were wasting away to nothing. He compared his state of mind and body to a shadow that grew fainter and fainter. "I am gone like the shadow when it declineth" (v. 23).

When a person gets this low, it is time for divine help and sometimes medical help. Though people had turned on David, his God was still there to help and heal him. "I will greatly praise the LORD. . . . For he shall stand at the right hand of the poor, to save him from those that condemn his soul" (vv. 30, 31).

I know how David must have felt when he said, "My heart is wounded within." I remembered one of my "dark valley" experiences as I wrote this devotional. I got out my journal and read a prayer I had written when I had my devotions that day. It was a prayer from a wounded heart: "Lord, if You're trying to break me completely, You're accomplishing the job. I can hardly move. . . . Today is the first time I ever wanted to quit—to get out of the ministry. I just feel I can't take any more hurts. I couldn't go to church tonight; I could hardly get out of bed; I have not eaten all day. I have no strength left except for the strength You are giving me. Help me to keep exchanging my strength for Your strength."

Do you have a wounded heart? Don't quit! Draw upon God's strength to keep going.

"The LORD said unto my Lord, Sit thou at my right hand, until I make thine enemies thy footstool" (Psalm 110:1).

DOES THIS sound like someone talking to himself: "The LORD said unto my Lord, Sit thou at my right hand, until I make thine enemies thy footstool" (v. 1)? Well, it wasn't. It was the Lord Jehovah talking to the Lord Jesus Christ, the King of Kings. Jehovah God told the Lord Jesus to sit at His right hand until He (Jehovah) made His (Christ's) enemies His footstool. Psalm 110 pictures Christ as both king and priest (vv. 2, 4).

This was new to David. No king in Israel was also a priest. Our King-Priest, Jesus Christ, is now seated in Heaven at the Father's right hand (Hebrews 10:12). One day every rebel will lie beneath His feet— "until I make thine enemies thy footstool"— and their final pursuit of evil will be over.

Isn't it comforting to know that the King-Priest Who reigns in Heaven was a man who faced the same struggles of life that we face?

Why is that so comforting? Because He can empathize with us. Everything we will ever experience, He experienced in some form. He knows how we feel when we cry out for help (Hebrews 4:14–16). I can sympathize with all people, but I can only empathize with those who are experiencing what I have experienced.

Do you ever wonder why God is allowing the trial you now have? Wait a few years; God will bring other people into your life who are passing through the same kind of trial. You will be able to comfort them (2 Corinthians 1:3, 4). Then you will begin to understand why God allowed the trial in your life. God takes us through the dark valleys so we will be able to say, "I know how you feel."

Store up comfort; someone will need it one of these days.

"The fear of the LORD is the beginning of wisdom: a good understanding have all they that do his commandments" (Psalm 111:10).

PEOPLE can never be truly wise and have good understanding until they begin to fear God. "The fear of the LORD is the beginning of wisdom: a good understanding have all they that do his commandments" (v. 10).

What does it mean to "fear" the Lord? It is the respectful reverence a child has toward a firm but loving parent. The child is careful to please the parent and fearful of offending the parent in any way. When we respect God's power and authority, we will not pull away from His commandments but want to obey them. Why? Because we know we will be blessed for our obedience.

The Biblical concept of wisdom is the application of moral and ethical principles that results in godly living. How do we get this kind of wisdom? Does it come by insight? No; we all know people who have good insight into various matters but they lack the principles that lead to godliness.

Does it come by learning? No; the learned Selden proved this. He said he had taken much pains to know everything that was esteemed worth knowing among men; but none of his learning and reading could comfort and help him when he came to the end of his life.

Does it come by experience? No; history has proven that people without God will not live godly lives.

How, then, do we get wisdom? It is so simple people stumble over it. "The fear of the LORD is the beginning of wisdom: a good understanding have all they that do his commandments." The truly wise person fears (respects) God and obeys Him.

Are you a wise person, fearing God and obeying Him?

"He shall not be afraid of evil tidings: his heart is fixed, trusting in the LORD"
(Psalm 112:7).

PSALMS 111 and 112 could have been written by the same person. Psalm 111 ends with the words "The fear of the LORD is the beginning of wisdom" (v. 10), and Psalm 112 starts with the same thought: "Blessed is the man that feareth the LORD" (v. 1). The fear of the Lord leads to a fearless life. The blessed man who fears the Lord in verse 1 "shall not be afraid of evil tidings: his heart is fixed, trusting in the LORD" (v. 7). The formula for fearlessness is simple: Fearlessness = a fixed heart, full of faith.

What is a "fixed" heart? It is a heart that is established or steadfast. The same Hebrew word is used in Psalm 40:2 and is translated "established": "He brought me up also out of an horrible pit . . . and *established* my goings." A fixed heart does not waver. It is not fearful because it is full of faith rather than doubt.

We live in a world of people filled with phobias. Here are just a few of them: algophobia—fear of pain; claustrophobia—fear of confined places; acrophobia—fear of heights; nyctophobia—fear of night. People are afraid of the dead, light, strangers, dogs, water, and many other things. One man said his wife had "burglarphobia." He told this story. He was awakened one night by his wife crying, "John, there's a burglar downstairs!" He went downstairs, and—sure enough—there was a burglar. He caught the man crawling out the window. He stopped the man and said, "Sir, before you leave, I want to take you upstairs to meet my wife. She has lain awake many nights in the past twenty years waiting for you to come."

Is your heart established? Are you full of faith or full of phobias?

"He raiseth up the poor out of the dust, and lifteth the needy out of the dunghill"
(Psalm 113:7).

THIS PSALM pictures the ministering grace of God that reaches down to the poor and needy. Amazing as it may seem, the King of Kings stoops down to lift up poor and needy creatures like you and me. This King is like no other; He is at home in His heavenly kingdom as well as at the side of the lowliest of His children. In His eyes our worth and value have nothing to do with our wealth or position on the social ladder. He is no respecter of persons (Ephesians 6:9). God loves the down-and-outer as well as the up-and-outer. "He raiseth up the poor out of the dust, and lifteth the needy out of the dunghill" (v. 7).

Many great servants of God were chosen from lowly or outcast positions. David the shepherd boy became a king; Joseph was taken from the prison to the palace; Peter went from catching fish to being a fisher of men; Abraham Lincoln went from country boy to president of the United States.

Are you feeling poor and needy? Reach out to the Lord, and He will lift you up. He may not lift you to a place of prominence in the eyes of men, but you are special to Him. You are His child; He shares His wealth with you.

I get excited when I think how rich we are as children of God. We have fellowship with God (1 John 1:7); a mansion in Heaven (John 14:2, 3); eternal life (John 10:28); an incorruptible, undefiled inheritance (1 Peter 1:4); great and precious promises (2 Peter 1:4); and all things that pertain to life and godliness (2 Peter 1:3).

Why not start enjoying your inheritance? Start living like a princess instead of a pauper.

"Tremble, thou earth, at the presence of the Lord, at the presence of the God of Jacob;
Which turned the rock into a standing water, the flint into a fountain of waters"
(Psalm 114:7, 8).

NOT ONLY do mountains tremble, but rocks give forth water when our mighty God decides it should be done. "Tremble, thou earth, at the presence of the Lord, at the presence of the God of Jacob; Which turned the rock into a standing water, the flint into a fountain of waters" (vv. 7, 8). The almighty God Who provided for the Children of Israel did some unusual things with rocks and water. On one occasion He turned water into walls so His people could cross the Red Sea on dry ground (Exodus 14:22). He provided water from a rock to nourish the people in the desert (Exodus 17:6). This same almighty God is our provider today!

As I was thinking about all the marvelous ways God has met our needs through the years, one day in particular came to my mind.

It was a cold wintry day years ago when we were struggling through Bible college and had three growing boys. The two older boys were getting on their snow boots, and I heard a ripping sound and "Oh no" coming from Dan's lips. The top of his boot had torn off. My first reaction was "Oh no" as well, because there was no money to buy another pair of boots. But how do you go without boots in the snow? Dan wore the torn boot to school because at least it covered the bottom of his shoe. That day a lady from our church called and asked if one of the boys could use a pair of boots. Guess what size they were? She didn't know our need, but God did! He supplied just what we needed, when we needed it.

❖

What has He done for you lately?

"But our God is in the heavens: he hath done whatsoever he hath pleased" (Psalm 115:3).

THE PSALMIST was evidently upset with the heathen who worshiped foolish idols made of wood and stone. They could see their gods, so they asked the psalmist where his God was. "Where is now their God?" (v. 2). The psalmist answered, "But our God is in the heavens: he hath done whatsoever he hath pleased" (v. 3).

The heathen gods dwelled on earth and were made from the earth. Our God created the earth and dwells in Heaven as the sovereign ruler of Heaven and earth. All the world is subject to His will, and nothing can stop His purposes from being accomplished. "He hath done whatsoever he hath pleased."

Does that thought bless you or bother you? I have a wall hanging that reminds me of the sovereignty of God each time I read it.

"There is nothing—no circumstance, no trouble, no testing—that can ever touch me until it has gone past God and Christ, right through to me. If it has come that far, it has come with a great purpose, which I may not understand at the moment. But as I refuse to become panicky, and as I lift up my eyes to Him, I accept it as coming from the Throne of God, for some great purpose or blessing in my own heart. No sorrow will ever disturb me and no trial will ever disarm me, no circumstance will cause me to fret, for I shall rest in the joy of what my Lord is" (author unknown).

Those thoughts are a blessing to me; how do they affect you?

"The heaven, even the heavens, are the LORD's: but the earth hath he given to the children of men" (Psalm 115:16).

THE SOVEREIGN, omnipresent God is in control of the whole universe, yet the Bible speaks of Heaven in particular as being His. "The heaven, even the heavens, are the LORD's: but the earth hath he given to the children of men" (v. 16).

Earth, this one little speck in space, is the home of the people God created. God is in control of all His creation, yet He allows men to have a free will to choose between right and wrong. He allows men to punish one another, break His laws, and even make their own idols (v. 4). God is in Heaven; the heathen gods of silver and gold are on this earth.

How many people do you know who worship "silver and gold"? I had a conversation with a man who had AIDS. He had $12,000 in his pocket, but he was miserable, and his future was dark and hopeless. I tried to tell him about the Sun of Righteousness Who could brighten the dreary days ahead, but he had no time for God. He was too busy trying to figure out how he could hold on to his "silver and gold" and not lose all his "things."

Christians are not exempt; they can be caught up with their "silver and gold" and let money and things become idols in their lives. One person described materialism like this:

"Possessions weigh me down in life;
I never feel quiet free.
I wonder if I own my things,
Or if my things own me?"

Are you managing your "silver and gold," or are they managing you?

"I love the LORD, because he hath heard my voice and my supplications" (Psalm 116:1).

THE PSALMIST'S personal love for God grew as he continued to experience God's goodness to him. The psalmist had been delivered in a time of distress and trouble. God had answered his prayer, and his heart was filled with love and gratitude. "I love the LORD, because he hath heard my voice and my supplications" (v. 1).

Charles Spurgeon said, "Answered prayers are silken bonds that bind our hearts to God." We love God because He loves us (1 John 4:19), and He continues to express His love to us in a multitude of ways each day, just as He did to the psalmist.

What are the first words that come from your mouth each day as you raise your voice to God in prayer? Do you say, "I love You, Lord"? You should! Before we make our requests, we need to tell God that we love Him and thank Him for what He has already done for us.

The story is told of two angels who came from Heaven each morning and went on their rounds all day. One was the "angel of requests"; the other was the "angel of thanksgiving." They each carried a basket. The basket of the "angel of requests" was always filled quickly; the basket of the "angel of thanksgiving" had only two or three contributions. This fictitious story reminds us that too many of us spend more time asking God for things than we do praising and thanking Him for His goodness and mercy.

How full is your basket of thanksgiving? Have you told the Lord today that you love Him?

October 12   Psalm 116:10–19

"Precious in the sight of the LORD is the death of his saints" (Psalm 116:15).

PSALM 116:3 pictures the psalmist being snatched from the jaws of death. "The sorrows of death compassed me" (v. 3). Was he full of fear? NO! He knew that the death of saints was precious in God's sight and would only come at God's appointment. "Precious in the sight of the LORD is the death of his saints" (v. 15).

God's children should be able to view death without fear and dread. Death frees us from the cares, uncertainties, and pains of this life. Even better is the fact that "we shall be like him; for we shall see him as he is" (1 John 3:2).

This poem was a favorite of missionary John Stam, who was martyred for his faith in the 1930s.

"Afraid? Of what?
To feel the spirit's glad release?

To pass from pain to perfect peace,
The strife and strain of life to cease?
Afraid—of that?

"Afraid? Of what?
Afraid to see the Savior's face,
To hear His welcome, and to trace
The glory gleam from wounds of grace?
Afraid—of that?

"Afraid? Of what?
To enter into Heaven's rest,
And yet to serve the Master blest,
From service good to service best?
Afraid—of that?" (E. H. HAMILTON).

Does the thought of your death fill you with fear or excite you?

"O praise the LORD, all ye nations: praise him, all ye people. For his merciful kindness is great toward us . . ." (Psalm 117:1, 2).

THIS IS the shortest psalm, and it is in the very center of the Bible. Because it is so short, some people think it might have been detached from the previous or following psalm, but the two verses stand alone as an invitation to praise the Lord. "O praise the LORD, all ye nations: praise him, all ye people. For his merciful kindness is great toward us . . ." (vv. 1, 2). Our worship of the Lord can be brief, as evidenced in Psalm 117, or extended, as shown in Psalm 119.

Each of us has reason to praise God for His "merciful kindness." One evidence of His kindness is the variety He put within His creation for us to enjoy. The animals are different; the flowers and trees are different. Life on earth would be dull and uninteresting if everything were exactly alike. I was reminded of this variety as I walked down a wooded pathway in the fall and observed all the different colors, sizes, and shapes of the glistening fall leaves. Soon the beauty of the fall gives way to winter, another evidence of God's variety in creation.

Make a list of God's "merciful kindness" to you; then take time to praise Him.

"The LORD is on my side; I will not fear: what can man do unto me?" (Psalm 118:6).

PSALM 118 celebrates a great deliverance, perhaps the return of the Jews from the Babylonian captivity. "The LORD is on my side; I will not fear: what can man do unto me?" (v. 6). It may be that the psalm was written at the completion of rebuilding the wall of Jerusalem (Nehemiah 6:15; 8:14–18). The psalmist was fearless because he knew God was on his side. God had brought His people back to their land; they were safe again.

I would choose to have some people on my side just so they wouldn't be against me. I am so thankful God is on my side! I sure wouldn't want Him against me. That would be a no-win situation. The most remarkable thing about having God on my side is that I didn't choose Him—He chose me! (See Ephesians 1:4.) Some people whom I thought were on my side have fallen by the wayside, but not my God. I am on His side, and He is on mine; we are a team.

I never have to fear rejection; God will never forsake me. I never have to fear things being out of control in my life; He always has everything under control. I never have to fear being inadequate; God will give me the strength to do whatever He asks me to do. I don't have to fear the future, sickness, or death; these come only at His appointment. With God on my side, I never need to fear again.

"Joyfully enlisting, By Thy grace divine, We are on the Lord's side—Savior, we are Thine!"

"I will praise thee: for thou hast heard me, and art become my salvation" (Psalm 118:21).

HOW DID the Lord become the psalmist's salvation? God saved him from his enemies! The heathen nations had encompassed, or swarmed around, him like bees (v. 12). He had felt their sting; he had felt they were crushing the life out of him and would surely destroy him. But the Lord helped him! "I will praise thee: for thou hast heard me, and art become my salvation" (v. 21).

I cannot tell you the number of times God has heard my cry for help and delivered me from a difficult situation. I faced a month that I knew would be particularly difficult. God gave me assurance from His Word that He would deliver me when I needed it. I was reading about Daniel in the lions' den, and these words especially caught my attention: "Is thy God, whom thou servest continually, able to deliver thee from the lions?" (Daniel 6:20). As I faced that difficult month, I realized that when my faith is weak, my all-powerful God looks weak as well. I find myself asking, "Is God able?" rather than affirming, "God *is* able!" Is our God able to deliver us? Yes; a thousand times yes!

When was the last time you said those words, "The Lord helped me"? You felt surely you couldn't make it, but the Lord helped you. In that moment of deliverance, the Lord became your salvation.

"This is the day which the LORD hath made; we will rejoice and be glad in it"
(Psalm 118:24).

THE FIRST twenty-one verses of this psalm describe a man reflecting on his circumstances: "I called upon the LORD in distress" (v. 5); "I will not fear: what can man do unto me?" (v. 6); "they compassed me about like bees" (v. 12); "I shall not die, but live" (v. 17); "the LORD hath chastened me" (v. 18).

The psalmist had passed through a difficult experience, but he was on the other side now. He was amazed at all the ways the Lord had helped him. "This is the day which the LORD hath made; we will rejoice and be glad in it" (v. 24).

Isn't it amazing what a difference a day can make? As I write this, my heart is light and full of joy. Yesterday was a different story; I would have had a hard time finding anything good about that day. I knew it was a day the Lord had made, but I sure had a hard time being glad in it. Things went from bad to worse. It was a terrible, no good, very bad, awful day.

I had just put four pretty flowers in a pot and set them by the pool. While I was cleaning the pool deck, the hose got caught around the pot and dumped all the new flowers and dirt into the pool. After cleaning up that mess, I went to the front yard where I was also planting some flowers. My shoe got caught on the edging around the flower bed, and I ripped my sandal and hurt my foot. While taking a shower and trying to get some of the dirt out of my foot, I soaked my hair, which I was not planning to wash right then. I felt like screaming, "Lord, give me a break!"

We can't always rejoice in our circumstances, but we can always rejoice in the Lord of our circumstances. He always does what is right.

In what are you rejoicing today?

"O that my ways were directed to keep thy statutes!" (Psalm 119:5).

THIS IS the longest psalm and the longest chapter in the Bible. It may have been written by David, or it could have been written by Ezra after the temple was rebuilt (Ezra 6:14–16). The psalm is divided into twenty-two sections, and almost every verse mentions God's Word.

Psalm 119 is a repetitive meditation on the beauty and value of God's Word to help us grow spiritually and keep us pure and clean. God's Word is the only sure guide we have in this wicked world to keep us from the sinful enticements all around us. Our hearts should yearn to keep God's Word as much as the psalmist's did. "O that my ways were directed to keep thy statutes!" (v. 5).

When is the last time you thanked the Lord for the value of His Word in your life? The only sure method of success is to know and obey the Word of God. "This book of the law shall not depart out of thy mouth; but thou shalt meditate therein day and night, that thou mayest observe to do according to all that is written therein: for then thou shalt make thy way prosperous, and then thou shalt have good success" (Joshua 1:8).

One day I tried a friend's cake recipe. When I got ready to make the cake, I realized I was missing one ingredient. Rather than take time to go to the store, I decided to use a substitute ingredient. The cake was a failure! It did not rise properly, and it tasted awful. In some ways, life is like baking a cake. If you follow God's recipe in His Word, it works. If you decide to make substitutions and do things your way, you can write "Spiritual Failure" over your life.

Do you want your life to be governed by God's statutes or your substitutes?

"Thy word have I hid in mine heart, that I might not sin against thee" (Psalm 119:11).

MANY YEARS ago Spurgeon wrote in the front of his Bible, "This book will keep me from sin, or sin will keep me from this book." The psalmist had the same thought in mind when he wrote, "Thy word have I hid in mine heart, that I might not sin against thee" (v. 11).

Most of us probably have more verses hidden in our hearts than we are aware of. When we hear a verse quoted or read, we can quote the verse in our minds. If we are wise, however, we will deliberately hide God's Word in our hearts as a preventative to sin.

I have struggled with an issue that I thought I would not face until later in my life. What has kept me from the sins of worry, anger, and fear? The Word of God! I will make it through this experience victoriously if I hide God's Word in my heart each day. What verses will I hide in my heart? I will memorize verses on the areas of need in my life. My big concern is fear of the future, so I am memorizing Jeremiah 29:11—"For I know the thoughts that I think toward you, saith the Lord, thoughts of peace, and not of evil, to give you an expected end." Whatever the area of need, I try to memorize a verse for that need.

In what areas of your life are you weak? Do you struggle with worry, greed, forgiveness, anger? Find some verses for your area of need and memorize them. God's Word will keep you from sin.

Psalm 119:17–24

"Open thou mine eyes, that I may behold wondrous things out of thy law" (Psalm 119:18).

AS YOU read this psalm, you realize that the psalmist did not read God's Word out of a sense of duty. He read with a desire to know more about God. He wanted the "spiritual blinders" lifted from his eyes. He wanted to see new and exciting things, "wondrous things," in God's Law. Notice the prayer of his heart: "Open thou mine eyes, that I may behold wondrous things out of thy law" (v. 18).

Someone once said, "It is not what we have, but what we know we have, that determines our material and spiritual wealth." That statement reminds me of a farmer who lived in Texas during the Depression. His finances were running out, and he was beginning to wonder how he was going to support his family. One day a man knocked at his door and asked if he would be willing to sell some of his land so the man's company could drill for oil. The Texan had many acres of land, but he could not afford to farm them. He decided he might as well sell some of his land to get money for seed to plant his crops. To the farmer's amazement, the company struck oil on the land, and he became a millionaire overnight. The farmer had always been a millionaire, but he just didn't know it.

We, too, are millionaires; we have a gold mine of treasure in the Word of God. But sometimes we act like we don't know it.

Are you digging for Biblical treasure each day? Are you finding new wealth, "wondrous things," in the Word of God that can enrich your life? Ask God to give you open eyes.

Psalm 119:25–32

"My soul melteth for heaviness: strengthen thou me according unto thy word"
(Psalm 119:28).

THE PSALMIST was evidently experiencing great grief as he recorded this portion of Scripture. He needed strength beyond himself to keep going. "My soul melteth for heaviness: strengthen thou me according unto thy word" (v. 28). The psalmist knew what God had promised; now he was trusting God to carry out His promise.

Great losses can cause great grief and heaviness in our souls. The loss of a mate, a child, a parent, our health, or our finances can put us into a state of distress and turmoil. If we stay in grief and sorrow for a prolonged period, life becomes a mere existence, leaving us feeling half dead or wishing we were.

Many books describe the emotions people experience as they move through loss to the point of acceptance. These books give us methods to follow that will help us in times of grief, but none of the authors comes with his or her book to give us personal help in carrying out the instructions. The Bible is the only book that comes with a private Tutor. "When he, the Spirit of truth, is come, he will guide you into all truth: for he shall not speak of himself; but whatsoever he shall hear, that shall he speak" (John 16:13).

Is it any wonder that the Bible is still the best-selling book in the world? Do you know the Author of the Bible as your personal friend and tutor? Or do you just know about Him?

"Teach me, O LORD, the way of thy statutes; and I shall keep it unto the end"
(Psalm 119:33).

IN PSALM 119:33–40 the psalmist prayed for help from on high. "Teach me, O LORD, the way of thy statutes; and I shall keep it unto the end" (v. 33). William Cowper translated the verse this way: "If thou continue a teacher of me, I shall continue a servant to thee." The psalmist had learned the secret of ending well; it involved three things: (1) teach me (v. 33)—he needed daily teaching from the Law of God; (2) give me (v. 34)—he needed to understand what he was being taught; (3) make me (v. 35)—he needed someone to make him do what he was being taught.

Do you know what it means to "practice the presence of God" in your life? This concept is related to abiding in Christ. It means to be in such close communion with Christ that we draw our strength from Him. Jesus Christ said He is the vine and we are the branches (John 15:1–11). A branch gets its sap, or strength for growth, as it stays united to the vine. If the branch is removed from the vine, it will soon wither and die because it has no strength in itself to keep growing.

The same principle is true in our lives. Only as we stay closely united to Christ, the Vine, will we have the strength to practice the presence of God in our lives and see spiritual growth. When we are abiding in Christ, we will pray as the psalmist did: "Teach me Your Word; give me understanding of Your Word; help me obey Your Word."

❖

Are these requests part of your prayer life?

"And I will walk at liberty: for I seek thy precepts. . . . My hands also will I lift up unto thy commandments, which I have loved; and I will meditate in thy statutes"
(Psalm 119:45, 48).

PSALM 119 repeatedly emphasizes the value of the Word of God in our lives. In these verses the psalmist tells us the Word of God gives us liberty. It sets us free from the fears and worries that bind us and imprison us. "And I will walk at liberty: for I seek thy precepts. . . . My hands also will I lift up unto thy commandments, which I have loved; and I will meditate in thy statutes" (vv. 45, 48).

Can you picture the psalmist lifting his hands to God, acknowledging that he welcomed God's precepts and commands in his life? As he meditated on them, he loved them more and more. They gave him peace in the storms of life, guidance when he was confused, strength when he was weary, and hope when the future looked dark. Oh, what liberty and freedom he enjoyed.

God's precepts and commands have also brought liberty to my life. They have taught me how to live a "palms-up" life. What is palms-up living? It is releasing one's grip on things and people; it is saying to God, "It all belongs to You, Lord; give what You want and take what You want." I can say this daily with no fear because I know God loves me and wants the very best for me. He wants me to be like His Son, and He knows the best way to accomplish His plan in my life (Romans 8:28, 29).

Are you walking in liberty and freedom, or is your life bound up with worries and fears? Why not try palms-up living? It can set you free!

"This is my comfort in my affliction: for thy word hath quickened me" (Psalm 119:50).

WHOEVER wrote this psalm knew something about affliction. If it was David, we know he lived many years of his life in turmoil. He experienced one problem after another. He often felt the need to be quickened, or revived. He needed courage to face the next day of uncertainty. He did not always have someone to comfort and encourage him in his afflictions and adversities. But he was never without comfort and encouragement. "This is my comfort in my affliction: for thy word hath quickened me" (v. 50). God's Word was not only the psalmist's survival kit, it was also his revival kit.

To whom or what do you turn in the midst of your troubles? A friend? If it is a spiritual friend, that person will turn you to the Word of God for the answers you need.

Do you turn to a Christian counselor? He or she, too, will direct you to the Word of God for help. Maybe you are saying, "I don't have a close friend or know a good counselor." My answer to you is, "Yes you do!" If you know Christ as your Savior, you have a friend Who sticks closer than a brother (Proverbs 18:24), and you have your own personal counselor (Isaiah 9:6). Furthermore, a Christian has the indwelling Holy Spirit, the Comforter (John 14:16, 17).

Some people have afflictions and no comfort. Those who know the Comforter have comfort in their afflictions.

Do you need comfort in your afflictions? Find a promise in God's Word and hang on to it. Here's a good starter, "I will never leave thee, nor forsake thee" (Hebrews 13:5).

"Thou art my portion, O LORD: I have said that I would keep thy words" (Psalm 119:57).

THE PSALMIST may have had many resources and treasures at his disposal, but he chose the Lord as his portion, his treasure. "Thou art my portion, O LORD: I have said that I would keep thy words" (v. 57). The psalmist's love for God resulted in a love for His Word. He preferred the Lord and His Word to the wealth of the world. If we are wise, we will follow his example!

We live in a materialistic age, a day when "things" are important to people. Not very many people choose spiritual wealth over material wealth. The more we get, the more we want.

I have a lovely home and everything I need. I love my home, and I am contented with it. However, I sometimes find myself battling discontentment. On one of our trips, we stayed in three homes that were larger and more beautiful than mine. In each home I found myself thinking, "It sure would be nice to build a new house." After I returned to my home, I soon overcame my discontentment. All I had to do was think about how much I have. It is more than I ever would have dreamed of and certainly more than I deserve. I also realize that if the Lord took away all my material wealth, I would still have all I need to be content. I would still have God and His Word. No amount of material wealth compares to my spiritual wealth. Truly, Christ is all I need! In Him I have everything I need to live a contented, godly life (2 Peter 1:3).

Can you say with the psalmist and songwriter, "Jesus Christ is made to me All I need, all I need; He alone is all my plea; He is all I need"?

"Before I was afflicted I went astray: but now have I kept thy word. . . . It is good for me that I have been afflicted; that I might learn thy statutes" (Psalm 119:67, 71).

THE PSALMIST stated that affliction was good for him. As he looked back on God's dealings in his life, he understood the reason for the affliction. "Before I was afflicted I went astray: but now have I kept thy word" (v. 67). He realized God had been good to him in disciplining him, so he declared, "It is good for me that I have been afflicted; that I might learn thy statutes (v. 71). Some lessons are only learned in sorrow and tears. The songwriter expressed it this way, "He wiped my eyes with tears that I might see."

Have you learned the value of trials in God's training program? The most beautiful wildflowers grow on the highest mountain peaks in spots that are exposed to the harshest weather. One man took flowers from a 10,000-foot summit and others from the wall of an old castle sheltered in a wooded valley. The flowers nurtured amid the storms on the mountain peak had a lovely primrose hue and were smooth in texture. The flowers nurtured amid the soft airs and the delicate showers of the lowland valley were a dim rusty color and rough in their texture. He went on to say, "Is it not so with the Christian who is afflicted, tempest-tossed, and not comforted? Till the storms and vicissitudes of God's providence beat upon him again and again, his character appears marred and clouded by selfish and worldly influences. But trials clear away the obscurity . . . and give brightness and blessings to his piety."

Again I ask you, Have you learned the value of trials in God's training program? I have!

"I know, O LORD, that thy judgments are right, and that thou in faithfulness hast afflicted me" (Psalm 119:75).

WE CAN learn valuable lessons in the school of affliction. The psalmist learned that God is faithful and that what God allows is right, even when it doesn't seem right. "I know, O LORD, that thy judgments are right, and that thou in faithfulness hast afflicted me" (v. 75). The psalmist knew that trials come from God's hand—either sent by Him or permitted by Him. Because God is in control, the psalmist could trust Him. Perhaps he knew the words of 1 Kings 12:24, "This thing is from me."

Have you learned that no circumstance is outside God's sovereign love? Everything He sends or permits is for our spiritual good and for His glory (Romans 8:28, 29). The question is, How much do we want to grow spiritually? How much do we really want to be like Christ? Warren Wiersbe wrote a book called *The Bumps Are What You Climb On.* He says we all respond in different ways to the rocks or difficulties in the paths of life. We complain about them; we kick against them and hurt ourselves; we try to push them aside and get rid of them; or we stop and go no farther. But some people are wise enough to use the rocky places as stepping-stones to climb higher.

What have you done with the rocks in your path?

"All thy commandments are faithful: they persecute me wrongfully; help thou me"
(Psalm 119:86).

THESE are the words of a hurting person: "they persecute me wrongfully." Can you sense the psalmist's disappointment with people? When he needed them, they had not been there, or they had turned on him and became his enemies. However, he knew one Person Who would never fail him. He knew God was faithful and trustworthy. He could depend on Him and His Word. "All thy commandments are faithful: they persecute me wrongfully; help thou me" (v. 86).

Are you faithful to your word? When you make a promise to someone, can that person be confident you will stay committed to your word? Our society, including the Christian world, is becoming more and more attached to the word "noncommitment." In fact, that attitude is epidemic in our western world. People refuse to be committed to their jobs, their marriages, or their churches.

Once we commit ourselves to take a task, big or small, we need to do everything in our power to be faithful to our word. A broken promise is hard to mend, and, in many cases, it can lead to a broken relationship. We need to remember what we learned in grade school:

> "If a task is once begun,
> Never leave it till it's done;
> Be the labor great or small,
> Do it well or not at all."

When you make a commitment, do you faithfully keep your word? God does!

"For ever, O LORD, thy word is settled in heaven" (Psalm 119:89).

WE LIVE in a world of changing people with changing loyalties. The psalmist had the same problem in his day. The people and circumstances in his life left him feeling insecure and unsettled. He needed support, but humanly speaking there was none. The only steadfast, settled, and unfailing thing he had in his life was the Word of God. He knew God never changed and neither did His Word. "For ever, O LORD, thy word is settled in heaven" (v. 89).

Some days everything seems to go wrong. The kids spill their milk at breakfast; they miss their school bus; then they call you at noon to let you know they forgot their lunch. We could call these minor irritations. But what about the major interruptions? Your job is insecure or your marriage is ending in divorce or your financial problems seem insurmountable. Times of prolonged anxiety leave us feeling faint, weary, and sometimes hopeless.

When we are ready to faint, we need to remember that our God never faints and never is weary (Isaiah 40:28). His Word has never failed. When we begin to waver and question if God will really keep His promises, we'd better start quoting Psalm 119:89: "For ever, O LORD, thy word is settled in heaven."

A farmer in England placed on the wind indicator on his barn the words "God is love." A friend looked at it and said, "Does that mean God is as changeable as the wind?" The farmer replied, "No; it means God is love no matter which way the wind blows."

God's Word is not shaky and changing like we and the people around us often are. The matter has been settled! God's Word is *always* true. Do you believe that?

"I have refrained my feet from every evil way, that I might keep thy word"
(Psalm 119:101).

IF DAVID wrote Psalm 119, how could he say, "I have refrained my feet from every evil way, that I might keep thy word" (v. 101)? Didn't he remember the sin of adultery with Bathsheba and the plot to murder her husband, Uriah?

Those memories may have challenged him to write these words. He never wanted to walk down that path again; he never wanted to feel that shame and guilt again. He loved God and His Word. He never wanted to bring that kind of dishonor to the Lord again. Yes, he walked in evil; yes, he failed. But he got up again. "Though he fall, he shall not be utterly cast down: for the LORD upholdeth him with his hand" (Psalm 37:24).

What tempts men? One person put it this way: Young fellows are tempted by girls. Thirty-year-olds are tempted with gold. Forty-year-olds are tempted with glory and honor. Fifty-to-sixty-year-olds say to themselves, "What a pious man I have become." This is a warning to those who feel they are beyond the years of temptation. David was about fifty years old and living in ease in the palace when he took his first look at Bathsheba.

We are all tempted to do evil, and sometimes we fail. However, no failure needs to be final. Here are some tips to help us when we are tempted to sin: (1) Expect temptation (1 Corinthians 10:12, 13); (2) Resist temptation (1 Peter 5:8, 9; James 4:7); (3) Identify your weaknesses (Proverbs 28:26); (4) Get away from tempting situations (2 Timothy 2:22; 1 Timothy 6:10, 11).

Remember, men are not the only ones who are tempted to sin; women have the same evil nature. Are you alert to your areas of weakness?

"Thy word is a lamp unto my feet, and a light unto my path" (Psalm 119:105).

IN BIBLE times an actual lamp was worn on the foot to lighten the path of the person walking. A tiny clay lamp was sometimes fastened to the sandal so that the rays of light cast from it were adequate to illuminate one step. As a person took that step, he or she then had light enough for the next step. Perhaps the psalmist had used one of these lamps on his sandal to guide him. He compared God's Word to a light: "Thy word is a lamp unto my feet, and a light unto my path" (v. 105).

We live in the age of artificial lights. We have headlights, streetlights, traffic lights, neon lights, electric lights, flashlights, strobe lights, and laser lights. In years past when people depended on lamps for their light, it seems God's Word was of higher value in people's lives. They used God's Word for guidance on the path of life. In our age of artificial lights, we see many "artificial" Christians who think they can get along just fine without the Word of God.

Have you replaced God's Word with some best-selling book that you think is more relevant? No artificial light can replace the true light, God's Word! Just as the lamp on the foot gave light for one step at a time, so it is with God's Word. We may not be able to see the whole path, but we'll be able to see the next step. And how much more do we really need?

Are you letting God's Word illuminate your steps along the path of life?

"My flesh trembleth for fear of thee; and I am afraid of thy judgments" (Psalm 119:120).

THE PSALMIST had seen the mighty hand of God destroy the ungodly and chasten the wandering believer. He had a reverential fear of God because he knew God's judgments were true. Therefore he cried out to God, "My flesh trembleth for fear of thee; and I am afraid of thy judgments" (v. 120).

When God gives a command, He expects obedience. When we don't obey, we can expect discipline from God. "It is a fearful thing to fall into the hands of the living God" (Hebrews 10:31).

Have you ever trembled in fear before God because of your sin? I have! When my husband told me he felt God was calling him into the ministry, I told him, "You'll be a pastor over my dead body! I'll never be a preacher's wife!" For five years I ran from God and tried to keep my husband out of the ministry. Near the end of those five years, God decided to take me at my word when I said, "You'll be a preacher over my dead body." I almost died twice. The second time it happened, I knew God was going to put a stop to my rebellion. I felt sure He was going to kill me if I didn't surrender my will to do His will. The next day I got down on my knees in my dining room and told God He was too powerful for me to fight against any longer; He had won the long battle. I told the Lord I was willing to do whatever He wanted me to do.

Are you running from God's will for your life? Are you afraid of God's judgments? You'd better be!

"Therefore I esteem all thy precepts concerning all things to be right; and I hate every false way" (Psalm 119:128).

DO YOU believe ALL God's Word is right for ALL the situations you pass through in life? The psalmist did. "Therefore I esteem ALL thy precepts concerning ALL things to be right; and I hate every false way" (v. 128). Every precept is right—however hard; every directive is right—however distasteful it is for us to obey.

Does God really intend for us to love our enemies (Matthew 5:44)? Does He really mean it when He says forgive or we won't be forgiven (Matthew 6:14, 15)? Yes, we are to obey ALL God's commands—even the hard ones.

Some of God's commands seem so diffi-cult, we might ask, "Is this coming from my kind and loving Heavenly Father?" When God's commands seem severe, our feelings are often unsettled. This is a dangerous place to be. Unsettled feelings lead to unsettled thinking—which can get us into trouble. It is good to keep reminding ourselves that ALL of God's precepts are right. Therefore we need to do right even if we don't feel like it. We must have the issue of obedience settled by faith, or else we will be unsettled by our feelings.

Do you believe ALL of God's commands are good for ALL situations?

"The entrance of thy words giveth light; it giveth understanding unto the simple"
(Psalm 119:130).

TO WHOM does the Word of God give understanding? The psalmist says "unto the simple." Not to those who are wise in their own eyes; not to the high-minded or the double-minded, but to the simple. "The entrance of thy words giveth light; it giveth understanding unto the simple" (v. 130). The simple submit themselves not to question but to hear, not to challenge but to believe.

A Chinese scholar was once asked to read Psalm 119:130 in the original language and then translate the verse into English. This is how he translated it: "God speaks; a light comes! This makes a dumb man a wise man."

William Gurnall said, "There are none so knowing that God cannot blind; none so blind and ignorant whose mind and heart His spirit cannot open." God can make the wise simple enough to understand His Word.

Many years ago two highly acclaimed men decided to expose what they termed the "imposture" of the Bible. They each chose a subject to criticize. Gilbert West chose the resurrection of Christ, and Lord Lyttleton chose the conversion of the apostle Paul. What was the result? They both were converted as a result of reading and studying the Word of God. Their findings were published, and they still stand today as valuable evidence to prove the truth of God's Word.

If you can't understand the Bible, it is probably because you have not read it enough.

Psalm 119:137–144

"My zeal hath consumed me, because mine enemies have forgotten thy words"
(Psalm 119:139).

THE PSALMIST was upset because people he had known had turned on him, and, more importantly, turned their back on God. "My zeal hath consumed me, because mine enemies have forgotten thy words" (v. 139). His enemies were not foreigners or heathen people living in Palestine. They were Israelites who had grown up knowing God's words but had forgotten them. The psalmist was consumed not because they had become his enemy but because they had become God's enemies.

Has someone in whom you've invested time and energy turned his or her back on you? I've had this happen a few times. It leaves me feeling wounded and helpless, asking, What did I do wrong? It devastates me even more if the person turns his back on God as well. I feel compelled to talk to him, but how do you talk to someone who doesn't want to talk to you? In one situation, a person had hurt me deeply, but I felt she was still salvageable. I asked for divine wisdom to know how to approach her. Sometimes I wondered if she really belonged to Christ.

How can we know if those who turn away from God are real or hypocrites? We can't; only God knows the heart. But we do know that a pious appearance is no guarantee of the real thing. The Municipal Museum of Amsterdam held a "Fake and Genuine" exhibit of art masterpieces. Fake copies of the originals were hung side by side with the genuine paintings. Visitors were asked to try to detect the genuine from the fake. Only 7 out of 1,827 visitors were able to do so!

Are you fake or real? God knows for sure!

"I cried with my whole heart; hear me, O LORD: I will keep thy statutes" (Psalm 119:145).

THE PSALMIST had cried for God's help many times; here he was crying out for help again: "I cried with my whole heart; hear me, O LORD: I will keep thy statutes" (v. 145). This passage of Scripture gives us a picture of the psalmist's prayer life.

How did he pray? With his whole heart (v. 145). He was not just moving his lips; his heart was moved as well. His mind, emotions, will, and heart were calling out to God.

What did he pray? Save me! (v. 146). He got right to the point of his need.

When did he pray? When he woke up, his first thoughts were of God (v. 147). He brought his needs to God while his surroundings were still calm and his mind was the clearest, before the thoughts and cares of the day crowded in upon him.

How long did he pray? Throughout the day he meditated on God and His Word (v. 148). As he closed his eyes in sleep, his final thoughts were of God.

What did he plead for? He wanted God to quicken, or revive, him (v. 149).

Why was he pleading for help? His enemies were drawing nearer (v. 150).

Did he feel he would be rescued? Yes! Because God was near (v. 151). No matter how near the enemy might be, God is nearer.

How did he view his situation? God's Word had stood the tests of time (v. 152). God would not fail him now.

Halfhearted people seldom get their prayers answered because they are usually double-minded as well. Are you wholehearted and single-minded for God, or halfhearted and double-minded? Are your prayers being answered?

"Consider how I love thy precepts: quicken me, O LORD, according to thy lovingkindness"
(Psalm 119:159).

WHAT ARE God's precepts? They are His commands to His children. The psalmist had come to love these precepts because he loved the One Who issued them. "Consider how I love thy precepts: quicken me, O LORD, according to thy lovingkindness" (v. 159). Many people like God's promises, but they do not like His commands. Perhaps that says something about their love for God.

Have you ever heard a parent give a child a command and the child responded, "Why do I have to do that?" The parent often answers, "Just because I said so!" God wants us to obey His commands "just because He said so."

The story is told of a college president who was invited to dine with the king of France. When the man arrived at the palace, the king was a bit surprised. "We did not know we were going to enjoy the pleasure of your company; you did not answer our invitation," said the king. The college president replied, "I thought the invitation of a king was to be obeyed, not answered."

God's precepts are to be obeyed—not questioned or rationalized. They have the voice of Royalty behind them!

Are you obeying God "just because He said so"?

"Seven times a day do I praise thee because of thy righteous judgments" (Psalm 119:164).

THE PSALMIST praised God several times a day. "Seven times a day do I praise thee because of thy righteous judgments" (v. 164). Devout Hebrews were accustomed to praising God twice in the morning before reading the Ten Commandments and once after reading them; they praised God twice in the evening before reading the commandments and twice after reading them. That's a total of seven times.

Do you praise God seven times a day? Do you even praise Him once in seven days?

Prayer and praise act as a cushion against the knocks and blows of everyday life. Daily irritations tend to make us tense and tired. They will wear us down unless we build some inner defense against them. We need quiet times each day to meditate on God's Word and praise God for Who He is. This gives us spiritual strength to face the irritations of life. Thinking about God and His goodness, beauty, and strength brings calmness to our countenance and puts peace that passeth understanding around our hearts and souls.

When we learn to practice the presence of God in our lives, we are able to let go of resentment, pain, and despair and find that life is good again. We begin to sense a change in being rather than an increase in our doing. We learn that quietness is as creative as action.

Prayer and praise change things, including you. How many times a day do you praise God?

"Great peace have they which love thy law: and nothing shall offend them"
(Psalm 119:165).

IN PSALM 119:164 the psalmist said he praised God for His Word. Verse 165 shows the result of loving God's Word: "Great peace have they which love thy law: and nothing shall offend them" (v. 165). Another benefit of loving God's Word is stability. The word "offend" in verse 165 is also translated "stumble." Loving God's Word keeps a person from stumbling.

When we keep our hearts and minds filled with precious promises that cause us to praise God, we can walk down dark, rocky roads without falling. We are not filled with panic but with peace because our hearts are filled with praise.

I have recently faced circumstances that could have filled me with panic. Instead, I had an unexplainable peace guarding my heart and mind. (See Philippians 4:6 and 7.)

I cannot muster up this peace in my own strength. God gives it to me as I keep my mind on Him. "Thou wilt keep him in perfect peace, whose mind is stayed on thee: because he trusteth in thee" (Isaiah 26:3).

"I cannot always understand,
    The way God leadeth me,
The why and when and wherefore
    Is oft a mystery.
But I can trust His wisdom,
    I know His way is best,
His heart knows no unkindness,
    And on His love I rest."

Has God called you to walk down a dark, rocky road? Are you filled with panic or peace? Rest on the pillow of God's precious promises and enjoy His perfect peace.

322

"I have gone astray like a lost sheep; seek thy servant; for I do not forget thy commandments" (Psalm 119:176).

WE HAVE heard the psalmist declare his love and respect for the Word of God in almost every one of the 176 verses in Psalm 119. We have heard him tell of the value of the Word in the valley and on the mountaintop; in the calm and in the storm. My, how he loved God's Word! Yet he knew his proneness to stray from God and His Word. "I have gone astray like a lost sheep; seek thy servant; for I do not forget thy commandments" (v. 176). If he did stray, he knew the Good Shepherd would seek him and draw him back to His side.

James H. McConkey told the following story. A lady was spending the summer in Switzerland. As she climbed a mountainside, she came upon a shepherd's fold. When she looked in the door, she saw a shepherd with his sheep lying around him. On a pile of straw she saw a sheep with a broken leg. She asked how it happened, and to her amazement the shepherd said, "Madam, I broke that sheep's leg; he was a wayward sheep. He would never obey my voice. He was constantly walking near the edge of the cliffs and leading other sheep astray as well. So I broke his leg. The first couple of days when I tried to feed him, he tried to bite me. I left him alone for a couple of days. Now he not only takes the food but licks my hand. When this sheep is well, it will be a model sheep. No sheep will hear my voice so quickly. None will follow as closely to my side."

Have you gone astray? Is the Good Shepherd trying to draw you back to His side?

"In my distress I cried unto the LORD, and he heard me. Deliver my soul, O LORD, from lying lips, and from a deceitful tongue" (Psalm 120:1, 2).

PSALMS 120 through 134 are called the "Songs of Ascent" or the "Pilgrim Psalms." They were sung by the people of Israel as they made their journey to the temple for the annual feasts. Psalm 120 was sung at the beginning of the journey, while the people were in a distant land and hostile surroundings. Psalm 122 pictures the people arriving in Jerusalem. In the other psalms they are moving toward the temple, mentioning different characteristics of God as they go.

David wrote Psalm 120, in which he bared his heart to the Lord concerning his hostile neighbors. "In my distress I cried unto the LORD, and he heard me. Deliver my soul, O LORD, from lying lips, and from a deceitful tongue" (vv. 1, 2).

Slanderous accusations are grievous and distressful to the soul. Jesus said, "In the world ye shall have tribulation" (John 16:33). One of the most piercing forms of tribulation we can undergo comes from lying lips. Lies suck away our life and character and are as destructive as razors and swords.

How can we protect ourselves? We can't! We must cry out to God to protect us. When the disciples wanted to know how to pray, Christ gave them an example in what we call the Lord's Prayer (Matthew 6:9–13). One of the requests in that prayer is "deliver us from evil." We need to pray, "Deliver us, Lord, from lying lips!"

In your distress, do you cry out to God or lash out at your offender?

"I will lift up mine eyes unto the hills, from whence cometh my help. My help cometh from the LORD, which made heaven and earth. He will not suffer thy foot to be moved: he that keepeth thee will not slumber" (Psalm 121:1–3).

MOUNTAINS had great significance in Bible times. They were considered places of security, for they often provided protection from invading enemies. In Psalm 121 one of the pilgrims traveling to Jerusalem looked at the mountains and said, "I will lift up mine eyes unto the hills, from whence cometh my help" (v. 1). He knew the hills couldn't help him, but the God Who made the hills could. "My help cometh from the LORD, which made heaven and earth" (v. 2).

One of the other travelers may have joined in and said, "He will not suffer thy foot to be moved: he that keepeth thee will not slumber" (v. 3).

A number of years ago the captain of an ocean liner was traveling from England to New York with his family. One night the ship sailed into a violent storm that tossed the boat on its side and awakened everyone on the ship. Many passengers quickly dressed, expecting the worst. The captain's eight-year-old daughter was also awakened and asked the frightened family what had happened. They told her a squall had struck the ship. She asked if her father was on the deck, and they told her he was. The child laid her on the pillow without a fear and was sound asleep in a few minutes.

"Fear not the windy tempests wild,
Thy bark they shall not wreck;
Lie down and sleep, O helpless child!
Thy Father's on the deck."

We can know His protection on an airplane, on a crowded highway, or on the streets of the inner city. Our Heavenly Father never slumbers or sleeps, so we can sleep in peace and perfect rest.

How are you resting these days?

"I was glad when they said unto me, Let us go into the house of the LORD" (Psalm 122:1).

A LARGE company of God's people was traveling with David to Jerusalem for the annual feast. The journey had been long and not without perils and problems. The people had traveled over high ranges of hills and now the sacred city was in full view. The excitement was mounting. As the people entered the gates of the city, they were invited into the house of God. "I was glad when they said unto me, Let us go into the house of the LORD" (v. 1). Can you imagine the whole group falling down and singing "The Holy City"?

Why such excitement about going to the house of the Lord? It was there that God was present with His people. In that place they heard the Word of the Lord, called upon His name, and found forgiveness for their sins.

Are you excited about going to the house of God each week? You should be! You may be saying, "My church is dead. I don't get anything out of it." If you only go for what you get out of it, you will always be disappointed. You need to go expecting to give not just receive.

We need to go to give our worship, honor, and obedience to God. He said, "Remember the sabbath day, to keep it holy" (Exodus 20:8). God set aside one day in seven for us to honor Him. We also need to give ourselves when we go to church. We need to be there to encourage others who are struggling.

Start going to church to give rather than to receive, and you'll find yourself eagerly waiting for the next opportunity to go. I can hardly wait for Sunday! What about you?

"Behold, as the eyes of servants look unto the hand of their masters, and as the eyes of a maiden unto the hand of her mistress; so our eyes wait upon the LORD our God, until that he have mercy upon us" (Psalm 123:2).

THE PEOPLE were in the temple, singing a prayer for God's mercy as they waited upon Him. "Behold, as the eyes of servants look unto the hand of their masters, and as the eyes of a maiden unto the hand of her mistress; so our eyes wait upon the LORD our God, until that he have mercy upon us" (v. 2).

An Eastern servant would stand with folded hands at the end of the room as he watched for his lord to direct him to his next duty. Often the master did not speak; he directed the servant with the movements of his hands. If the servant did not keep his eyes on the master, he might miss his sign and fail to obey him.

How wise we are to readily submit to the mighty hand of God. However, if we do not keep our eyes on the Lord each day, we will miss His guidance in our lives. He knows so much better than we do where we should go and how we should get there (Proverbs 3:5, 6). In addition, He has promised to supply *all* our needs (Philippians 4:19).

We must faithfully fix our eyes on God and put our cares into His sovereign hand. He will reward us for our faithfulness. Remember, payday is not always on Friday!

> "Leave to His sovereign sway
> To choose and to command,
> So shalt thou wondering own His way,
> How wise, how strong His hand."

Are you willing to watch and wait for God's sovereign hand to direct your life?

"If it had not been the LORD who was on our side, when men rose up against us: Then they had swallowed us up quick, when their wrath was kindled against us" (Psalm 124:2, 3).

MORE THAN one time the Israelites had faced Red Sea experiences when their enemies were behind them and no way of escape was in sight. They knew that if their God had not rescued them, they would have been swallowed up and destroyed. This was the song coming from the psalmist's lips: "If it had not been the LORD who was on our side, when men rose up against us: Then they had swallowed us up quick, when their wrath was kindled against us (vv. 2, 3).

"Heavier the cross, the heartier the
   prayer;
The bruised herbs most fragrant are.
If sky and wind were always fair,
The sailor would not watch the star;
And David's Psalms had ne'er been sung
If grief his heart had never wrung."

If God never took us to the edge of the abyss, we would never know how to praise Him for His deliverance. Unsaved people turn to drugs, alcohol, perverted sex, psychiatrists, or pills for help when they feel they are being swallowed up by their problems. Aren't you glad you know the Lord is on your side, always ready to help you? He is stronger than any tranquilizer; He is wiser than any psychiatrist; He is more faithful than your closest friend.

Sometimes we take God's help and deliverance for granted because He has always been there for us. We need to ask ourselves occasionally, "If it hadn't been for the Lord, where would I be today?"

Take a minute and rehearse what great things God has done for you.

"As the mountains are round about Jerusalem, so the LORD is round about his people from henceforth even for ever" (Psalm 125:2).

THROUGHOUT Psalms we see the Lord compared to many things; for example, "But thou, O LORD, art a shield for me" (3:3); "The LORD is my rock, and my fortress, and my deliverer" (18:2); "The LORD is my shepherd" (23:1). Now the psalmist says God is like a mountain. "As the mountains are round about Jerusalem, so the LORD is round about his people from henceforth even for ever" (v. 2).

In Biblical times, when there was no dynamite or earth-moving machinery, a mountain was considered immovable. It was a picture of stability, security, and steadfastness. It would always be there; it would never change. This is how the psalmist described his God.

Would you like to have more stability, security, and steadfastness in your life? I would! How can it happen? By learning to trust God more. As we develop a more confident trust in God, we find ourselves feeling more stable in our faith and in other relationships. This confident trust also gives us a deeper sense of security; all is well, God is in control. And it fosters a steadfastness in our faith; we don't doubt in the dark what we know in the light.

I was humbled by a statement a friend made to me. She said, "Juanita, you are a solid standard by which I can always gauge my spiritual life. When I'm with you, I know if I am drifting too far in one direction or another. You are always solidly planted just where you have always been." I praise God for the stability, security, and steadfastness He has brought into my life.

Do you need more stability, security, and steadfastness in your life? Trust God more!

"When the LORD turned again the captivity of Zion, we were like them that dream. . . .
The LORD hath done great things for us; whereof we are glad" (Psalm 126:1, 3).

THE PEOPLE in this psalm were saying, "This is too good to be true! The people had been captives in Babylon, and now they were free. "When the LORD turned again the captivity of Zion, we were like them that dream" (v. 1). They never dreamed the mighty Babylonian Empire would collapse. God restored His people to their homeland as He had promised (Jeremiah 32:36–38). Their hearts were overflowing with praise and thanks to God for delivering them. "The LORD hath done great things for us; whereof we are glad" (v. 3).

On other occasions in the Bible, God did something so spectacular the people involved could hardly believe it. One example is the widow of Zarephath. When Elijah asked her for food, she had only enough left for one meal. She gave it to Elijah, and God provided flour and oil for the duration of the famine (1 Kings 17:10–16).

Many years ago my husband was training for the ministry at Moody Bible Institute in Chicago. At the same time, he was preaching at a little storefront church in the city on the weekends. The church decided to collect food for a needy family for Christmas. We were leaving to go home for Christmas, so we took all the food in our cupboards to church that night for the needy family. Little did we know: We were the needy family! When we got in our car after church, the back seat was filled with the food! God provided for us in a way that seemed too good to be true—we thought we were dreaming!

Thanksgiving Day is only about a week away. Be ready to share with someone else what great things God has done for you.

"They that sow in tears shall reap in joy" (Psalm 126:5).

ONE DAY we're laughing; the next day we're crying. This describes the Jews in Psalm 126. They had escaped the captivity of Babylon and were returning to the Land of Promise after seventy years of exile. But the joy of deliverance turned to tears of sorrow when they reached their beloved country and found it a wilderness wasteland. Jerusalem and the temple were in ruins. (Read Ezra 1 and Nehemiah 1 and 2.) The people began to sow their fields, but often in tears, hoping they would reap a harvest. "They that sow in tears shall reap in joy" (v. 5).

"Our tears can be seeds that will grow a harvest of joy." Oh, how I needed to read those words while our family was going through a difficult time. I kept thinking, "Lord, when will this ever be over?" The trial had gone on and on. But there was always grace and strength for each new day. I know God allowed this trial to stretch our faith. Because we waited so long and sowed so many tears, I had every reason to believe we would reap a great harvest of joy.

"God is in every tomorrow,
Therefore I live for today,
Certain of finding at sunrise,
Guidance and strength for the way;
Power for each moment of weakness,
Hope for each moment of pain,
Comfort for every sorrow,
Sunshine and joy after rain."

Don't give up! There is a great harvest of joy coming!

"Except the LORD build the house, they labour in vain that build it" (Psalm 127:1).

GOD DID not allow David to build the temple because David had been a man of war (1 Chronicles 22:7–10). However, God promised David that his son Solomon, a man of peace, would build the temple. Even though David had knowledge, manpower, and material to build the temple, he did not have God's blessing. He knew it would be a waste of time without God's blessing. Solomon was aware of all of this, so he could write, "Except the LORD build the house, they labour in vain that build it" (v. 1).

A young couple can draw up the most elaborate plans and hire the finest contractor to build their new home, but whether they realize it or not, they are dependent on God for its completion. God is the producer of the raw materials, the giver of strength for the workers, and the One Who provides favorable weather conditions.

A couple can marry and start their family, but unless their home is built upon the solid Rock, Christ Jesus, there is only a 50 percent chance their marriage will survive. "Therefore whosoever heareth these sayings of mine, and doeth them, I will liken him unto a wise man, which built his house upon a rock: And the rain descended, and the floods came, and the winds blew, and beat upon that house; and it fell not: for it was founded upon a rock. And every one that heareth these sayings of mine, and doeth them not, shall be likened unto a foolish man, which built his house upon the sand: And the rain descended, and the floods came, and the winds blew, and beat upon that house; and it fell: and great was the fall of it" (Matthew 7:24–27).

Are you building your house on shifting sand or the solid Rock?

"Blessed is every one that feareth the LORD; that walketh in his ways" (Psalm 128:1).

THIS PSALM, like Psalm 127, is a family psalm. In my Bible the heading over this psalm reads, "Blessing on the House of the God-fearing." The prosperity of our families depends upon the blessing of God. The way to obtain that blessing is to fear God and obey Him. "Blessed is every one that feareth the LORD; that walketh in his ways" (v. 1).

This psalm may have been sung at the marriage of Israelites, at a birth, or on any day in which a happy household met together to sing praises to God. The six verses of the psalm could be summarized like this: "Happy is the man who fears God, has meaningful work, and a fruitful family."

A God-fearing husband is a strong tower of support and strength for his wife and children. This man produces a happy family.

A godly wife loves and honors her husband because she first loves God and wants to obey His commands. Her obedience to God makes her obedience to her husband a delight. God-fearing children will honor and obey their parents. To be sure, it is a happy home when the reverential fear of God is the standard on which the home functions.

A good, happy, harmonious family is the reward for following and fearing God. If you are not married, you are not excluded from this blessedness. It is for "every one that feareth the LORD" (v. 1).

Is your life hectic or heavenly? If you need to make some changes, start reading and obeying God's Word so you can start walking in His ways.

"The plowers plowed upon my back: they made long their furrows" (Psalm 129:3).

IN THIS psalm the poet lamented the years of trials the Israelites had endured. The people had suffered one disaster after another. The nation was constantly tormented by foreign enemies.

The psalmist remembered these continual attacks from the time of his youth (v. 2). He looked back on these afflictions as one who was lying face down on the ground as the plowmen cut deep furrows into his back. "The plowers plowed upon my back: they made long their furrows" (v. 3). The picture is that of a farmer who tears up the ground from one end of the field to the other.

But as bad as these trials had been, the psalmist did not dwell on them. Instead, he remembered the Lord, Who had always delivered His people: "The LORD is righteous: he hath cut asunder the cords of the wicked" (v. 4).

How do you handle your trials? Do you dwell on all that has gone wrong, or do you dwell on the Lord, Who is righteous? The Lord *will* cut asunder the cords of the wicked, but the question is, When? If He doesn't do it right now, you can still make something beautiful out of a bad situation. God often plants His flowers among rough rocks.

An old man had a beautiful garden, but he could never enjoy it because a huge boulder was in the middle. He tried to blast it out, but it wouldn't budge. When he died, his son moved into the home and began to care for the garden. He, too, tried to remove the boulder, but with no success. Since he couldn't move it, he decided to convert the the area into a rock garden with ferns, flowers, and vines. It soon became a point of interest and beauty in the garden. The man made defeat work for him, not against him.

Has God planted you among some rough rocks? "Bloom where you're planted," and let the beauty of Jesus be seen in you.

"If thou, LORD, shouldest mark iniquities, O Lord, who shall stand? But there is forgiveness with thee, that thou mayest be feared" (Psalm 130:3, 4).

PERHAPS this psalm was written by Hezekiah, king of Judah, as he recovered from a time of sickness (2 Kings 20:1–7; Isaiah 38). Whoever the writer was, he wanted God to hear his prayers. "Lord, hear my voice: let thine ears be attentive to the voice of my supplications" (v. 2).

The psalmist wanted God to be attentive to his voice, but not to all his sins. "If thou, LORD, shouldest mark iniquities, O Lord, who shall stand? But there is forgiveness with thee, that thou mayest be feared" (vv. 3, 4). It's as though the psalmist said, "Lord, if You kept track of every lie I told, every unkind word I said, every word of gossip I repeated, every evil thing I thought, every evil deed I've done, I could never stand before You. But You don't! You forgive me when I confess my failures." To know we are forgiven gives renewed hope and joy.

Are we as merciful to others in extending undeserved forgiveness? I read of a young man who had been in prison for two years, and he wanted to return home. He had had no contact with his parents during those years. Three weeks before his release, he wrote his parents and told them how sorry he was that he had disappointed them. He asked them to forgive him. He said he would understand if they couldn't forgive him. He suggested that they tie a white ribbon on the old apple tree in the front yard if they wanted him to return. If he didn't see a ribbon, he wouldn't get off the bus. As the bus neared his house, he was afraid to look out the window for fear of being disappointed. But when he looked, he saw that the entire tree was covered with white ribbons.

To forgive others as God for Christ's sake has forgiven us is the Biblical command (Ephesians 4:32). Are you obeying it?

November 21   **Psalm 131**

"Surely I have behaved and quieted myself, as a child that is weaned of his mother: my soul is even as a weaned child" (Psalm 131:2).

THIS IS one of the shortest psalms to read but the longest to learn. It is a lesson on humility. No doubt David had a crying child in mind when he wrote these words, "Surely I have behaved and quieted myself, as a child that is weaned of his mother: my soul is even as a weaned child" (v. 2). No child wants to be taken from the breast or the bottle. He wants his own way, not his mother's way.

Oh, how childish we act when we fight and struggle for our will and our way. When God chooses to take something out of our lives that He feels we no longer need, we kick and scream like a little child being weaned from her mother's breast.

God will not adjust to our will when He wants His will to be accomplished in our lives. We can get angry, blow off steam, and act like foolish children; but sooner or later, after we are exhausted, we must come to grips with the fact that God is not going to move. He is in charge; He will have His way! Humble Christians do not have a problem with this. Proud, self-willed Christians resent it and become more and more angry with God. Only as we humbly submit to God's will can we enter into the great joy and freedom He has planned for His children. The self-willed Christian is always restless and dissatisfied.

Are you still acting like a child, kicking and screaming, wanting your own way? Or have you grown up and learned to humbly submit to the Father's will?

"I will not give sleep to mine eyes, or slumber to mine eyelids, Until I find out a place for the LORD" (Psalm 132:4, 5).

HAVE YOU ever heard someone say, "I will not rest in peace until I find out who . . . ," or, "I can't think about anything else until I. . . ." Was that the way David was feeling when he said, "I will not give sleep to mine eyes, or slumber to mine eyelids, Until I find out a place for the LORD" (vv. 4, 5)?

What was the driving ambition behind these words? David wanted to build a temple for the Lord. When David became king, he built a beautiful palace, but this did not satisfy him. He wanted a permanent place for the ark of the covenant, the symbol of God's presence among His people (Exodus 25:10–22); the tent, or tabernacle, was not good enough (2 Samuel 6:17; 7:1–7). This bothered David so much that he became consumed with his plans to build the temple. However, God did not allow David to fulfill his plan. Solomon, his son, built the temple instead. How did David react to this disappointment? Naturally, he was hurt at first, but there were no screams of "this is unfair." He said in effect, "If this is the will of God, I will accept it" (2 Samuel 7:18–29).

How do we react to our disappointments? Do we ever think or say, "God, this isn't fair. I did nothing wrong, but I'm the one who gets hurt"? Sometimes God isn't fair—as we perceive fairness. God is merciful and just. He always does what is right. Why doesn't God work things differently? Because He is working things together for His purposes not ours. What reaction does He expect from us? A childlike trust, remembering this period of "child training" on earth is preparing us for eternity.

God may not always seem fair—but He is always right! Will you quit crying, "Lord, this is not fair"?

"Behold, how good and how pleasant it is for brethren to dwell together in unity!"
(Psalm 133:1).

THE PSALMIST wrote, "Behold, how good and how pleasant it is for brethren to dwell together in unity!" (v. 1). He compared the unity of believers to precious ointment, or oil, and the morning dew (vv. 2, 3).

At first, these comparisons may seem strange, but take a closer look. The precious ointment was used to anoint the head of the high priest. This oil had a pleasant scent, and everyone in the room could smell it. The morning dew has a refreshing effect on the grass and flowers. A body of believers with a sweet, refreshing spirit of love and unity gives the world a positive message for God's glory.

If you sense such a spirit is missing in your church, what should you do? Should you leave, or should you face the problem and try to do something to help change the spirit? The easy thing would be to leave and keep looking for the perfect church. However, there are no perfect churches, because churches are filled with imperfect people like you and me. Instead, start working to be an instrument to bring about love and unity in your church. Whom could you go out of your way to show love to this Sunday?

By the way, if the spirit of love and unity has left your church, your pastor may appreciate your encouragement. If he truly loves his flock, he feels responsible to keep a spirit of love and unity among the brethren, and it must hurt him to realize that unity is missing.

What can you do to help your church be a good and pleasant place?

"Lift up your hands in the sanctuary, and bless the LORD" (Psalm 134:2).

THIS IS the last of the fifteen psalms that are known as "Songs of Ascent." (They started with Psalm 120.) The people sang as they made their way to the annual feasts in Jerusalem. This is the psalm the people sang on their way home from the temple. It is a song of benediction, or blessing. "Behold, bless ye the LORD, all ye servants of the LORD, which by night stand in the house of the LORD. Lift up your hands in the sanctuary, and bless the LORD. The LORD that made heaven and earth bless thee out of Zion" (vv. 1–3).

What did the people do while they were in the temple? They lifted their hands in praise and blessed the Lord. When they lifted their hands, they acknowledged the blessings they expected to receive as well as the ones they had already received.

What do you do when you go to church? Do you look around to see if so-and-so is there? Do you check out what Sally is wearing? Do you keep looking at your watch to see when the service will be over? Do you ever think about why you are there and what you should be doing? We should be in church to worship and praise the Lord and to learn new truth from His Word. We may not raise our hands in praise, but we should be lifting our hearts in praise for past blessings and for the blessings we expect to receive.

When is the last time you really worshiped the Lord when you went to His house?

"For I know that the LORD is great, and that our Lord is above all gods. Whatsoever the LORD pleased, that did he in heaven, and in earth, in the seas, and all deep places"
(Psalm 135:5, 6).

THE LEVITES may have sung this psalm when they opened the gates of the temple in the morning and again in the evening when they shut the gates. The people had much for which to praise the Lord, but I think verses 5 and 6 give the basis for their praise: "For I know that the LORD is great, and that our Lord is above all gods. Whatsoever the LORD pleased, that did he in heaven, and in earth, in the seas, and all deep places."

Truly the Lord is great! He has everything under control. He does as He pleases, when He pleases, where He pleases. We sit back in awe and worship Him for His greatness. Does that mean we are always pleased with what He allows in our lives? No, it does not.

Joni Eareckson Tada is an example of this. She is a quadriplegic, confined to a wheelchair. Did she happily accept what God had allowed in her life? No. But once she was finally able to see God's sovereign hand working in her life, God began to use her. In fact, she has accepted her condition with such sincerity and grace that her life has been used to transform thousands of other lives. God has undoubtedly used her in a more significant and effective way from her wheelchair than she could have ever been used under normal circumstances.

At this Thanksgiving season, praise the Lord for His greatness and sovereignty. The Lord is great! You can trust His wisdom and power.

Psalm 135:15–21

"The idols of the heathen are silver and gold, the work of men's hands" (Psalm 135:15).

WHY WOULD men serve idols instead of the living God? Why serve a God that cannot hear, see, or speak, a god made of silver or gold? "The idols of the heathen are silver and gold, the work of men's hands" (v. 15). Why? Because these gods were men's invention; they could manipulate and control these gods. They could touch and see these gods. The psalmist said the "heathen"—people with no knowledge of the living God—served these gods.

Men and women today are still serving idols of silver and gold. In our society the idol is money. The consuming drive of some people is to have more and more of it.

Verse 18 says that people who worship idols and trust in them become like their idols: "They that make them are like unto them: so is every one that trusteth in them." The idols cannot see, hear, or speak; people who worship them cannot see, hear, or speak of the living God because they are so consumed with their gods.

When people come to know the living God and His Son, Jesus Christ, they have new desires that drive and consume their lives. Once they were consumed with getting more and more money; now they are consumed with getting to know God better and better.

Which do you want the most: more money or more knowledge of the living God?

"O give thanks unto the LORD; for he is good: for his mercy endureth for ever"
(Psalm 136:1).

IF REPETITION is the basis of learning, then we know the one thing God wanted us to learn from the twenty-six verses of Psalm 136: "His mercy endureth for ever." Every verse ends with those same words. "O give thanks unto the LORD; for he is good: for his mercy endureth for ever" (v. 1).

In order to comprehend the beauty of this psalm, we have to remember it was sung in the temple by two groups of priests or by the leader of the congregation and the people. It was sung in the same way we would do a responsive Scripture reading; the leader sang a line, and then people responded, "for his mercy endureth for ever."

During this Thanksgiving season, we have much for which to praise the Lord. We can praise Him that He never runs out of mercy. He will always be kind, loving, and faithful because the well of His love and mercy never runs dry! Ours often does, but not God's. He has all that we need for each day's needs.

"He giveth more grace when the burden
  grows greater,
He sendeth more strength when the
  labors increase;
To added affliction He addeth His mercy,
To multiplied trials, His multiplied
  peace. . . .
His love has no limit, His grace has no
  measure,
His power no boundary known unto men;
For out of His infinite riches in Jesus
He giveth and giveth and giveth again"

(ANNIE JOHNSON FLINT).

Will you thank the Lord right now for His boundless supply of love and mercy?

"And gave their land for an heritage: for his mercy endureth for ever"
(Psalm 136:21).

IN PSALM 136 the psalmist gave a history lesson. He started with Creation and then told the history of the nation of Israel. The Israelites were not only a chosen people but also a unique nation. What other nation has had her history recorded from beginning to end: how she started, how she grew, what is happening today, and what will happen in the future?

As the psalmist reviewed this history, he was constantly reminded of God's mercy in three major ways: God brought the people OUT of slavery (vv. 10, 11); He brought them THROUGH the wilderness (v. 16); and He brought them INTO their inheritance, the Promised Land. "And gave their land for an heritage: for his mercy endureth for ever" (v. 21).

God wants to do the same things for us today. He wants to free us OUT of the bondage of sin (John 8:32–36), take us THROUGH our wilderness journey on earth (Isaiah 43:2; 1 Corinthians 10:13), and bring us INTO the land He has promised to us, Heaven (John 14:2, 3). God leads us out of sin by faith, through this world by hope, and into Heaven by love.

Have you taken that first step of faith, believing God has freed you from the bondage of sin? Just as you believed God for salvation, now believe He wants to deliver you from the power of sin's control in your life.

Christ came not only to deliver you from future punishment, but also to deliver you from present bondage. Have you claimed everything God has promised for you?

". . . We wept, when we remembered Zion. We hanged our harps upon the willows in the midst thereof" (Psalm 137:1, 2).

TO THE Israelites, Jerusalem, or Zion, was the place where God met with His children. But they were not there; they had been taken captive by the Babylonians; they were in a strange land. The people were filled with sadness as they thought of home. They were too sad to sing. It is hard to weep and sing at the same time. The people hung their harps on the willow trees to indicate they had lost their song. ". . . We wept, when we remembered Zion. We hanged our harps upon the willows in the midst thereof" (vv. 1, 2).

I once asked a lady if she would sing a solo at a luncheon. She answered, "It is hard to sing with a lump in your throat." She was passing through some difficult experiences and felt like crying much of the time.

How can we keep our song when we are in a "strange land" experience, an experience we have never passed through before? The Jews remembered what they had in the past and hung up their harps. It is better to keep our minds on the future and forget the disappointments of yesterday. Each new day must be filled with faith, hope, and love. And each new day we must be filled with the Spirit to experience faith, hope, and love. The result of a Spirit-filled life is "singing and making melody in your heart to the Lord" (Ephesians 5:19).

Have you hung your harp on the willow? Why not take it down and get it back in tune?

"Though I walk in the midst of trouble, thou wilt revive me: thou shalt stretch forth thine hand against the wrath of mine enemies, and thy right hand shall save me" (Psalm 138:7).

IF EVER a man walked in the midst of trouble, it was David. Yet he never gave up in utter despair; he was always revived when he remembered the greatness of his God. "Though I walk in the midst of trouble, thou wilt revive me: thou shalt stretch forth thine hand against the wrath of mine enemies, and thy right hand shall save me" (v. 7). David remembered how God had delivered him in the past, and that gave him new light and hope for the future.

Godliness does not shelter a person from the troubles of life. Like Job, we are sometimes almost overwhelmed with our troubles. We have diseases and afflictions in the body, trials and losses in family relationships, difficulties in financial matters, spiritual conflicts, and enemies who haunt us. I have walked in the midst of troubles many times, but I have always been revived. I have always been able to take my harp off the willow tree (see Psalm 137:2) and get a song in my heart again. I lose my song when I look back in regret. I regain my song when I rehearse God's greatness in the past and, by faith, imagine all He will do in the future.

Do you need to be revived? Then it's time to "Count your many blessings—name them one by one, And it will surprise you what the Lord hath done."

December 1 Psalm 138

"The LORD will perfect that which concerneth me: thy mercy, O LORD, endureth for ever: forsake not the works of thine own hands" (Psalm 138:8).

SOMETIMES when we are in the midst of trouble, as David was, we feel as if God has forsaken us. David gave himself a quick reminder that God had not forsaken him. Why? He still had a work to do in David's life. The job was not yet perfect, or complete. "The LORD will perfect that which concerneth me: thy mercy, O LORD, endureth for ever: forsake not the works of thine own hands" (v. 8).

Have you ever felt abandoned by God in the midst of your suffering? I have! However, it is just a *feeling; we know*, deep down in our soul, God would not and could not ever forsake us.

Does God ever give up on us? No! What He starts, He finishes (Numbers 23:19; 1 Thessalonians 5:24). If He started to build something and didn't finish it, that would be a dishonor to His name. When you see a house that is unfinished for years, do you always wonder why? Did the builders run out of resources? Did they die? Did they change their mind? It makes us wonder, doesn't it.

What God starts He will perfect, or finish. "The LORD will perfect that which concerneth me." He never runs out of resources; He never dies; and He never changes His mind about what He planned to do.

Feel forsaken? You're not! Remember Who You belong to!

December 2

Psalm 139

"O LORD, thou hast searched me, and known me. Thou knowest my downsitting and mine uprising, thou understandest my thought afar off" (Psalm 139:1, 2).

FOR THE next two weeks these devotionals will focus on Psalm 139. Why so many days on twenty-one verses? I want you to know this psalm very well. Please read the entire psalm each day, meditating on the thoughts and memorizing some of the verses. If we could more fully comprehend and believe the depth of this psalm, we would begin to understand the greatness of our God.

In this psalm we see God's omniscience: He knows everything about everything and everyone. "O LORD, thou hast searched me, and known me. Thou knowest my downsitting and mine uprising, thou understandest my thought afar off" (vv. 1, 2). We see that God is omnipresent: He is everywhere, all the time. We see His omnipotence: He can do anything!

Sometimes we have a hard time being transparent with people, letting them really get to know us. Why? Are we afraid they will see something they will not like and reject us? Isn't it amazing that God knows everything about us—even those thoughts we would not share with anyone—and He still accepts us and loves us? Henry Ward Beecher said, "Before men we stand as opaque beehives. They can see the thoughts go in and out of us, but what work they do inside of a man they cannot tell. Before God we are as glass beehives, and all that our thoughts are doing within us He perfectly sees and understands."

Would you want God to know your secret thoughts and fantasies? Well, He does!

"Thou compassest my path and my lying down, and art acquainted with all my ways"
(Psalm 139:3).

DID DAVID feel like a prisoner, hemmed in by God? No, he felt free as he moved down the pathway of life, and yet he knew he could not escape God. Wherever he went, God went with him. "Thou compassest my path and my lying down, and art acquainted with all my ways" (v. 3). The fact that God knew everything about him and went everywhere he went did not turn David's world into a prison. On the contrary, it gave him a great sense of comfort, assurance, and freedom.

Is it possible to go to a place where God can't find you? Jeremiah 23:24 says no. "Can any hide himself in secret places that I shall not see him? saith the LORD. Do not I fill heaven and earth? saith the LORD." Jonah tried to run away from the presence of God, but ended up in the belly of a big fish. Even there, God knew exactly where His runaway servant was (Jonah 1).

I remember a miserable five years in my life when I tried to run from God. I did not want His will and way in my life. I, like Jonah, thought God was going to kill me, only to find out He wanted to bring me to a place where He could bless me and use me.

An atheist wrote on the chalkboard, "GOD IS NOWHERE." A Christian stepped up to the board and made a slight change, so the board read, "GOD IS NOW HERE."

If you have been trying to run from God, would you drop to your knees right now and tell the Lord you are tired of running? Surrender your will to do His will. Remember, He wants to bless you and use you!

"Thou hast beset me behind and before, and laid thine hand upon me" (Psalm 139:5).

DAVID was hemmed in by God. Wherever he turned, God was there. God surrounded David. "Thou hast beset me behind and before, and laid thine hand upon me" (v. 5). God was before him, preparing the way to provide all his needs. God was behind him, blotting out all his sins as quickly as they were confessed. David couldn't turn back and escape God; he couldn't go forward and outrun Him. He was like a man with security agents surrounding him.

Did David resent being hemmed in by God? Of course not! Who resents that kind of protection?

Do you feel hemmed in or confined in a circumstance or relationship? No matter what you do, you can't escape? You know God is all-powerful and could change the situation, so you wonder why He doesn't. Have you ever thought that what you are enduring may be designed to prepare you for helping others in a more effective way? God wants to bring you to the place that you can say, "My will is no longer important. I want Your will to be done in and through me. I no longer want to live my life just to be comfortable. I am more concerned with developing character—Your character. Whatever You choose for my life it is okay because I know You will give me the grace and strength to handle it."

Do you have the faith to pray that prayer?

"Whither shall I go from thy spirit? or whither shall I flee from thy presence?"
(Psalm 139:7).

DID DAVID want to run away from God? No; he wanted nothing more than to be near God. David was talking to himself and to God. Do you ever do that? I do! David was saying, "Suppose I was foolish enough to think I could flee from Your spirit and Your presence (v. 7). Where would I hide? Could I go so high in the sky You could never see me? Could I dig deep enough in the earth to hide from You?" David knew he couldn't. He could not escape the all-seeing eye and the all-encompassing arms of his God.

Why would a child want to run away from home? Why would he want to leave his provider, protector, and caregiver? I can think of only two reasons: (1) He doesn't want to obey the commands of the loving parent; or (2) the parent is not loving but abusive, unkind, and cruel. When we try to run way from God, we have only one reason: we don't want to obey His commands. We can be sure He is never abusive, unkind, or cruel. He is our loving provider, protector, and caregiver.

> "I know not where His islands lift
> Their fronded palms in air;
> I only know I cannot drift
> Beyond His love and care."

Does it comfort you or frighten you to know that around every corner you turn you will face God?

"For thou hast possessed my reins: thou hast covered me in my mother's womb"
(Psalm 139:13).

EACH TIME a baby is born, a miracle takes place. How could that tiny baby be so perfect—no missing parts, just the right color, and everything working just like clockwork? Occasionally, a baby is born who has a missing part or in whom everything doesn't function properly. This baby is not an accident, because He comes from God's creative hand.

Even in the womb, we were not hidden from God. We were hidden from our parents, but were surrounded by God. "For thou hast possessed my reins: thou hast covered me in my mother's womb" (v. 13).

Yes, new life is a miracle we can hardly fathom, and yet we believe it because we have seen it. But an even greater miracle is the new birth, our salvation experience (John 3:1–16). Physical birth is natural; the new birth is supernatural. The new birth is possible because of another supernatural birth: the virgin birth of Jesus Christ (Luke 1:26–35). There would be no new birth if there had not been a virgin birth.

When was the last time you rehearsed your salvation experience? Let me share mine with you. I was in a little country church with my boyfriend (now my husband). We were sitting in the back of the church. While the congregation sang the closing song, my boyfriend's dad walked to the back of the church and said, "Little lady, wouldn't you like to get saved tonight?" I had been under conviction for several weeks, and I guess he sensed it and knew I just needed a little encouragement. I knelt by the front pew with him and invited Christ into my life to be my Savior. I was born again that night.

When were you born again? Share your experience with someone else.

"I will praise thee; for I am fearfully and wonderfully made: marvellous are thy works; and that my soul knoweth right well" (Psalm 139:14).

DAVID realized he was a unique creation of God. No other person he knew looked just like him, acted like him, or thought like him. "I will praise thee; for I am fearfully and wonderfully made: marvellous are thy works; and that my soul knoweth right well" (v. 14).

This is the way I express how I feel: I am God's one-of-a-kind creation.

"Lord, thank You for making me a unique, one-of-a-kind creation. It is overwhelming to realize there is no one else in this whole world just exactly like me. No one else has fingerprints just like mine; no one else acts just like me. Lord, don't You ever run out of ideas?

"Lord, thank You for creating me with a plan for my life. Before I was born, You planned for me to be like Your Son. You want me to be a reflection of Christ on this earth. Lord, only You would set such high expectations for Your children. Had I planned my life, I would just be drifting aimlessly.

"Lord, thank You for making me feel so special! You are my Elohim—my Creator; I am made in Your image. You have chosen me; You told me I have infinite, eternal value. Wow! Am I special! No longer do I have to search for significance; I am significant in Your sight."

Does it excite you to realize you are a one-of-a-kind creation?

December 8

Psalm 139

"My substance was not hid from thee, when I was made in secret, and curiously wrought in the lowest parts of the earth" (Psalm 139:15).

OUR SUBSTANCE, or our bodies, was curiously woven together in a secret place: our mothers' wombs. "My substance was not hid from thee, when I was made in secret, and curiously wrought in the lowest parts of the earth" (v. 15).

God wondrously wove together our veins, our arteries, our tissues, our organs, and our nerves. They were shaped and twisted together day by day until everything was in working order. It generally takes about nine months for this project to be completed. David did not understand how all of this happened, but he knew he had been fearfully and wonderfully designed by God.

Do you understand all that God does to keep your body working right day after day? Thousands of things have to work together simultaneously. Consider these facts about the complexity of the heart alone. At rest, the heart pumps about 2 ounces of blood per beat, making a total of 5 quarts per minute! The heart contracts, or beats, 4,000 or more times an hour. So every hour over 300 quarts of blood pass through the heart. Other parts of our bodies are just as complex and just as amazing.

Do these facts help you more fully appreciate God's creative work? He is the master designer!

"Thine eyes did see my substance, yet being unperfect; and in thy book all my members were written, which in continuance were fashioned, when as yet there was none of them" (Psalm 139:16).

DAVID'S words in verse 16 are translated as follows in the New American Standard Bible: "Thine eyes have seen my unformed substance; And in Thy book they were all written, The days that were ordained for me, When as yet there was not one of them."

God superintends the union of the sperm and the egg, attaches it to the wall of the uterus, and watches as the tiny life begins to develop. No matter what the circumstances might be, the human embryo is not the result of some biological accident. Because God is in control of human reproduction, all life has meaning and purpose.

Before an architect ever puts his drawing on paper, he has sketched it in his mind. He can see each wall, each door, each window. Before we ever were born, God determined what every part of our bodies would be. Before we ever were completely formed, God saw us as complete. In addition, He had already determined—before we were born—what the length of our lives would be.

More than 21 million babies have been killed in the womb since the Supreme Court legalized abortion in 1973. Medical science calls the fetus a product of conception, a mass of tissue. God calls it a human being whom He formed in His image. God has a plan and a purpose for every person He creates; He never tosses a person aside as trash. Every person, whether in the womb or old and gray, is valuable to God.

You are valuable to God! Do you feel special?

"How precious also are thy thoughts unto me, O God! how great is the sum of them!"
(Psalm 139:17).

DAVID was not bothered by the thought that God knew him inside out. In fact, it was a great comfort to David to realize God knew him so personally. "How precious also are thy thoughts unto me, O God! how great is the sum of them!" (v. 17).

God's thoughts toward us are precious as well. "For I know the thoughts that I think toward you, saith the LORD, thoughts of peace, and not of evil, to give you an expected end" (Jeremiah 29:11). God planned how we should look in the womb and how we should walk in this world.

"When I stand at the judgment seat of
    Christ,
And He shows me His plan for me,
The plan of my life as it might have been

Had He had His way; and I see
How I blocked Him there, and I checked
    Him here,
And I would not yield my will.
Will there be grief in my Savior's eyes,
Grief, though He loves me still?
He would have me rich, and I stand
    there poor,
Stripped of all but His grace,
While memory runs like a hunted thing
Down the path I cannot retrace. . . .
Oh, Lord of the years that are left to me,
I give them to Thy hand;
Take me, and break me, mold me to
The pattern that Thou hast planned"

(MARTHA SNELL NICHOLSON).

Are you following your plan or God's plan?

"If I should count them, they are more in number than the sand: when I awake,
I am still with thee" (Psalm 139:18).

SOMETIMES a person will say, "I just cannot get that person out of my mind." Continually thinking about a person will have a positive or negative effect on us, depending upon our feelings about the person. If we have anger and bitterness in our minds, it only increases as we dwell on that person. Feelings of love and compassion have the same effect, only in a positive way.

David probably wished he could forget some people, and I am sure he wished his enemies would forget about him. But he was glad God would never stop thinking about him. "If I should count them [God's thoughts, v. 17], they are more in number than the sand: when I awake, I am still with thee" (v. 18).

Have you ever thought on something so long you heard yourself saying, "This is driving me crazy"? Have you ever talked to someone who *was* driving herself crazy with her thoughts? I remember a lady who called me late one evening. As I listened to her, I realized that everything she was saying was a figment of her imagination. She had rehearsed this story so many times in her mind she actually now believed the bizarre story; it was driving her out of her mind. She was at the breaking point because no one would believe her or try to understand her imagined circumstance. Her wrong thoughts had led to mental instability. Wrong thoughts can be dangerous. Positive thoughts give us security and stability, mentally and spiritually.

God never stops thinking about us. If we want to stay mentally stable, we must never stop thinking about Him.

If you need some positive Scripture verses to think on, start memorizing the "Why Sink When You Can Swim" verses on pages 377 and 378 of this book.

"Surely thou wilt slay the wicked, O God: depart from me therefore, ye bloody men. For they speak against thee wickedly, and thine enemies take thy name in vain" (Psalm 139:19, 20).

VERSES 19–22 almost seem out of place in this beautiful psalm that magnifies the greatness of our God. Would this great God Who tenderly cares for the unborn baby actually kill a wicked man?

This is not the first time David prayed a prayer like this. In at least six other psalms David prayed for violent judgment on his enemies. These are called "imprecatory prayers" because David was calling for God's judgment on people. David's hatred of the wicked was not an emotion but a principle. God hates the sinner who loves his sin, and David felt the same way. "Surely thou wilt slay the wicked, O God: depart from me therefore, ye bloody men. For they speak against thee wickedly, and thine enemies take thy name in vain" (vv. 19, 20).

God will judge the wicked in His time and in His way. "Be not deceived; God is not mocked: for whatsoever a man soweth, that shall he also reap" (Galatians 6:7).

Often we get tired of waiting for God's judgment, and we decide we need to take the judgment of the wicked into our hands. How unwise! Why? We only see what is happening outwardly—God sees the heart. God is the only One Who can judge rightly. Here are just three reasons why we need to leave the judging to God:

Only God can be impartial. He cannot be manipulated by human reasoning.

Only God is holy. He is always more interested in holiness than happiness.

Only God sees the motives of the heart. People can fool us, but no one can pull the wool over God's eyes.

"Shall not the Judge of all the earth do right?" (Genesis 18:25). Will you be patient and see what God will do?

"I hate them with perfect hatred: I count them mine enemies" (Psalm 139:22).

DAVID hated his enemies with a "perfect hatred." "I hate them with perfect hatred: I count them mine enemies" (v. 22).

How in the world could hatred be perfect when we are told over and over again to love our enemies? David's hatred was "righteous indignation." Notice what motivated his anger: "Do not I hate them, O LORD, that hate thee? and am not I grieved with those that rise up against thee?" (v. 21). Because of David's love for God, those who were God's enemies were his enemies.

"Perfect hatred" is the same kind of hatred Christ demonstrated in the temple when He drove out the moneychangers (Mark 11:15–19). When our hatred is against sin, our motivation for justice is that God's name be honored. When our hatred is against the sinner, our motivation for justice is that our name be honored.

When we think about the way sinners treat our Savior, we, too, have a right to feel "righteous indignation." His authority is ignored. His name is cursed. People exploit His name for personal gain. His children are abused and mistreated just because of Who their Father is. He is blamed for famines, wars, and diseases. His standards for godliness are considered old-fashioned. He has been forgotten, slandered, and hated. Yet the rain still falls on the just and the unjust.

In spite of how they treat Him, God is patient and merciful to ungodly, wicked men. What is our attitude?

"Search me, O God, and know my heart: try me, and know my thoughts: And see if there be any wicked way in me, and lead me in the way everlasting" (Psalm 139:23, 24).

DAVID started this psalm with these words: "O LORD, thou hast searched me, and known me" (v. 1). Why did he pray, "Search me, O God, and know my heart: try me, and know my thoughts: And see if there be any wicked way in me, and lead me in the way everlasting" (vv. 23, 24)?

Perhaps David was saying, "Lord, I have searched myself, and I didn't find any hidden sin. I think I hate what You hate, but Your sight is clearer and deeper than mine. Can You see some sin I have missed? Is there some wicked way I haven't seen? Is there some pride I am hanging onto? Is there selfishness I haven't sensed? Is there a desire for worldliness that I haven't faced? Is there disobedience I haven't corrected? If there is any sin I have missed, test me and try me until I see it and correct it."

David was a man of courage—he had killed a lion and a giant as a young man and was a warrior for many of his adult years. However, this kind of prayer demands a giant step of faith and a lot of courage. David wanted God to do whatever He had to do to make David the man God wanted him to be.

Would you be afraid to have God perform exploratory surgery on your heart? Would you want Him to search every nook and cranny? Would you want Him to know every thought, every motive, every desire, every sin? I have good news and bad news for you. The good news is, God doesn't have to do exploratory surgery on you. The bad news is, He doesn't have to do exploratory surgery because He already knows you inside out.

If you have a sincere desire to be the kind of person God wants you to be, will you take a giant step of faith and courageously pray like David prayed?

"They have sharpened their tongues like a serpent; adders' poison is under their lips"
(Psalm 140:3).

WICKED people had told malicious lies against David, hoping to ruin his reputation. "They have sharpened their tongues like a serpent; adders' poison is under their lips" (v. 3). David compared the words of the wicked to that of the bite of an adder, which is one of the most poisonous snakes.

As you read this psalm, you sense David venting his emotions and praying another imprecatory prayer, a curse on the wicked. David prayed for justice to be done and for protection from the wicked. He cursed the wicked whose tongues were poisonous, whose minds plotted to kill him, and whose hands did evil things against him. David's prayer was marked by honesty. He was filled with fear, and his emotions were churning. He didn't deny his internal pressures. David had been in situations like this before and was always able to come out on top with God's help. He and God were a majority!

Someone has said, "The tongue is the only instrument that doesn't get dull from constant use. It stays sharp." When angry people attack you verbally—keep still! When your feelings are hurt—keep still! When trouble is mounting—keep still until your emotions settle down. Things always look different when you are not so agitated. Be careful not to write someone when you are angry. If you feel you must write down your feelings, do it; but keep the letter until your anger is gone. You may decide not to send it after all. Time works wonders! Wait until you can speak with a calm voice, and you may find you do not need to speak at all. Someone once said, "Silence can be a great peacemaker."

The next time you want to lash back with harsh words, remember these two words: KEEP STILL!

"O GOD the Lord, the strength of my salvation, thou hast covered my head in the day of battle" (Psalm 140:7).

A CAPTAIN or a prince always had an armor-bearer beside him when he battled the enemy. His job was to ward off the blows that were aimed at his master's head. The armor-bearer used his shield to accomplish this job.

David was in a battle; he was being chased and hunted like an animal. The words in the psalm come from the heart of a hunted, hurting man. David didn't have an armor-bearer beside him, holding a shield to protect his head, but he had an Armor-bearer above him Who protected him. "O GOD the Lord, the strength of my salvation, thou hast covered my head in the day of battle" (v. 7). David sensed God's protection covering him like a shield.

Ephesians 6:13 tells us to put on the whole armor of God. Verses 14 through 17 describe each piece of the armor. Why do we need to put on a whole set of armor each day? To fight our enemy, Satan. "Put on the whole armour of God, that ye may be able to stand against the wiles of the devil" (Ephesians 6:11).

When you read about the different pieces of armor in Ephesians 6, you will notice that nothing is provided for the back. We are not to turn our backs on our enemy; we must face him head-on. I have a friend who says she and her husband mentally put on each piece of the armor every day when they first get out of bed. They are mentally prepared for any of Satan's tricks and schemes.

That sounds like a pretty good idea. I think I'll try it! What about you?

"Set a watch, O LORD, before my mouth; keep the door of my lips" (Psalm 141:3).

IN TIMES of adversity and persecution, we can easily say things we will regret later. David was in that kind of situation. He didn't want to say anything to dishonor the Lord or himself. As a king, he was accustomed to doorkeepers who guarded the palace doors. No one could pass through those doors without the guard's permission. David was asking the Lord to be the doorkeeper of his lips. "Set a watch, O LORD, before my mouth; keep the doors of my lips" (v. 3).

How wise we would be to pray this prayer when we know we are in situations where we could say something we would be sorry for the rest of our lives.

"In every life
There's a pause that is better than
    onward rush,
Better than hewing and mightiest doing;
'Tis the standing still at Sovereign will.
There's a hush that is better than ardent
    speech,
Better than sighing or wilderness crying;
'Tis the being still at Sovereign will.
The pause and the hush sing a double
    song
In unison low and for all time long.
O human soul, God's working plan
Goes on, nor needs the aid of man!
Stand still, and see!
Be still, and know!"

Are you sure you should give someone a piece of your mind, or should you be quiet and have peace of mind?

"Bring my soul out of prison, that I may praise thy name: the righteous shall compass me about; for thou shalt deal bountifully with me" (Psalm 142:7).

Are you open and honest with people? Are you transparent enough for them to see when you have real needs? David was! He was in trouble—probably running from Saul and hiding in a dark cave—when this psalm was written. David felt abandoned by everyone; "no man cared for my soul" (v. 4).

Not only was David imprisoned in a cave of darkness, but his spirit was overwhelmed and imprisoned in darkness and despair. "Bring my soul out of prison, that I may praise thy name: the righteous shall compass me about; for thou shalt deal bountifully with me" (v. 7).

All prisons do not have iron bars! When you look within, do you feel imprisoned in a body that doesn't work as it once did? When you look around, do you feel imprisoned in loneliness, having no one who cares about your struggles? When you look up, do you feel imprisoned in silence, as if God isn't hearing your prayers? When you look ahead, do you feel imprisoned in circumstances you fear will never change?

How can you get out of your prison? Keep looking up! The clouds will eventually part; the silence will end; and you will be released to enjoy life again. "Thou shalt deal bountifully with me." Aren't you glad David was honest with us? We would never be able to appreciate the great confidence he had in God if we had not known how low he had sunk.

If you are imprisoned in some way, let people know you are hurting. God often works through other people.

"Hear me speedily, O LORD: my spirit faileth: hide not thy face from me, lest I be like unto them that go down into the pit" (Psalm 143:7).

THE LOWEST part of David's life was not when Saul wanted to kill him, but when his son Absalom was pursuing him with the intent to kill him. David had hit bottom; he was more than discouraged—he was depressed. He felt he would surely die if God didn't help him quickly. "Hear me speedily, O LORD: my spirit faileth: hide not thy face from me, lest I be like unto them that go down into the pit" (v. 7).

One of the signs of depression is a person who is consumed with self. We see the words "I," "me," "my," and "mine" thirty-six times in the twelve verses of this psalm. David was depressed, but his depression was not so severe that he had lost hope. Severe depression puts a person in such a pit of darkness that the light of faith is shut out and all hope is gone. David could still see God, even though he was not sure God saw him: "hide not thy face from me." There was still a glimmer of hope in his prayer: "deliver me" (v. 9), "teach me" (v. 10), "quicken me" (v. 11). David still had hope God would deliver him from his miserable circumstances and do a work in his life.

If all your thoughts and prayers are filled with "I," "me," "my," and "mine," get your eyes off yourself and back on the Lord and others. Don't lose hope! God loves to do the impossible! You can start climbing out of that pit today, or you can help someone else climb out.

"My goodness, and my fortress; my high tower, and my deliverer; my shield, and he in whom I trust; who subdueth my people under me" (Psalm 144:2).

IN THIS psalm we see David, the warrior, the conquering hero. He was the General MacArthur of his day. He sang praises to God for being his strength and protector. "My goodness, and my fortress; my high tower, and my deliverer; my shield, and he in whom I trust; who subdueth my people under me" (v. 2).

David started his praise by calling God "my goodness." In a thousand different ways God was good and merciful to him. David went on to exalt God's goodness in expressing the different ways God demonstrated His goodness to him. God was David's strong and safe refuge, "my fortress"; God was David's tower of strength, "my high tower"; God was David's rescuer, "my deliverer"; God was David's protector, "my shield." When David rehearsed in his mind all God was to him and could do for him, it gave him great confidence and continual reasons to trust Him.

What God was to David He is to us as well. To every believer He is a fortress, a wall we can hide behind where the darts of the evil one cannot touch us. He is our high tower; in Christ we can rise above our circumstances so we can dodge the arrows of the enemy. He is our deliverer when we must be exposed to the enemy. He is our defender, rescuer, and shield. Wherever we go, we carry His protection with us. Yes, in a thousand different ways He expresses His goodness to us each day.

Have you thanked God for His goodness lately?

"I will sing a new song unto thee, O God: upon a psaltery and an instrument of ten strings will I sing praises unto thee" (Psalm 144:9).

BECAUSE God's mercies were new every morning, David could continually sing new songs of praise to God. He used an instrument with ten strings to aid him in his praises as he sang this psalm. "I will sing a new song unto thee, O God: upon a psaltery and an instrument of ten strings will I sing praises unto thee" (v. 9). This musical instrument probably looked something like a harp, but it was smaller and more portable.

I once heard someone make this comment on this verse, "We have ten strings with which we can praise God: two hands, two feet, two ears, two eyes, one heart, and one mouth." I cannot play a musical instrument, but my body can be an instrument of praise for my great God.

How can we use our ten strings to praise God? With our two hands we can write notes of encouragement to people, telling them about the greatness of God. With our two feet we can visit people who need to hear praises instead of discouraging words. With our two ears we can listen to God each day and learn new songs of praise to share with others. With our two eyes we can look for new mercies and expressions of God's goodness to share with hurting people. With our one heart we can love God so much that our lives radiate praise and thanks wherever we go. With our one mouth we can "sing of the mercies of the LORD for ever" (Psalm 89:1).

Are you using your ten "strings" to praise God?

"Every day will I bless thee; and I will praise thy name for ever and ever" (Psalm 145:2).

THE JEWS said that anyone who could pray this psalm from the heart three times a day was preparing himself best for the world to come. "Every day will I bless thee; and I will praise thy name for ever and ever" (v. 2). The members of the early church reportedly read this psalm at their midday meals.

As we awake in the morning, our early thoughts should be on God. We should already have a plan to spend time with God, getting our spiritual food for the day and thanking Him for His goodness. "Every day will I bless thee; and I will praise thy name for ever and ever." God wants our daily praise—whether things are good or bad.

Someone has said that each week has two golden days, carefree days when we never need to worry. These two days are free of fear and apprehension. One of these days is *yesterday*. It is gone; we cannot change any of the pain, mistakes, or blunders. We cannot undo an action or unsay a word. Worry cannot change it. Yesterday the day was mine; today it is God's.

The other golden day is *tomorrow*. It is as far beyond my control as yesterday is; in fact, it may not even come. All the possible adversities, failures, and mistakes we are dreading may never happen. Tomorrow belongs to God alone.

Only one day in the week is left, and that is *today*. Today I will bless the almighty and all-loving Lord, Who takes care of yesterday and tomorrow.

Will you journey just one day at a time so you can bless the Lord each day?

"The LORD upholdeth all that fall, and raiseth up all those that be bowed down"
(Psalm 145:14).

CERTAINLY David knew what it was to fall down and to be bowed down with burdens. But he knew God had been faithful to him. "The LORD upholdeth all that fall, and raiseth up all those that be bowed down" (v. 14). David never fell so far that, with God's help, he could not get up again. Though David was burdened with cares, sometimes to the point of wishing for death, he always raised his head and looked to the Lord for the strength to keep going. It is not a failure to fall; it is a failure not to get up and try again.

Are you burdened down physically with disease or pain and suffering? Are you burdened down mentally with the cares of this world? You can transform your troubles into triumphs. That's how Christians become beautiful jewels.

Before a pearl is a beautiful jewel, it is an irritating grain of sand. The grain of sand gets under the oyster shell. To relieve the continual irritation, the oyster spins a gummy substance around the trouble spot. This is what produces a pearl. We can let God surround our troubles—our sandy grains of irritation—with His love and peace, and in so doing transform troubles into blessings. We don't have to be the victims of circumstances; we can be the victors!

"For all the heartaches and the tears,
For all the anguish and the pain,
For gloomy days and fruitless years,
And for the hopes that lived in vain,
I do give thanks, for now I know
These were the things that helped me
    grow!"

Is God making some pearls in your life?

"The LORD shall reign for ever, even thy God, O Zion, unto all generations.
Praise ye the LORD" (Psalm 146:10).

THE PSALMIST understood the promise that Messiah would come someday and reign forever. "The LORD shall reign for ever, even thy God, O Zion, unto all generations. Praise ye the LORD" (v. 10). What he didn't know was that the Messiah would be Jesus Christ, Who would be a suffering Savior before He would be a reigning King.

Mary understood that Messiah was coming, but she didn't know God would choose her to be the vehicle through whom He would enter the world. How would you have felt if you had been young and unmarried and heard the angel of the Lord speak these words, "Fear not, Mary: for thou hast found favour with God. And, behold, thou shalt conceive in thy womb, and bring forth a son, and shalt call his name JESUS. . . . and the Lord God shall give unto him the throne of his father David" (Luke 1:30–33)?

Mary was confused. "How shall this be, seeing I know not a man" (v. 34). The angel said, "The Holy Ghost shall come upon thee, and the power of the Highest shall overshadow thee: therefore also that holy thing which shall be born of thee shall be called the Son of God. . . . For with God nothing shall be impossible" (vv. 35, 37). Mary may not have understood what God was doing in her life, but she believed what He said because she shared with Elizabeth what had happened and said, "For he that is mighty hath done to me great things; and holy is his name" (v. 49).

Is the Lord doing some things in your life that you don't understand? Can you trust Him even though it doesn't make sense? If you will, one day you may also say, "For he that is mighty hath done to me great things."

"Sing unto the LORD with thanksgiving; sing praise upon the harp unto our God"
(Psalm 147:7).

DECEMBER 25 was just another day in the psalmist's life. Christ had not yet been born; there was no such thing as Christmas.

Is Christmas just another day in your life? Is it just a day of presents, food, and relatives? Or is it the day you celebrate the birthday of your Savior? When you sing Christmas carols, are you just singing words you memorized years ago, or is your heart full of praise to the Lord? "Sing unto the LORD with thanksgiving; sing praise upon the harp unto our God" (v. 7).

Many people have a distorted view of Christmas—perhaps as distorted as little Tommy's. Tommy was a mean, selfish boy. His "Dear Santa" letter before Christmas was ten pages of requests for expensive gadgets and toys. In an attempt to teach him a lesson, his father sat him in the family room in front of the nativity scene. "I want you to sit here until you remember what Christmas is all about and then write a letter to Jesus," said his father. After a short time, Tommy began to write, "Dear Jesus, if You will bring me all the things I want, I will be good for a whole year." But he soon tore up the paper. Next he wrote, "Dear Jesus, if You will bring me everything on my list, I will be good for a whole month." After a few minutes he tore up this paper too. Then he picked up the figure of Mary, took it to his room, put it in a shoe box, and hid it in his closet. He wrote, "Dear Jesus, if You ever want to see Your mother again. . . ."

How did the true meaning of Christmas ever get so distorted? How did Santa ever become as popular as Christ?

Let us never forget the true meaning of Christmas. It is the birthday of Jesus Christ, Who was born to die so that we might live.

"He healeth the broken in heart, and bindeth up their wounds" (Psalm 147:3).

THE PSALMIST began this psalm with a command: "Praise ye the LORD" (v. 1). Why? Because it is good, pleasant, and comely (beautiful). The psalmist went on to list more reasons why people should praise the Lord. One reason was because the Lord was building Jerusalem and regathering the dispersed people (v. 2). Another reason is seen in verse 3: "He healeth the broken in heart, and bindeth up their wounds." No doubt in the dispersion some people were separated from their families and never returned to Jerusalem. Broken families leave people with broken hearts. God takes a special interest in brokenhearted, hurting people.

No medicine, no therapy, no operation can heal a broken heart. I have felt the pain of a broken heart several times in the past few years, but nothing can compare to the pain I experienced when our family unit was broken by divorce. The rejection, loneliness, pain, and confusion that family members experienced was like a knife sticking in my heart.

I have found out this statement is *not* true: "Given time, all things will work out." But this statement *is* true: "He healeth the broken in heart." God has healed me, and I am learning to live with the pain in my heart. "In acceptance lieth peace."

God will heal you if you will stop resenting what He has allowed in your life. You need to rely on Him to heal rather than resist what He is doing.

"He telleth the number of the stars; he calleth them all by their names. Great is our Lord, and of great power: his understanding is infinite" (Psalm 147:4, 5).

IN VERSES 4 and 5 of this psalm the psalmist gave more reasons to praise the Lord: "He telleth the number of the stars; he calleth them all by their names. Great is our Lord, and of great power: his understanding is infinite."

What an astounding passage! Could God really know how many stars there are and have a name for each one? That's what the Bible says! But there are millions upon millions of stars; could He really know each one? "His understanding is infinite." How many people are on this earth? Several billion. Can God know each one by name? Yes; "His understanding is infinite!"

Sometimes we feel no one understands us; sometimes we feel as if we don't even understand ourselves. We ask questions like, Why do I feel this way? What do I want? What's wrong with me? What should I do about this situation? But *God understands* because His understanding has no limit; it is infinite.

"God understands your sorrow,
He sees the falling tear,
And whispers, 'I am with thee,'
Then falter not, nor fear.
He understands your longing,
Your deepest grief He shares;
Then let Him bear your burden,
He understands, and cares" (OSWALD J. SMITH).

If you struggle with the feelings that no one understands, remember God does! He not only understands, He cares.

"The LORD taketh pleasure in them that fear him, in those that hope in his mercy"
(Psalm 147:11).

THE PSALMIST'S fear of God was not "shaking in your boots," but rather a reverential fear that brought him to his knees in awe and trust. "The LORD taketh pleasure in them that fear him, in those that hope in his mercy" (v. 11). When he was reminded of the power, majesty, and mercy of His God, he was renewed with confident trust and hope.

God is pleased when we trust Him. On the other hand, I'm sure our lack of trust brings sorrow to His heart. How would you feel if you promised your children something but they were constantly filled with anxiety because they didn't believe you would keep your promise? I dare say you would be hurt!

Make a list of all the qualities you would expect from an earthly father who truly loved his children. Do you think your Heavenly Father—Who has no human limitations or sinful nature—would do less for His children? Oh, how our Heavenly Father must be grieved when we fail to trust Him. He is full of love, wisdom, and integrity, but we often treat Him as if He were mean, unwise, and dishonest. I need to pray in the words of the songwriter, "O for grace to trust Him more!"

Have you found that it is sweet to trust in Jesus? God takes pleasure in His children who trust Him!

"Let them praise the name of the LORD: for he commanded, and they were created"
(Psalm 148:5).

THIS PSALM is a call for all the universe to praise God. The song has two stanzas. The first stanza is verses 1–6. The psalmist calls the heavenly creation to praise God because He is creator and controller. The second stanza is verses 7–14, in which the psalmist calls things on the earth to praise God because of the excellency of His name and His glory.

"Let them praise the name of the LORD: for he commanded, and they were created" (v. 5). God commanded and everything came into being just as He ordered, and everything stays in order just as He commands. If God withheld His control of the universe and you and me, everything would immediately become chaotic and confusing. The oceans would cover all the land, and all the planets in the universe would crash into one another.

No wonder everything in the universe has reason to praise the Lord! How sad it would be to stand before the Lord and hear Him say, "The trees and animals gave more praise to My name than you did."

We'd better start practicing our praising now, because we're going to be doing it throughout all eternity!

"Praise ye the LORD. Sing unto the LORD a new song, and his praise in the congregation of saints" (Psalm 149:1).

SOMEONE has said, "Praise is the rent we owe to God, and the larger the farm, the greater the rent." These great praise psalms at the end of the book of Psalms are calls to the saints to praise God. In this psalm we are urged to sing a new song unto Him.

I like to sing the old hymns, but I also like many of the new songs and choruses. Recently I found an old song (written in the 1800s) that was new to me. It is my prayer as I approach the end of the year.

"More holiness give me, More striving
    within,
More patience in suff'ring, More
    sorrow for sin;
More faith in my Savior, More sense
    of His care,
More joy in His service, More purpose
    in prayer.

"More gratitude give me, More trust in
    the Lord,
More pride in His glory, More hope in
    His Word;
More tears for His sorrows, More pain
    at His grief,
More meekness in trial, More praise
    for relief.

"More purity give me, More strength
    to o'ercome,
More freedom from earth-stains, More
    longings for home;
More fit for the kingdom, More used
    would I be,
More blessed and holy, More, Savior,
    like Thee" (PHILIP P. BLISS).

Why not find this old song in a church hymnal? Ask the music director to teach the congregation an old song, which will probably be a new song to most people.

"Let every thing that hath breath praise the LORD. Praise ye the LORD"
(Psalm 150:6).

THE FIRST and last psalms have only six verses each, but each psalm gives important instruction. Psalm 1 reminds us that we should meditate on the Word of God daily. Psalm 150 tells us that we should praise God daily. "Let every thing that hath breath praise the LORD. Praise ye the LORD" (v. 6). Thirteen times in six verses we are told to praise the Lord.

If the book of Psalms is the hymnbook of the Bible, then Psalm 150 is the "Hallelujah Chorus." One of the things I love about Christmas cantatas is the "Hallelujah Chorus" at the end. Tears come to my eyes when I see every person standing in honor of the King of Kings.

I feel like rising to my feet and shouting "Hallelujah!" right now. It is not Christmas, but it is a special day for me. I have finally finished this book! My heart is praising God for helping me with this task. I feel drained and yet full, tired but ready to jump up and down. This has been a three-year project. I have passed through many valley experiences during this time; often I was so discouraged I felt this book would never be completed. But God is good! Every time my strength was gone, God would renew my strength. It was as though I could hear Him say, "Get up and try again. You're not done! You haven't crossed the finish line yet."

Oh, by the way, you haven't crossed that line yet either, so don't quit! A new year begins tomorrow. Determine to meditate on God's Word and praise Him daily. He is waiting to do great things in your life!

Why Sink When You Can Swim

26 VERSES TO ENCOURAGE

Job 23:10—"But he knoweth the way that I take: when he hath tried me, I shall come forth as gold."

Psalm 18:30—"As for God, his way is perfect: the word of the LORD is tried [proved]: he is a buckler to all those that trust in him."

Psalm 31:15—"My times are in thy hand. . . ."

Psalm 91:1, 2—"He that dwelleth in the secret place of the most High shall abide under the shadow of the Almighty. I will say of the LORD, He is my refuge and my fortress: my God; in him will I trust."

Proverbs 3:5, 6—"Trust in the LORD with all thine heart; and lean not unto thine own understanding. In all thy ways acknowledge him, and he shall direct thy paths."

Isaiah 26:3—"Thou wilt keep him in perfect peace, whose mind is stayed on thee: because he trusteth in thee."

Isaiah 40:31—"But they that wait upon the LORD shall renew their strength; they shall mount up with wings as eagles; they shall run, and not be weary; and they shall walk, and not faint."

Isaiah 43:2—"When thou passest through the waters, I will be with thee; and through the rivers, they shall not overflow thee: when thou walkest through the fire, thou shalt not be burned; neither shall the flame kindle upon thee."

Jeremiah 31:3—". . . Yea, I have loved thee with an everlasting love. . . ."

Jeremiah 33:3—"Call unto me, and I will answer thee, and shew thee great and mighty things, which thou knowest not."

Luke 1:37—"For with God nothing shall be impossible."

Romans 8:28, 29—"And we know that all things work together for good to them that love God, to them who are the called according to his purpose. For whom he did foreknow, he also did predestinate to be conformed to the image of his Son, that he might be the firstborn among many brethren."

Philippians 4:4—"Rejoice in the Lord alway: and again I say, Rejoice."

Philippians 4:6, 7—"Be careful [anxious] for nothing; but in every thing by prayer and supplication with thanksgiving let your requests be made known unto God. And the peace of God, which passeth all understanding, shall keep your hearts and minds through Christ Jesus."

Philippians 4:11—"Not that I speak in respect of want: for I have learned, in whatsoever state I am, therewith to be content."

Philippians 4:13—"I can do all things through Christ which strengtheneth me."

Philippians 4:19—"But my God shall supply all your need according to his riches in glory by Christ Jesus."

1 Thessalonians 5:18—"In every thing give thanks: for this is the will of God in Christ Jesus concerning you."

2 Timothy 1:7—"For God hath not given us the spirit of fear; but of power, and of love, and of a sound mind."

Hebrews 13:5—". . . I will never leave thee, nor forsake thee."

James 1:2, 3—"My brethren, count it all joy when ye fall into divers [various] temptations; knowing this, that the trying of your faith worketh patience."